The Power of Blackness

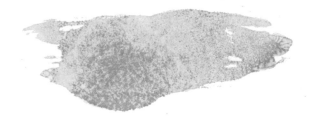

BOOKS BY HARRY LEVIN

Harry Levin

THE POWER
O F
BLACKNESS

Hawthorne

Poe

Melville

OHIO UNIVERSITY PRESS

Chicago   Athens, Ohio   London

Copyright © 1958 by Harry Levin
All Rights Reserved
Printed in the United States of America

Originally published by
Alfred A. Knopf, Inc., 1958
First paperback edition published by
The Ohio University Press
1980

ISBN 0-8214-0581-0
Library of Congress Catalog Card No. 80-83221

Preface

To begin a book with a personal word is, as I have learned from Hawthorne, rather an act of diffidence than of presumption. It would be presumptuous indeed for me to venture, without the preliminaries of explanation or apology, into a field which is being so expertly and so intensively cultivated today. One who is by profession a student of literature, and by birthright a citizen of the United States, would be doubly remiss if he were not keenly interested in the work of the major American writers; but he might well be deterred from commenting on them at any length by the current reorganization of American Studies into a specialized academic discipline. This is a logical and productive consequence of that movement toward self-examination and rediscovery which has been under way since the First World War, and which has gained particular momentum since the Second. During the course of the forty-year discussion, which has sensitively reflected the course of contemporary history, the tone has gradually tended

to change from the self-critical to the self-congratula-
tory. To observe both of these tendencies in a single witness, we need only juxtapose the earlier and later writings
of Van Wyck Brooks. It should be added, in fairness to
Mr. Brooks, that his two positions have been neither
mutually inconsistent nor untypical. Rather, they have
represented a cultural progression which, in moving
from the rebellions of youth to the consolidations of
middle age, has replaced an old-fashioned colonial viewpoint with an up-and-coming sense of national importance.

In practice, of course, that happened a hundred years
ago. In theory the lag was so protracted that, if you
look up Melville in the four-volume *Cambridge History
of American Literature* (1917–21), you will find that he
occupies less than four pages. Graduate schools have recently been doing their utmost to compensate for previous neglect; and the investigation of *Moby-Dick* might
almost be said to have taken the place of whaling among
the industries of New England. Through the ground-
work laid down by such scholars as M. C. Tyler and
V. L. Parrington, American literature has long been
utilized as a source of historical documentation. Yet it
has largely remained for non-academic men of letters,
most perceptively in the case of D. H. Lawrence, to
stimulate the process of critical revaluation. The contribution of the late F. O. Matthiessen was based on his
capacity to span those broad areas of differing awareness,
to assimilate the relevant findings of scholarly research
and esthetic criticism, and therewith to give us our most
comprehensive view of our classic writers, in their relationship with one another and with their age. As it
happens, it was my good fortune, while an undergradu-

ate in Harvard College, to have been among Matthiessen's first students. I wish I could go on to claim the
benefits of the broadening curriculum that was signalized by his arrival. But my interests then, I must
confess, were all too narrowly bound to the classical
and the European. When our minds met, it was usually upon the common ground of the English Renaissance.

An older mentor, nearing the end of his teaching
career, was Irving Babbitt who used to say: "America is
where Europe goes when it dies." A snobbish and—I
would now agree—shallow dictum, and not the best
measure of Babbitt's approach to comparative literature; but it served a purpose if it reversed our inherent
provincialism, and taught us whence America drew its
vitality—the direction to which my appendix will revert.
It was in the year after graduation, while browsing at
the British Museum, that I started to read Henry James
and to learn that, if one looks far enough, the horizons
of culture are all-embracing; the important matter is the
whole continuum, given one's particular connection at
some point. Returning to my university, I found myself
becoming conscious of the traditions it exemplifies, as
they have been chronicled by some of my senior col-
leagues. I had the privilege, which I mention by way of
ever-grateful acknowledgment, of following *American
Renaissance* from draft to draft. If I also mention the
fact that I suggested the title, as the author has characteristically attested in my copy, it is because I think that
should be deprecated. Matthiessen had wanted to call
his book, after an apt phrase from Whitman, *Man in
the Open Air.* The publisher wanted something more
descriptively categorical. My groping formulation may

4

have caught Matthiessen's liberal idealism, his warm feeling for the creative potentialities of American life. But it left out that "vision of evil" which clouds the hopeful picture from time to time, that note of anguish which foreshadowed the tragedy he was himself to enact.

My belated wanderings homeward, so to speak, have met with much other stimulus and encouragement. My largest debt, which I do not specify here because it continues to enlarge, is at least declared in my dedication. The generosity of the John Simon Guggenheim Memorial Foundation, during the year 1943-4, provided me with the leisure to accumulate a backlog of reading upon which I have been subsequently relying. A seminar, open to graduate students at Harvard University and Radcliffe College, has provided a beneficial testing-ground for some problematic ideas. Occasion to lecture on Hawthorne, Poe, and Melville came with a course offered at the University of Paris during the winter trimester of 1953, as a part of the program for the *Agrégation d'Anglais,* and again in the summer of that year at the Salzburg Seminar, where America finds Europe so alive. The present volume is the direct outgrowth of a series of public lectures which I delivered in Berkeley during the spring semester of 1957, as first incumbent of the Mrs. William Beckman Professorship of English Language and Literature at the University of California. For the honor of that invitation and the pleasure of that experience, I cannot sufficiently express my gratitude—especially to Professors James D. Hart, Vice-Chancellor of the University, and Henry Nash Smith, Chairman of the English Department, both distinguished authorities on American literature. I should express further thanks to Mr. Alan Pryce-Jones, Editor of the London *Times Literary Supplement,* for his kind permission to reclaim my anonymous article, "Castles and Culture," from the issue of September 17, 1954.

The three authors I have studied are amply surrounded with a secondary literature, from which I have profited in such ways as are indicated by the highly selective bibliography. The respective biographical facts, condensed to the barest chronological outline, are appended for cross-reference. It should become evident, if it is not already, that the actual substance of this book is incidental to its method of interpretation. My central concern is with the workings of the imaginative faculty, particularly in what may be called fabulation: man's habit of telling stories as a means of summarizing his activities and crystallizing his attitudes. These fantasies, as projected by modern fiction through its principal vehicle, the novel, have been more and more consciously regulated by the conditions to which they have owed their existence. I have tried elsewhere to analyze a few examples of this realistic trend, beginning with Cervantes and continuing with certain French novelists of the nineteenth century. Some years before, I devoted a monograph to the strategic example of our time, James Joyce, whose writing oscillates so ambiguously between realism and symbolism. Following the symbolistic undercurrent, I am now led back to our nineteenth century. "At heart, the American novelists were all transcendental. The scene was a symbol; they scarcely had the patience to describe it; they were interested in it only because it pointed to something more important. Even Poe, who sneered at Concord, was equally an imaginative Trancendentalist: *Mardi* and 'The Fall of the

House of Usher' and *The Scarlet Letter* were all of one brood."

So Lewis Mumford recognized in his pioneering study, latterly reprinted, *The Golden Day*. Yet interpretations persistently stress the American scene for its own sake, discuss our literature in the framework of ideology more often than art, and treat the romance as an anachronism retarding the full development of Critical Realism. Misunderstanding has been abetted by the notorious lack of adequate tools for dealing systematically with prose fiction. Novels, unlike poems, are bulky and seemingly amorphous objects. Hence critics tend to ignore their form except on the level of style, regarding virtually everything else as content, rehearsing the story rather than criticizing it, and moralizing over the behavior of the characters. We have just begun to understand that themes lend a work its structure as well as its subject-matter, and that patterns created by images are no less significant than patterns created by words. In an essay published separately under the title of *Symbolism and Fiction*, sketching some of the methodological problems which confront—and sometimes confound—the interpreter, I looked forward to the possibility of a literary iconology. This book is a very tentative effort toward the approximation of that possibility. The theme has greatly facilitated the undertaking; for it would be hard to find a simpler image conveying a more universal idea, designated so explicitly and elaborated so variously. The body of writing examined sets the procedure for the examination: Hawthorne with his historical consciousness, Poe with his analytic rigor, Melville with his archetypal imagery.

The demonstration required that they be presented

on their own terms and, as far as possible, in their own words. Thus, while tracing configurations of symbolism, I have respected the integrity of the symbols; I have not attempted to reduce them to a literal plane, though there are points at which psychological inference can hardly be avoided. Much depends on the original language, quoted directly or echoed in paraphrase; but, since none of our writers was wholly consistent in spelling and punctuation, I have slightly regularized the texts. Since these are available in many forms, and so many of them are short, it has not seemed necessary to include specific page-reference. A fairly close familiarity with the material is taken for granted. Perhaps the reader should be warned that, when I retell a tale, my version may not be well rounded; it may be designed to emphasize latent elements, for reasons which should be discernible from the context. Some of the minor and marginal illustrations may scarcely seem to be worth allusion in passing; yet they play their part by revealing how pervasively their authors were obsessed by the power of blackness. Lest I seem to be superimposing an obsession of my own upon them, I might add that much more textual evidence accumulated than I could finally use. However, I was looking for thematic significance rather than for statistical incidence. I did not expect to discover a key that explains everything, but rather a touchstone that brings out characteristics.

The resulting triptych—to shift to a closer metaphor —may resemble a set of photographic negatives. But we stand in slight danger of forgetting that black is merely one side—the less popular side—of a famous polarity. The union of opposites, after all, is the very basis of the American outlook: the old and new worlds, the

past and present, the self and society, the supernatural
and nature. Those concepts will be the coordinates of
our study, an arbitrary but convenient scheme for testing its range and relevance on the dramatized levels of
place, time, characterization, and plot. Each of these,
in turn, forms a kind of archetype, an elemental shape
assumed by the collective imagination: a journey, a
house, an alter ego, a dream. "Following darkness like
a dream," the value of the pursuit will probably lie in
the detailed applications we are able to make along the
way. Our theme will concretely link two broad assumptions: the symbolic character of our greatest fiction and
the dark wisdom of our deeper minds. Together they
constitute what I would rather describe as an antithesis
than as a thesis, since they act in opposition to more
publicized influences, blandly materialistic. Which is
the true voice of America? Tolstoy's opinion may pertinently be cited in this regard. In a letter to an American
correspondent, he speaks of Emerson, Thoreau, Whitman, and others among our compatriots who have inspired him. Why, he asks, do we Americans pay so
little heed to our poets and moralists, and so much to
our millionaires and generals?

H. L.

Berkeley
June 4, 1957

Contents

For Perry and Betty Miller

The Power of Blackness

I

The American Nightmare

TRAVELERS on stormy roads at night—or so the tale goes—sometimes encounter a stranger in old-fashioned garb, driving a large black horse and accompanied by a child. Always he inquires the way to Boston; usually his open carriage seems to be heading in the wrong direction. Gradual curiosity discovers that the wayward driver set out for his destination many years ago and, caught in a thunderstorm, made an equivocal vow: "I will see home tonight . . . or may I never see home!" There is a sequel which follows him to the end of his ghostly predicament. Finally he arrives at Boston, only to witness his ruined estate being auctioned off. When he tries to establish his identity, he is admonished by a voice from the crowd: "Time, which destroys and renews all things, has dilapidated your house and placed us here . . . You were cut off from the last age, and you can never be fitted to the present. Your home is gone, and you can never have another home in this world." This story of "Peter Rugg, the Missing Man," published first in 1824, may well serve as the starting point for an attempt to discriminate what is unique in American fiction. Its author, William Austin, is scarcely remembered in any other connection; but, for a while, his shadowy hero became a quasi-proverbial harbinger of the storm; so it may be that, in this particular instance, Austin hit upon some latent impulse of the teeming Over-Soul. A later generation would express that impulse in the succinct inscription: "Kilroy was here."

Peter Rugg, to be sure, had an immediate predecessor in Rip Van Winkle, who also figures as a displaced person, dislocated temporally if not spatially. Voyaging heroes of legend, ever since Odysseus, have been delayed and deflected from their homecoming. Folklore abounds in such prolonged condemnations and such ironic releases. The Wandering Jew remains an unregenerate nomad; the Flying Dutchman gains redemption at last through the sacrifice of another. It is not because Peter Rugg keeps moving, because he pledges his will against the elements, or because he brings his curse down upon his own head, that he seems so uniquely American. Rather it is because the missing man, having left his home behind, keeps looking homeward: because he exists in a state of suspense between wanderlust and nostalgia. Thus, although the narrative offers little more than a sketchy roadside encounter or two, it outlines a sequence of themes which more serious writers will develop: an extraordinary journey, straying from its course like the cruise of the Pequod; an illusory dwelling, like the House of Usher sinking into its black and lurid tarn; a homeless man turned into a fiend by egoism, estranged like Ethan Brand from the magnetic chain of humanity. Above all, like so many other figments of the American

imagination, it passes marvels off as actualities, so that
we disengage ourselves from its nocturnal atmosphere
with the sensation of waking up from a nightmare, and
with the Raven's eternal negation ringing in our ears.

Given the circumstances, it is no wonder that voyages
of discovery have served as real or imaginary vehicles for
our literature, from John Smith to Ernest Hemingway,
or that its prevailing movement has been westward.
This accords with its inherent yearning to construct,
and at other times to demolish, local habitations,
whether at Walden Pond or on the water side of Beacon Street. A chapter on "Time and Temples" in *Mardi*
pauses to argue that architecture represents duration,
whereas travel is the measure of space. But journeys,
taken one way or another, are universal conditions of
existence; and so are the houses to, or from, which they
may lead a restless protagonist. Even more native is the
tendency to communicate his adventures at first hand,
either as he tells them himself or as they are retold by
a close eye-witness. Any personage conceived by any
writer must—to a certain extent—be an alter ego, a
personal surrogate, a composite figure standing somewhere between the writer's experience and his impressions of others; of that relationship Henry James has
drawn a diagram in "The Jolly Corner," where the abandoned house conceals the missing man, who turns out
to be the self that might have been: "A black stranger!"
It is the business of fiction to explore what might have
been, what may be, what is not; and, in this respect, our
story-tellers are no less prone than those of the Middle
Ages to remind us that they are recounting dream-
visions.

Moreover, they often insist that our lives are com-

pounded of the same insubstantial stuff. It is not a
mystic nor a metaphysician, it is the rambunctious
Mark Twain, who reproves us through his *Mysterious
Stranger*: "Strange, indeed, that you should not have
suspected that your universe and its contents were only
dreams, visions, fiction!" If life itself is no more than
a dream, then works of imagination must constitute
"a dream within a dream." Yet the fact that Longfellow
borrowed this very phrase from Poe and applied it to
Hawthorne suggests that such a fantasy may be shared,
through conscious imitation or unconscious plagiarism,
if not through the workings of racial memory. On the
most overt plane of self-consciousness, we all participate
in an ideology which is commonly known as the American dream. This takes its dramatic aspect from the terrain; and since the place is a new world, the time is the
present, imminently verging upon the future. The leading character ought to be nothing less than society as
a whole, and the plot should be the fulfilment of nature
through material progress. Such, at all events, is the
benign and familiar ideal. But dreams not only drama-
tize our wishes; they also mock our anxieties; and though
our daylight selves may conform to a public vista of
bland perfection, on the night-side we are not exempt
from the visitations of insecurity. Americans tend to
suffer from "an ambivalence of anguish," according to
Jean-Paul Sartre, who may be regarded as a specialist
on the subject of comparative anguish.

The justification of M. Sartre's comment is that, having been relatively free from those political calamities
which Europeans have borne, we seem to face our conflicts internally. Wanting to believe in a national credo,
we have found ourselves declining to accept one that

seems more and more self-evidently composed of eupeptic half-truths. Consequently, our most perceptive minds have distinguished themselves from our popular spokesmen by concentrating upon the dark other half of the situation, and their distinctive attitude has been introspection, dissent, or irony. Where the voice of the majority is by definition affirmative, the spirit of independence is likeliest to manifest itself by employing the negative: by saying *no* in thunder—as Melville wrote to Hawthorne—though bidden by the devil himself to say *yes*. The rhetoric of the Everlasting Yea, the rhapsody of the eagle-screaming orator, and the note of self-praise have clangorously predominated, affecting the mood of attempts to interpret our culture and aggravating the suspicions of our foreign critics. But even Whitman continually glanced backward, saluted the old world, aired his cosmic doubts, and emphasized the cult of personality as against the principle of *en masse*. And if we take the common man for our hero, we must balance Walt's idealization against Poe's "Man of the Crowd," that gas-lit portrait of a besotted vagrant stumbling down mean streets into obscurity. "All was dark yet splendid —as that ebony to which has been likened the style of Tertullian."

Without necessarily likening our writers to Fathers of the Church, we are bound to see darkness combining with splendor in their depiction. Clearly, the whole truth is large enough to encompass both extremes. That is why, at every level, our loyalties waver so ambivalently between two different worlds: the new and the old, the present and the past, society and the self, nature and the supernatural. However, our official reputation is grounded upon a series of one-sided platitudes.

Therefore our freest spirits have voiced their denial by stressing the opposite side, expressing themselves in paradoxes, and confronting each standard assumption with its dialectical alternative. Against the received opinion that Americans are uniformly pragmatic and utilitarian, they would set a transcendental worldview, variously stated in religious or philosophical terms. In response to the widespread notion of American gregariousness, they would urge the counterclaims of individualism, not infrequently carried to the point of isolation and alienation. They have brought us to realize that, collectively speaking, we are no longer young; that the United States may be considered the oldest country in the world today, if we date its coming-of-age by the after-effects of technological development.

> A voice from out the Future cries,
> "On! on!"—but o'er the Past
> (Dim gulf!) my spirit hovering lies
> Mute, motionless, aghast!

Poe is by no means alone in this dilemma; and Main Street has a fourth dimension for Hawthorne, if not for Sinclair Lewis. Most of our modernists have been less concerned with novelty than with tradition, investigating the resources of what they like to term "the usable past." Most of our regionalists, in their turn, have made their transatlantic pilgrimages and paid their retrospective tributes to Europe. History has latterly been conspiring to neutralize the differences of geography, while social commitment and ultimate belief are problems which now do more to unite the hemispheres than to divide them.

In short, when we refer to the American way of life,

we simply mean the human condition, accelerated, am-
plified, and projected on a wide screen. "Settled by the
people of all nations," Melville declares in *Redburn*,
America may lay claim to a truly international culture.
"We are the heirs of all time, and with all nations we
divide our inheritance. On this Western Hemisphere all
tribes and people are forming into one federated whole;
and there is a future which shall see the estranged children of Adam restored as to the old hearthstone in
Eden." Out of the many reverberations touched off by
these excerpted sentences, mankind itself emerges as a
sort of Peter Rugg, pushing his search for home into virgin territory. Simultaneously, as he looks ahead to
Utopia and to the millennium, he glances back toward
the idyllic revery of his lost innocence. This continent
has held so strong an appeal for Europe because it presented, in Tocqueville's phrase, *une feuille blanche*: a
blank page in the book of the historians, an uncharted
region on the map of the geographers. But that white
hope was early overshadowed by the probability that any
fresh chapter would be a continuation of those which
had preceded it. "What does Africa,—what does the
West stand for?" asks Thoreau; and, through the home-
spun metaphysics of *Walden*, the outer darkness finds
its counterpart in a wilderness within. "Is not our own
interior white on the chart? black though it may prove,
like the coast, when discovered."

The continuity of human awareness, for Thoreau, was
convincingly attested by the universality of its means of
expression. The fable, the most elemental phase of story-
telling, was the poetic outgrowth of natural wisdom.
Since it could pass from one environment to another
without essentially changing, in a process which folk-

lorists would call diffusion, it could become a constant factor, an irreducible unit of what Jung would call the collective unconscious. And since astronomers still gave classical names to newly discovered planets, as Thoreau pointed out in *A Week on the Concord and Merrimack Rivers,* science itself reaffirmed the vitality of ancient myth:

> By such slow aggregation has mythology grown from the first. The very nursery tales of this generation were the nursery tales of primeval races. They migrate from east to west, and again from west to east; now expanded into the "tale divine" of bards, now shrunk into a popular rhyme. This is an approach to that universal language which men have sought in vain. This fond reiteration of the oldest expressions of truth by the latest posterity, content with slightly and religiously retouching the old material, is the most impressive proof of a common humanity.

Melville viewed his subject-matter in this perspective, and formulated his viewpoint during a trip to Greece, where he renounced "innovating wilfulness" in favor of "reverence for the archetype." His sometime neighbor, Hawthorne, from his porch overlooking the hills of western Massachusetts, had evoked the Greek myths in his *Tanglewood Tales* and his *Wonder-Book for Boys and Girls.* Yet Hawthorne, honest Puritan that he was, confessed that he might have Gothicized the Pantheon. Certain stories seem congenial to his temperament: Proserpina dividing her life-cycle between the alternations of sunlight and shadow, Pandora and Epimetheus losing their little paradise like a juvenile Adam and Eve.

Others, in Hawthorne's version, are revealingly modified. The poor Minotaur is so lonely in the confinement of his labyrinth; Ariadne, refusing to be seduced by Theseus, chooses to stay with her father like a good New England spinster; Hercules, by intercepting all contact between Antaeus and the earth, exercises a spiritualizing influence over the giant; Hecate, dazzled by the radiance of Phoebus, mutters that he ought to wear a black veil. Midas has an apocryphal daughter who, like Beatrice Rappaccini, becomes the victim of her father's experiment.

Such modifications, slight as they may be, register changes of intellectual climate, leaving us with something less than Ovidian metamorphoses. More opportunely, they demonstrate how the archetypes, when transmitted by a markedly individual talent, are individualized in the act of transmission. "Eclaircize the myths Asiatic, the primitive fables," the poet invites his soul in "Passage to India." But the mysteries of the East seem to wither away under the harsh light of Whitman's *éclaircissement*, just as the pagan gods fade before Hawthorne's austerity. We need not search far for the reason why Hellenism failed to adapt itself; it was precisely because Hebraism had made so complete an adaptation. Satan himself had been naturalized under the nickname of Old Scratch. The Yankee had his mythology in the Old Testament, which fully prefigured everything that would or could happen to him, and out of which he accordingly named his children. To cite that most primary of sources, the *New England Primer*, his education began with Adam's fall, the primordial mistake. How deeply those acrostic jingles and woodcut emblems were engraved in his conscience, we may judge by turning the pages of the primer to the letter R:

> Rachel doth mourn
> For her first-born.

This distich naïvely echoes a strain of maternal lamentation from both Jeremiah and Matthew. But it is re-echoed, as we then recollect, in the final cadence of *Moby-Dick*, where Rachel is the name of the ominous whaling-ship that seeks a missing child and picks up an orphan. The name of that orphan has already identified the narrator in the arresting first sentence ("Call me Ishmael"), while the habit of scriptural prefiguration is used as a technique of characterization throughout the book (" . . . and Ahab of old, thou knowest, was a crowned king"). Ahab, who worshiped Baal in the Book of Kings, "did more to provoke the Lord God of Israel to anger than all the Kings of Israel that were before him."

A well-known anecdote illustrates how specifically the Puritan apprehension of daily events was guided by cross-reference to the Bible. When a snake intruded upon a meeting of the Synod at Cambridge, Massachusetts, in 1648, the identification with its prototype was all but automatic. John Winthrop recorded in his journal: "The serpent is the devil." When Hawthorne sought to conjure up the devil two centuries afterward, as the Black Man in "Young Goodman Brown," he armed his character with a staff which resembled—and which, ambiguously, might have been—a black snake. There was likewise an unnoted resemblance to the caduceus of the classic Mercury, which had survived as an apothecary's sign and would reappear as the Brazen

Serpent in Hawthorne's posthumous fragment, *The Dolliver Romance*, where it is said to resemble "a Manichean idol." Perhaps the most noteworthy use to which Hawthorne put that enigmatic device was to embody it in the walking-stick of Westervelt, the diabolical mesmerist of *The Blithedale Romance*. Now the distance is considerable between a suggestive allusion of this kind and the animism that accepts a small reptile as a supernatural being. When Melville described the paradisiacal qualities of his South Sea islands, he was careful to indicate that they contained no snakes or venomous reptiles—motifs of ill omen which were to decorate the walls of the gambling hell in *Redburn*. When Dr. Holmes wrote his "medicated", novel, *Elsie Venner*, he sought to diagnose the evil nature of his heroine; yet, scientific rationalist though he was, he could do no better than trace her symptoms back to a pre-natal snake-bite. "The things"—the chattels that encroach upon mankind, in Emerson's warning—"are of the snake."

Hence the serpent is never cast out; "the envious marplot of Eden" winds its ubiquitous way among Melville's images; and the ever-present danger of corruption is hinted there and elsewhere by a side-glance at its basic symbol. The symbol itself, we need no Freud to observe, is even more deeply and universally rooted in man's imperfect control of his own body. But though this helps to explain its potency, we do not need to stray beyond the Judeo-Christian tradition for an explicit vocabulary of symbols adequate to the situations that met the English colonists. It did not occur to them that the land might have an indigenous lore of its own, imagined by its aborigines; for, by virtue of the colonial mythos, the Indians played the part of devils in a transplanted garden; and though Longfellow would belatedly try to domesticate their legends, the Sunday-school tone of *Hiawatha* itself is the clearest proof of Protestant ascendancy. "Here," wrote Cotton Mather, "hath arisen light in darkness." Christianity, tested anew by primitive conditions, had renewed its fabulous outlook, its faith in miracles, its interest in portents, oracles, and "wonders of the invisible world." The ministry of New England had been enjoined, by the President and Fellows of Harvard College, to note and collect "remarkables" and "memorables", and to preach on providential design as revealed in shipwrecks, thunderbolts, and other "preternatural occurrences." Their chronicler was not the romantic Mrs. Radcliffe but the credulous and all-too-credible Mather—as Melville would add in "The Apple-Tree Table," a satire which compounds original sin with latter-day spiritualism.

Orthodoxy presupposed that the visible universe was animated by a divinity which showed its hand in "remarkable providences," in meaningful interventions as well as in marvelous works. Transcendentalism, shifting its base from the inscrutable to the scrutiny, still retained the premise that matter was the mere external manifestation of spirit. Revelation was no longer based upon dogma, but upon the mystical intuition or the poetic insight that could scrutinize the welter of appearances and discern the presence of hidden realities. To read those hieroglyphics, to interpret the analogies whereby the soul of man might link itself with the physical world, such was the imaginative challenge that Emerson's *Nature* held for the generation that grew up with it. For them, as for their French contemporary,

Baudelaire, nature was a temple where the pillars were trees, the priest was a poet, and language was related to perception through the doctrine of correspondences. For the writer who accepted the Emersonian metaphysic, there was no choice but to be a symbolist.

> It is not works only that are emblematic; it is things which are emblematic. Every natural fact is a symbol of some spiritual fact. Every appearance in nature corresponds to some state of the mind, and that state of the mind can only be described by presenting that natural appearance as its picture. An enraged man is a lion, a cunning man is a fox, a firm man is a rock, a learned man is a torch. A lamb is innocence; a snake is subtle spite; flowers express to us the delicate affections. Light and darkness are our familiar expression for knowledge and ignorance; and heat for love.

The moral qualities listed here by Emerson have some innate connection, in each case, with the stock metaphors that represent them. Nothing more would be needed to create a fiction of the very simplest type: let us say, the perennial beast-fable of the lion and the fox. Whereas, with the enraged man and the cunning man of Emerson's dramatis personae, the potential drama should be a morality; and whereas attributes are personified in the beast-fable, personalities are abstracted in the morality. Animals, of course, may be treated anthropomorphically; Brer Rabbit would be endowed with all the patient sagacity of Uncle Remus. Conversely, human beings might be framed by the rigidities of an inhuman system of values; instead of springing organically from the image, the idea might be superimposed upon it. This is both the theme and the technique of *The Scarlet Letter,* where the *donnée* is the literal application of an ethical label to the heroine. The *New England Primer* could not have spelled out the lesson more didactically if it had begun with a couplet reprehending adultery. Yet Hawthorne, in "Endicott and the Red Cross," wonders whether the A on the breast of another young sinner might not conceivably stand for "admirable." His entire development is comprehended within that ambiguity.

In the sketch that introduces *The Scarlet Letter*—where he discusses the book he will not be writing, a novel concerning the daily routine and political intrigue of the Salem Custom House—Hawthorne visualizes the black-browed ghosts of his puritanical ancestors, frowning upon his frivolous avocation: "A writer of storybooks!" Nonetheless, he is able to recognize some of their strong traits in his own temperament. Distrusting the arts, they had found a story acceptable only when it served a didactic purpose. But the art of story-telling could never be repressed; in the Middle Ages it had even mounted the pulpit, when the sermon was illustrated by an *exemplum,* an anecdotal object-lesson. Hawthorne, whose career recapitulates this formative stage, once sketched a youthful self who had left the guardianship of stern old Parson Thumpcushion in order to become an itinerant story-teller. He was to range afield; yet he would often revert to the clerical background; and many of his stories preserve the cautionary twang of homilies. In his introduction to *Mosses from an Old Manse,* he speaks of the late clergyman who preceded him in that house as living there enveloped in "a veil woven of intermingled gloom and brightness." This figurative mask had been literally displayed and moralized over as "a type and symbol" in "The Minister's Black Veil," an earlier tale explicitly subtitled "A Parable." It was as if the author were reenacting the role of a preacher, and directly exhorting his congregation of readers to behold "an ambiguity of sin and sorrow."

From the strategic vantage-point of a gifted Anglo-American man of letters today, W. H. Auden would generalize: "Most American novels are parables; their settings, even when they pretend to be realistic, symbolic settings for a timeless and unlocated (because internal) psychomachia." This is a good example of critical paradox, in contradicting the usual emphases on local color and timely relevance. But Mr. Auden is not being overemphatic when he directs us back to the center of consciousness, and revives the early Christian concept of a debate between the soul and the body. It is true that we could apply the same generalization to many Russian novels. "God and the devil are always fighting, and the battlefield is the heart of man"—the stage upon which Dostoevsky arranges the struggles of *The Brothers Karamazov*. But, in this very similarity, the Russian and American novelists are equally to be distinguished from the English and French, and from the novel's habitual preoccupation with manners rather than morals. That distinction, as between the more speculative creations of Hawthorne and the solidities of English realism, was generously accorded by Anthony Trollope. "On our side of the water," Trollope concretely testified, "we deal more with beef and ale, and less with dreams." And the difference was not just the Atlantic Ocean, as Dickens proved by crossing it with *Martin Chuzzlewit*.

Tocqueville, the most clairvoyant of all our European observers, ventured what was to be one of his major prophecies, when he announced that American literature would deal less with actions and characters, and more with passions and ideas.

If Tocqueville's prediction seems to herald poems rather than novels, many of our novelists have been poets at heart. As a matter of fact, it is an anachronism for us to talk about the novel at all in the context of mid-nineteenth-century America. If the novel meant "a picture of real life," then Poe wanted none of it; realism was "pitiable stuff." Poe's genre was the tale, with one full-length exception; and that exception would fall into Melville's category, the narrative. That again—if the narrative was fictitious—belonged in a more inclusive category, the traditional medium of American fiction, the romance. This word itself carries with it an aura of medieval legend, as opposed to the brisk suggestion of novelty in the novel. The line between the two forms is a sharp one, as Hawthorne meticulously drew it in his prefaces, where he claimed a romancer's privilege to set his scene on middle ground between the actual and the imaginary. The line broke down and the actual prevailed after the Civil War, when Howells and James adopted the novelistic approach, although James remained more American than Howells in this regard. It would be all too easy to assume that a rough-and-ready young democratic culture, when it found its level of expression, would naturally express itself by naturalistic means. But naturalism, which is nowhere a spontaneous growth, came to this country as a late and sophisticated importation from France, with a Frank Norris exploiting the methods of an Emile Zola. The cultural lag had perpetuated older ways of thought; the apogee came too late for rationalism and too early for realism; our cherished Renaissance was inspired by European romanticism. Consequently, symbolism h.. been the intrinsic mode of American writing.

If we were traversing the annals of prose fiction, our earliest landmark would be a book so rare that it has not yet been discovered by literary historians of the United States, although it was well reprinted in a limited edition ten years ago. This is *The History of the Kingdom of Basaruah*, printed at Boston in 1715 and attributed by its modern editor to a Calvinist minister, Joseph Morgan. It purports to be a traveler's account of a visit to a homeland "north of America." Since its name is glossed as a compound of the Hebrew for "flesh" and "spirit," its topography opens up a wide field for psycho-physical parallels, and the tract becomes a sort of psychomachia as well as an imaginary journey. The natives of Basaruah, constituting mankind, rebel against their covenant with their king, who is God. Though they must be exiled into the wilderness, the King's son goes among them and petitions on their behalf. An end to their wanderings is finally promised via the River of Palingenesia, or regeneration; however, there seems to be some argument over the use of its waters—some controversy, in other words, over baptism. The narrator has obviously been guided at every step by the memorable precedent of Bunyan, who will be instanced again and again by Hawthorne and hailed as a precursor by Melville. Given the importance of *The Pilgrim's Progress* as the determining link between English literature and our own, some of its archetypal ele-

ments are worth our passing recall: the dream, the
protagonist who is another self, the pilgrimage and its
goal, a celestial home.

Thus American fiction sprang from religious allegory,
a form which gave ample scope to the moralistic impetus. This ran through the eighteenth century on the
taut thread of the philosophical tale. Fashions were set
by more worldly English novels, picaresque or sentimental, masculine or feminine; but the remove was far,
and the reflection dim. A change of pace in Europe,
which coincided with a period of revolutionary storm
and romantic stress, was marked by the augmenting
sensationalism of the tale of terror. Poe, whose apprenticeship was an imitation and parody of that school as
popularized by *Blackwood's Magazine,* would protest
that his own terrors originated not in Germany but in
the soul. The substance of his claim is a genuine sense
of the affinity between the American psyche and Gothic
romance. The revival of the romance, in countries where
the novel had matured, was bound to seem an artificial
contrivance like Horace Walpole's pseudo-Gothic castle. Doubtless the vogue of the Waverley Novels responded to a vicarious longing for adventures and wonders and beauties which had little place in so highly
developed a civilization. In America, on the other hand,
where the Middle Ages had not been lived through, un-
expressed meanings could be fitted to unconsummated
fantasies. The oriental tale of *Vathek,* written in French
by an English dilettante, William Beckford, seems no
more than an oddity, with its underground chambers
and its sadistic gestures. Yet Poe quotes it as a warrant
for his own architectural imaginings; and Melville is

known to have received a copy of it while he must have
been brooding upon demonic possession.

Our first master of fiction, Charles Brockden Brown,
started where the Gothicists of the old world left off,
professing himself "a story-telling moralist." An admirer of William Godwin and a fellow citizen of Benjamin Franklin, he was completely committed to the
postulates of the Enlightenment; and light itself is an
almost compulsive source for his imagery. Ironically but
.not illogically, the consequence is an intensification of
shadow. One of his heroes speaks for them all when he
says, "The darkness suited the color of my thoughts."
With his *Edgar Huntly*, we seem to be sleep-walking;
but when we awaken, in a dark pit, it is to a reality
which is worse than a nightmare; and we soon become
involved in a secret pursuit by an evil genius, following
the pattern of Godwin's *Caleb Williams* and Brown's
other books. Brown not only solves the mysterious
crimes his villains perpetrate; he delights in rationalistic
explanations of apparently supernatural phenomena,
not stopping short at spontaneous combustion. The
voices that drive the fanatic to madness and murder in
Wieland are produced by a ventriloquist, whose avowed
intent has been to test his victim's credulity. This raises
questions of motivation more terrifying in their purport than the superstitions they undermine; for Wieland's voices are easily discredited; but Carwin, the
malevolent rationalist, is prompted by that "mischie-
vous demon" who will subsequently instigate Dostoevsky's *Possessed*. Brown's intellectual curiosity, restlessly
probing into obscure relationships, clearly foreshadows
Poe. His anticipation of Fenimore Cooper, in fictional

exploitation of the redskins, is a further stroke of pioneering ingenuity.

Hawthorne assigned "an obscure and shadowy niche" in his "Hall of Fantasy" to Brockden Brown—an appropriate but inadequate commemoration for the most penetrating and sensitive mind among Hawthorne's forerunners. Brown's successors, Cooper and Washington Irving, gathered much greater reputations by depending heavily upon their raw material. Irving ranged across both worlds in his lifelong quest for romantic associations, from an arabesque castle in Spain to the fur trade in the Far West; and if the sketch is a literary genre, we owe it to his casually pictorial talent, which was more at ease with places than with people, especially with distant places. He never quite succeeded in detaching himself from the mouthpiece of Jonathan Oldstyle; and when he celebrated his natal New York, he was happiest with characters who were long dead and had been of Dutch extraction. If his typical hero was Rip Van Winkle, the man of another day who survives himself through the gift of indolence, his villain was Ichabod Crane whose fault is enterprise, and whose expulsion from Sleepy Hollow is the prologue to success i1 politics and business. Irving's light-hearted portfolio ncludes at least one sketch which reflects the darker side of things, rendered in the quick pencil-strokes of the *Salmagundi* papers: the Little Man in Black, half sinister, half pathetic, and wholly outcast. But there was so much surface to be covered, and Irving managed to cover it so deftly, that he did not get beyond the descriptive stage.

Cooper was far from being so skilful a writer, but he struck the ore that was in widest demand. Though the red man might be a devil incarnate, he also embodied the myth of the noble savage. Indian-haters would make him the most implacable of villains, such as the Black Vulture in R. M. Bird's *Nick of the Woods*. And Cooper himself was no apologist; his good Indians are exceptional; they fight for a losing cause and belong to a dying tribe. His authentic hero, Leatherstocking, is a grizzled frontiersman at the outset, soundlessly moving from the pathless forest to the western prairie. Later volumes, retrospectively written, restore him to youth and retreat with him toward the pastoral. But if he is a "philosopher of the wilderness," his philosophy has less in common with the primitivistic idyll of Rousseau than with the brute strife of Darwin. Leatherstocking may swear blood brotherhood with Indian John, yet he prides himself on "white gifts"; he is " a man without a cross," no half-breed; and between the paleface and the darker breeds, the feud is endless. This racial tension even extends to the erotic sphere, where it discriminates against the creole, Cora, to the advantage of the fair-haired Alice in *The Last of the Mohicans*. Here we touch on the well-established preference of Anglo-Saxon romancers for blonde heroines, along with their suspicion that every brunette may be a *femme fatale*. Thackeray poked fun at Scott for this prejudice in his burlesque, *Rebecca and Rowena: A Romance upon Romance*; but in *Vanity Fair* he draws the same invidious comparison between the sensual Becky Sharp and the pure Amelia Sedley.

Balzac prized Cooper above all other novelists, not so much for his exotic scenery as for his exposure of naked violence—a feature of our fiction which continues to influence its continental adherents. He essayed many

other themes, but on the whole vainly; for they lacked
the crudely compelling force of the frontier antagonism; and in the cosmopolitan domain of polite letters,
Cooper was just another genteel colonial. Irving, not
unlike a Scottish or an Anglo-Irish writer, won assimi-
lated status in England. What both Americans offered,
to appreciative publics in both worlds, was landscape-
painting rather than true portraiture. It was certainly
not that "original relation to the universe" which Emerson prophesied for *homo americanus*. But "the new in
art is always formed out of the old," as Emerson allowed; and the transition is normally affected by imita-
tive artists who give more or less conventional treatment
to hitherto untried subjects. Furthermore, as James
Russell Lowell affirmed, a truly creative epoch must be
preceded by critical endeavor. As the nineteenth century was reaching its middle years, criticism grew clam-
orous in its demands for a national literature commensurate with the size of the country itself, a great American novel which would confound the over-emulated
British, a native author who would out-Shakespeare
Shakespeare. Whether he would be recognized when
he arrived was the moot point of Hawthorne's quizzical
parable, "A Select Party," where a youthful and poorly
dressed newcomer with glowing eyes is scornfully ig-
nored by the abstract celebrities.

And who was he?—who but the Master Genius for
whom our country is looking anxiously into the
mist of Time, as destined to fulfil the great mission
of creating an American literature, hewing it, as it
were, out of the unwrought granite of our intellectual quarries? From him, whether moulded in

the form of an epic poem or assuming a guise altogether new as the spirit itself may determine, we are to receive our first great original work, which shall do all that remains to be achieved for our glory among the nations.

Melville read these lines even while he was composing his review of the book in which they appeared, *Mosses from an Old Manse*. What is more important, he was also then composing *Moby-Dick*; and the "parity of ideas" between what he was reading and what he was writing, between those expectations he held with Hawthorne and his own endeavors to realize them, occasioned that famous "shock of recognition" which registers the impact of one master genius upon another. The book that Melville would dedicate to Hawthorne lives up to his grandiose formulations better than Hawthorne's own book; while the elder writer, in retrospect, seems to be somewhat less of a kindred spirit than Melville hoped. But his review, which mirrors the sunlight and shade of the Edenic countryside where it was written, six miles from Hawthorne's Tanglewood, was a manifesto for "a plurality of men of genius." And since it was signed pseudonymously "by a Virginian," perhaps we may include Poe in that plurality, and entertain the conjecture that Poe's death the year before may be commemorated in Melville's epitaph for Bulkington, the solitary Virginian adventurer. Melville's essay, on the positive side, is a declaration of independence and a plea for originality, which echoes the patriotic argument for the second coming of Shakespeare. Yet it diverges from the messianic hopefulness of the professionally democratic critics by heavily underlining the

Shakespearean torment, the melancholy and madness, the intuitive truth that flashes forth from the mouths of the darkest characters—Hamlet, Timon, and particularly King Lear.

Applying the touchstone of Shakespeare's tragedies to Hawthorne's tales, the crucial trait that fixed and fascinated Melville was what he designated the "power of blackness"—a power which "derives its force from its appeals to that Calvinistic sense of Innate Depravity and Original Sin, from whose visitations, in some shape or other, no deeply thinking mind is always and wholly free." Melville might not have isolated this essence "ten times black" or summed it up so decisively, had it not been omnipresent among the shades and contrasting lights of the work before him. Yet, though it is a virtual obsession with Hawthorne, as we shall be constantly aware, though it became Hawthorne's trademark after Melville had pointed it out, it is hardly less characteristic of Melville himself and—in greater or lesser degree, as he asserts—of all other thoughtful intellects. "The blackness of darkness," that intensive phrase from the epistle of Jude, which he uses here and twice in *Moby-Dick*, was also invoked by Poe in both "The Pit and the Pendulum" and *The Narrative of Arthur Gordon Pym*. It was even used by the western writer, James Hall, who celebrated "The Black Steed of the Prairies" and was to teach Melville the ethics of Indian-hating, in *The Wilderness and the War Path*. In the other direction, as charted by D. H. Lawrence's dynamic *Studies in Classic American Literature*, we are apprised that the Pilgrim Fathers were "black, masterful men" who had crossed a "black sea" in "black revulsion" from Europe. Wherefore, Lawrence warns us, we must somehow learn to "look through the surfaces of American art, and see the inner diabolism of the symbolic meaning. Otherwise it is all mere childishness."

Most of us owe our acquaintance with it to childhood, and to the irony of ironies that has consigned such bedevilment to the schoolroom, on the fairly safe assumption that pedagogy would never reach the depths at which the artistic intention lay buried. Nevertheless, like Poe's moribund heroines, it can be exhumed to embarrass our optimism. Superficially Melville's chief illustration, "Young Goodman Brown," is artless as "Goody Two-Shoes"; whereas, to the alerted reader, "it is deep as Dante." Brockden Brown was an untypical namesake; the Browns of this world, in every-day observance, are neither more nor less than the average decent people; yet the couple in Hawthorne's story are led astray into a witches' sabbath, a black mass. The heart-cry of the husband, recognizing his wife as a participant, resounds beyond Dante; for her name is Faith, and it is faith itself which is being called into question. The guide to the forest at midnight has been the devil himself, present here in the person of a black man; more commonly he is conspicuous, in his absence, through something black exhibited as a clue to the symbolic meaning. This association of idea and image is much too general to be the hallmark of American fiction alone; indeed what we characterize as the Gothic novel is denoted in French, more broadly, as *le roman noir*. Nor is it irrelevant for us to notice that a series of fictional shockers, mostly translated—as their French publisher will have it—"from the American," is currently advertised as *La Série noire*.

It may be that blackness stands out more, for our

writers, because of its continual interplay with a not
less pervasive sense of whiteness: *la feuille blanche, le
roman noir*. The running contrast between them sets
forth all our dilemmas as inevitably as black print upon
a white page. The iconology of whiteness, pondered
over by Melville, has furnished one of the farthest-rang-
ing chapters in our literature. The theme of blackness,
enunciated by Melville, surpasses the mighty scope of
the whale itself; the soundings that exemplify it here,
accordingly, must be references *passim*. Melville's literary model was Rabelais' chapter, "Of that which is
signified by the colors white and blue." But Rabelais
could not define white, the color of bridal joy, without
mentioning its antithesis, the funeral garb of grief. Curiously enough, the same inspiration prompted Poe, in
"A Chapter of Suggestions," to substitute blue for
black, though he was a connoisseur of blackness—
"*nigrum nigrius nigro*." One of his letters refers to a
similar substitution, as handled by one of his predecessors in Gothic romance:

> Monk Lewis once was asked how he came, in one
> of his acted plays, to introduce *black* banditti,
> when, in the country where the scene was laid,
> black people were quite unknown. His answer was:
> "I introduced them because I truly anticipated that
> blacks would have more *effect* on my audience than
> whites—and if I had taken it into my head that, by
> making them sky-blue, the effect would have been
> greater, why sky-blue they should have been."

For Poe too, the main consideration was the esthetic
effect. But such effects do not pre-exist in a vacuum, although the artist may obtain them subconsciously; he

chooses one shade, rather than an alternative, because it bears some connotation for him and for others. As Poe could have learned from Emerson, "the artist must employ the symbols in use in his day and nation to convey his enlarged sense to his fellow men." Sky-blue banditti would have been pointlessly far-fetched, and white ones less effective than black, for reasons which Poe thoroughly apprehended, even if he did not want to verbalize them. To be strict, as he now and then liked to be, black and white were not really colors at all; and if white was rather a synthesis of all colors, black was "the no-color." How, then, could it accumulate such a vast burden of connotations? Why should melancholy be the black humor? Why should magic be the black art? Why should it be pitch that defiles? And how is it that—for the thinking man, *Il Penseroso* —black is "wisdom's hue"?

This takes us back to the very beginning of things, the primal darkness, the void that God shaped by creating light and dividing night from day. That division underlies the imagery of the Bible from Genesis to the Apocalypse, and from the word of life to the shadow of death. It is what differentiates the children of light from the children of darkness in the Dead Sea Scrolls. The Puritans were fond of invoking it to distinguish themselves from the other sects; and it reverberates with an added poignance in the lines of their blind laureate, Milton. But all religions, in accounting for the relation of the earth to the sun and for the diurnal and seasonal cycles, seem to posit some dichotomy, such as the Yin and Yang of the Orient or the twin paths of the *Bhagavad-Gita*. The interconnection of white and black with well-being and malaise, as Jakob Grimm perceived, was

too recurrent to confine itself within the limits of any
single mythology. In the ensuing conflict, ethical sympathies have naturally adhered to the brighter side; yet
certain heresies have ascribed an equal power, if not a
predominance, to the contending forces of darkness;
and the uncompromising dualism of the Manicheans,
engendered out of the limbo between Zoroastrianism
and Christianity, has exerted its fascination over some
of our thinkers. Orthodox Christian ethics would permit Satan, the prince of darkness, to have his frequent
triumphs in this world; but the radiant afterlife would
be the kingdom of Jesus, whose garments the Vulgate
describes as *"alba sicut lux."* At the polar extreme,
through the perspective glass of *Paradise Lost*, we contemplate "black Gehenna . . . the type of hell," which
corresponds to the pagan underworld, the tenebrous
realm of Dis. Homer's description of pain as dark is
consistent with our view of the Greeks as champions of
brightness and conquerors of the unknown—to whom
we are indebted, as Jefferson put it, "for the lights which
originally led ourselves out of Gothic darkness."

Here a shift is implied from religious illumination to
philosophical enlightenment. Kant was playing upon
the same implication, and progressing from Olympian
fire toward modern electricity, when he compared
Franklin with Prometheus. Although civilization moves
on, its respective colors of good and evil are still re-
ducible to light and dark. Yet, whenever we allude to
a black sheep or a whited sepulcher, we acknowledge
the dangers of confounding one hue with the other. "If
pleasure and pain, good and evil, were black and white,
then justice and injustice, right and wrong, might depend upon this distinction," William Hazlitt remarks

in his *Life of Napoleon*, where he deplores the injustice done by such phraseology to members of the so-called colored races. But usage is stubborn, and the best that Blake can say for "The Little Black Boy" is that his soul is white. If right and wrong were always clearly labeled, if devils were as black as they are painted and angels as fair, the problem of evil would be easily solved. When Shakespeare first addressed himself to tragedy, he made his villain a black man, Aaron the Moor in *Titus Andronicus*. Later, with more understanding of life's complexities, he could make a noble Moor his hero, and portray Othello victimized by a white villain known as "honest Iago." In the murky air of *Macbeth*, fair is foul and black is white—or so it seems until we realize the tragic upshot of ambiguous choices. The issue is as old as the black snow of Anaxagoras, and as enigmatic as Rilke's image of black milk.

The Romance philologist Leo Spitzer, noting this union of opposites in Poe, has surmised that the pattern may be more extensive. Students of Hawthorne, beginning with Melville, have had to confront it in its most consciously articulate form. There is nothing arcane about its recurrence; it was amply rationalized by the esthetics of the day, which made a catchword out of *chiaroscuro* and encouraged such word-painting as the battle-scene between the Serapis and the Bonhomme Richard in *Israel Potter*. But since the highlights and shadings go so much deeper and farther back, a few brief citations from earlier writers and other forms of writing may fill out the broad dimensions of the picture. To begin with the pioneer defender of freedom of conscience, Roger Williams: when he denounces the "Tenent of Persecution," he calls it "black" as well as "bloody." He calls its proponent, John Cotton, a "deformed Ethiopian," who—by inference—will persist in iniquity until he is exposed to the sun of righteousness, Jesus. Such is the idiom of scriptural metaphor, serving as ammunition for theological controversy. Whereas when we turn to the notebook of Jonathan Edwards, suggestively titled *Images, or Shadows of Divine Things,* we can watch the process of symbolization at work as graphically as in Hawthorne's notebooks. Earthly observations are systematically reduced to a collection of otherworldly emblems, a typology. Since holiness comprehends all the other virtues, it is typified by white, which is also the type of purity because it signifies mothers' milk and childish innocence. As for black:

> Ravens, that with delight feed on carrion, seem to be remarkable types of devils, who with delight prey upon the souls of the dead . . . devils are spirits of the air. The raven by its blackness represents the prince of darkness. Sin and sorrow and death are all in Scripture represented by darkness or the color black, but the Devil is the father of sin, a most foul and wicked spirit, and the prince of death and misery.

This might cast an interesting light—or rather, shadow—on Poe, suggesting a possible answer to the inquiries so cryptically dismissed by his ominous bird. Poe does not make his entrance as an outsider into a tradition of poetry which, from Michael Wigglesworth through William Cullen Bryant, was essentially a graveyard school. Poets of all schools have hymned the night; but Philip Freneau's "House of Night" is a colloquy with sable-winged Death himself, a dream-vision in the meter of Gray's elegy, "painted with fancies of malignant power." Those fancies are not less powerful because they forego immortality to concentrate, as Poe will do, upon the psychic sensations of the charnel house. Whitman would be more of a sun-worshiper; yet he did not flinch when the "black murk" of Lincoln's assassination hid the star of the republic; and the specter of "Black Lucifer" raises its ugly head in one version of *Leaves of Grass*, to be exorcised by further revision. But let us cite our poetic text from Emerson, overtaken at a moment of unwonted perplexity, in the *Ode* inscribed to his abolitionist friend, W. H. Channing:

> Foolish heads may mix and mar;
> Wise and sure the issues are.
> Round they roll till dark is light,
> Sex to sex, and even to odd;—
> The over-god
> Who marries Right to Might,
> Who peoples, unpeoples,—
> He who exterminates
> Races by stronger races,
> Black by white faces,—
> Knows to bring honey
> Out of the lion;
> Grafts gentlest scion
> On pirate and Turk.

Cosmic optimism will win out over skeptical irony, and all contradictions will be resolved in the long run, but not before disclosing the abysses of lawless competition, imperialistic expansion, and racial aggression. Emerson's tropes, now Biblical, now Delphic, catching the

tensions that threaten to turn the dream into a nightmare, bring home the very worst of national problems,
the evils resulting from the peculiar institution of slavery. This was blackness with a vengeance, as the humanitarian Dickens noted on his visit to the southern
states, "the darkness—not of skin, but mind—which
meets the stranger's eye at every turn." Dickens' figure
of speech reverses the typical sequence of attitudes,
since it proceeds from a social actuality through a psychological impression to a moral judgment; nevertheless, it sums up the principal lines of interpretation in
a typology of blacks which will have some bearing upon
the authors whose books now lie before us.

The selection of these particular authors for detailed
study hardly needs any additional warrant; for once the
topic is entertained, they will have selected themselves.
Two of them would occupy central and closely adjoin-
ing niches in any annex we might erect to the Hall of
Fantasy; while the third, though situated very much by
himself, must be conjured with in any discussion of
what he characteristically styled the "management of
imagination." All three have been grouped together by
a recent Italian historian of American literature, Luigi
Berti, under the expressive epithet, *I Triumviri dell'
Inquietudine*, the triumvirs of disquietude. In a republic—or, should we say, an empire?—which presses for
assent, conformity, and even quietism, we may seem to
have left their disturbing mood far behind. Ideally, as
Emerson balances the duties of the artist, he should
render "the gloom of gloom and the sunshine of sunshine." Actually, at least since the age of Howells, writers have been under pressure to dwell on "the smiling
aspects of life." Their "darker musings"—to hark back

to Bryant's phrase—have been further obscured by the reluctance of readers to look beneath surfaces and face diabolic meanings. But the adaptable devil, as Melville conceived him, tempts men to say *yes*; hence to defy him was to be a nay-sayer. Taking for granted the obvious American thesis, the cheerfully confident trend of a practical and prosperous culture, it is the antithesis that we find in our greatest writers. Visionaries rather than materialists, rather symbolists than realists, the vision they impart is not rose-colored but somber, and the symbols through which they impart it are charged with significations that profoundly justify the most searching analysis.

II

Camera Obscura

THE notion of the writer as a recluse, sitting apart from all involvements with his fellow beings, was never more self-consciously embraced than by Nathaniel Hawthorne. Marcel Proust, in his cork-lined apartment, was not so solitary as Hawthorne in that haunted chamber which he describes on a wistful page of his notebooks, and which—he says—should loom large in his biography. There, in his mother's house at Salem, this fatherless and brotherless young man shut himself up for a twelve-year period between college and marriage; there he struggled with himself to bring forth his lonely imaginings; and there, through insomniac hours, "the nightmare of the soul" brooded over "The Haunted Mind." While other minds were formed by worldly experience, Hawthorne was glad to have so long avoided it, since the seclusion endowed his own reactions with a virginal freshness and purity. His mind itself became a *camera obscura*, a dark room which sensitively registered the infiltration of light from outside. Later years were to involve him in journalism, public service, politics, diplomacy, even a socialistic community; but, in each of those sociable pursuits, his participation was mild and marginal; and the personal trait that impressed others most was reserve. During his sojourn in England he was visited by a recurrent dream, which brought him back to college or to school with "a feeling of shame and depression," a guilty consciousness of having stayed at home while friends and classmates had "moved onward" toward fame in the great world. So they had; they had careers in the army and the navy and the Congress; Longfellow was the most famous of poet-professors; Franklin Pierce was President of the United States.

The question of moving onward—or not moving onward—sets the rhythm of Hawthorne's development, regulating the outward flights and the homeward impulsions of his art, and wavering between ideas of progress on the one hand and pieties of tradition on the other. The cult of the antithesis, which he so assiduously practiced, is bound to influence any endeavor to characterize his thought. But this is simply a stylistic indication of the key role he played in that dialectic of loyalties which, as we have seen and shall see, each American artist seems to face in his own way; and this is why the outgoing Melville made such a hero of the retiring Hawthorne. Melville, his warmest admirer, also found him a "sequestered man." In his calm aloofness, in the esthetic distance from his subject at which he placed himself, Hawthorne could not have differed more strikingly from Melville's engagement with his own material, and from the subsequent trend of American prose toward immediacy and empathy. Hawthorne sustained his detachment by cultivating the literary elegances of

the day, which was the heyday of ladies' books and
genteel magazines, of the polite euphemism and the
facetious circumlocution. Yet his bookish archaisms are
not unsalted by Yankee colloquialisms; and his special
irony often springs from the tension between an urbane
manner and a soul-searching matter. Much of his original piquancy must have come—like Irving's—from the
incongruity of handling autochthonous themes with an
old-fashioned craftsmanship, which stands securely in
the line of the eighteenth-century English essayists.

Hawthorne was ruefully amused that the mask he
donned for purposes of "intercourse with the world"
should present it to such a split personality; that, as he
wrote in the preface to a new edition of *Twice-Told
Tales*, "the obscurest man of letters in America" should
have "the style of a man of society." Poe criticized him
for being too much the essayist and not sufficiently the
teller of tales; indeed, his talent is descriptive and speculative rather than narrative. Nor was characterization
his strongest point; he candidly admits that the hero of
"Feathertop: A Moralized Legend," charlatan and
scarecrow though he be, is no less convincing than some
of the same author's other fictive personages. The
trouble, he confessed to Longfellow, was that—having
lived in a dungeon and thrown away the key, as it were
—he had little to create from except thin air. His notebooks attest his belief in pictorial art as a form of
magic more potent than poetry; and, as we might have
suspected, he was dazzled by the highlighted faces and
the black backgrounds of Rembrandt's portraiture; but,
though we naturally think of Hawthorne's work in
visual terms, we speak more appropriately of delicate
shading than of rich coloring. His instinct seems to have

led him toward that principle which Verlaine's *Art
Poétique* would enunciate: *"Pas la couleur, rien que la
nuance."* Disarmingly, Hawthorne emphasizes the pallor, the coolness, and the evanescence of *Twice-Told
Tales*; the pages will look blank if the book is opened in
the sunshine; it must be read "in the clear, brown, twilight atmosphere in which it was written."

This is precisely the atmosphere in which Melville
read *Mosses from an Old Manse*, the half-light of a
shady New England barn; and it harmonized with Hawthorne's lyric description of the moss-covered parsonage
at Concord where he had begun his married life. The
blackened walls of the Old Manse had been painted,
and the blacker portraits replaced; the garden, so near
a neighbor to Thoreau's Walden, was bright as Eden.
In the study where Emerson had pondered the opti-
mistic philosophy of *Nature*, Hawthorne conceived the
stories that overpowered Melville with their burden of
"Puritanic gloom." Why should this blackness, which
lifted for the philosopher, have settled again so heavily
on the romancer? The year he spent measuring coal in
the port of Boston will not suffice to explain it. According to Henry James, it was superimposed by Hawthorne's surroundings. His life was as blameless, almost
as colorless, as the uneventful lot that James discloses
in "The Beast in the Jungle." But the Puritan conscience was Hawthorne's by legitimate inheritance. "It
projected from above, from outside, a black patch over
his spirit, and it was for him to do what he could with
the black patch." What he did, by transposing it to
the plane of imagination, was to objectify it and—so
James would argue—to exorcise it. If so, the catharsis
was incomplete; the ghost kept returning to haunt the

claustral premises; and if theology no longer lent it support, then psychology might reckon with it. Hawthorne was well aware that the sense of sin is more intimately related to inhibition than to indulgence; that the most exquisite consciences are the ones that suffer most; that guilt is a by-product of that very compunction which aims at goodness and acknowledges higher laws; and that lesser evils seem blacker to the innocent than to the experienced.

But James was in no position to allow for the morbid exaggerations of unduly prolonged adolescence, with its prurient curiosities, its shrinking modesties, and its narcissistic explorations. Furthermore, his admirable life of *Hawthorne*, in eagerness to demonstrate that an American could be an artist, may have gone too far in repudiating the vestiges of earlier didacticism. What Poe had called the didactic heresy was based, of course, on the purest orthodoxy: the old assumption, which would not be seriously challenged today, that esthetics depends upon ethics. It followed, for the Puritans— and, to a more qualified extent, for their progeny—that art could justify its existence only by serving a moral intent. Art was edification, not entertainment. As at the Custom House, so in the Old Manse, Hawthorne imagined his forbears reproving him for being a mere fiction-monger; facing the heavy shelves of tracts and treatises, he promised himself "at least to achieve a novel that should evolve some deep lesson." Perhaps he could seek through imaginative fiction what they had sought through religious speculation, an awareness of some controlling pattern in human destiny. On a window-pane his wife inscribed: "Man's accidents are God's purposes." This was an invitation to allegorize, to look through nature toward the supernatural, to gather tangible images which might serve as types or emblems of spiritual ideas, as Mather had done with his "remarkables" and Edwards with his "shadows." But Hawthorne's gathering of such hints in his *American Notebooks* is more than a handbook of symbols; it is a germinal process for the best of his tales and romances.

He is somewhat apologetic about his "blasted allegories"; but he claims to have always started with a meaning, though it was sometimes lost along the way. Actually, he is inclined to overstate his moralistic intention, to limit his story to the barest hint, which is then developed into a sort of essay. He is conscious of a certain lack of substance, an elusiveness which prompted Poe's suggestion that Hawthorne get himself a bottle of visible ink; and he frequently feels called upon to remind us that his scenes are set in some ethereal half-world, somewhere between dreamland and reality. But the allegorical habit of thinking is true to itself in its distrust of mundane things and its appeal to transcendental sanctions. "I can never separate the idea from the symbol in which it manifests itself," the narrator of "The Antique Ring" declares, refusing to state a moral, but stating one in the end. If Hawthorne's landscapes contain their sermons in stones, it is because he has taken care to implant them; but it is also because his discerning glance has fixed upon the exemplary detail; and this double concern of the moralist and the artist is aptly formulated in one of his sketches, "The Old Apple Dealer," when he identifies himself with "the lover of the moral picturesque." In his youthful project, "The Story-Teller," the tales told as object-lessons were to be accompanied by verbal pictures of their natural settings. Something of that project was realized in "The Seven Vagabonds," where the wandering story-teller meets six motley entertainers; together they head for a camp-meeting, but disband upon learning—from a traveling preacher dressed in rusty black— that it has broken up.

Hawthorne, like his story-teller, did not altogether put the ministry behind him when he rejected it as a possible calling; the possibility often rearises; and if it does not break up his entertainment, it gives his stories their homiletic undertone. "The Minister's Black Veil" is a sermon rather than a story; the self-isolated protagonist is a preacher who preaches on behalf of the author; and nothing happens except for his one symbolic gesture, his *exemplum*, which incidentally leads him to the rejection of earthly love. It is a far cry from this rarefied apologue to the anecdote that Dickens was currently narrating in *Sketches by Boz* under the heading of "The Black Veil"—a grimly realistic confrontation of pathos and crime, in the persons of a mad widow and her criminal son. By comparison, Father Hooper's veil seems the most tenuous of material objects, and Hawthorne fully intended that it should; while the secret sin, which it obscurely typifies, remains an eternal secret. But, if Father Hooper is not an effectual actor, he is an intensive spectator. "Perhaps," we are told, "the pale-faced congregation was almost as fearful a sight to the minister, as his black veil to them." Turning the other way, we can look back through its ambiguous tissue, and join the narrator in assuming a spectatorial point of view. This was the habitual outlook for one who had cloistered himself during manhood's most vigorous years, who had looked out at life—so he sighed

—through a peephole. In "Sights from a Steeple" he sighs for the vantage-point of Asmodeus, the lame devil of Le Sage, who entered houses invisibly through chimneys. Or, better still:

> The most desirable mode of existence might be that of a spiritualized Paul Pry, hovering invisible round man and woman, witnessing their deeds, searching into their hearts, borrowing brightness from their felicity and shade from their sorrow, and retaining no emotion peculiar to himself.

Now a spiritualized Paul Pry, a high-minded eavesdropper, might seem to be a contradiction in terms. Yet Hawthorne could instance a living example in "Wakefield": an Englishman who walked out of his house and lived on a neighboring street for more than twenty years, disguised and incognito, peering through a window at his own wife. As a projection of an author's relationship to his characters, this has a parallel in Balzac's *Honorine*. But Wakefield is in worse plight than a mere *voyeur*; Hawthorne designates him the "Outcast of the Universe" because he is a self-displaced person; he is more like Proust's Marcel, who—attempting to imprison his mistress—becomes the prisoner of his own suspicions. At that extreme stage of solitude, nothing is left but the mirror of introspection, to which —in the absence of flesh-and-blood characters—Hawthorne has frequent and literal recourse: an intermittent dialogue with himself as "Monsieur de Miroir." By gazing into the glass, with his peculiar concentration of fantasy, he peoples the empty room with vicarious emotions. "What is Guilt?" he asks at the beginning of "Fancy's Show Box," and answers, "A stain upon the

soul." Then, after a paragraph of further questioning:
"Let us illustrate the subject by an imaginary example."
Thereupon we are shown a sequence of pictured situations, almost as if a modern psychologist were putting
us through one of his tests in thematic apperception.
The lingering question is whether an author must not
be a villain himself, when he contrives a story involving
villainy; whether he does not share the guilt by conceiving it, conspiring with his evil characters in a kind
of Dostoevskian complicity.

Hawthorne's son would trace this mood of self-accu-
sation back to a misunderstanding, over a Salem co-
quette, which nearly eventuated in a duel between
Hawthorne and a friend. Hawthorne's readiness to fight
on that occasion may have encouraged another friend,
Jonathan Cilley, to engage in the duel that cost him his
life a few years later; or so the penitent Hawthorne
might have thought; and "Fancy's Show Box," in Julian
Hawthorne's opinion, is the expression of his father's
remorse. The biographical episode, as Julian Hawthorne
recounts it, seems to bear a closer resemblance to the
early tale of "Alice Doane's Appeal." This is a fragmentary scenario, evoked by the historic associations of a
visit to Gallows Hill in contemporary Salem; and the
personal wrong, a fatal rivalry between two brothers
over a maiden who turns out to be their sister, is somehow associated with the mass delusion of witchcraft
and with the victims whose unmarked graves make the
hill a monument. That persecution was the blackest
patch of all for Hawthorne, all the blacker because it
emanated from the New England conscience itself; and
if he had no heinous sins to repent, he could do penance for his witch-hanging ancestors. Having grown up

in so tragic a neighborhood, he was a haunter of cemeteries from boyhood, and had filled a home-made newspaper with talk of worms and graves and epitaphs. The note of *memento mori* sounds, with medieval insistence, in "Graves and Goblins," the monologue of a ghost; and "Fragments from the Journal of a Solitary Man" expresses a wish to promenade down Broadway in a shroud. There lurks a hidden exhibitionist in every *voyeur*.

Hawthorne brushes aside such funeral trappings and touches a more thoughtful level of tragedy, after a Hamlet-like interview with a philosophic tombstone carver in "Chippings with a Chisel," which leaves him meditating "whether the dark shadowing of this life, the sorrows and regrets, have not as much real comfort in them . . . as what we term life's joys." The shrine of happiness, in "The Lily's Quest," is likewise a sepulcher. Viewing "The Procession of Life," in a companion piece, he sees it as a *danse macabre* marshaled by Death. From the position of the inveterate bystander, he is able to watch more cheerful processions; in "Sunday at Home" he reveals himself as no church-goer; but his sympathies go out to a group of Negroes promenading churchward to whiten their souls. The viewpoint of Hawthorne's sketches is that of the onlooker, reacting to whatever may come along, however trivial; in "A Rill from the Town Pump," it is identified with that centrally located public facility, through the rhetorical device of prosopopeia. A more ingenious treatment of a similar theme is the "pictorial exhibition" of "Main Street," where the author introduces himself as a showman, who turns the crank to exhibit successive scenes in the growth of the community, "somewhat in the nature of a puppet-show." We readers are the spectators, watching his show-box, as we were the minister's congregation; and just as the minister thumped upon his cushion, so the showman does not hesitate to point. Hawthorne, in the one part or the other, is there to moralize the spectacle. His mode of presentation is illustrative and indicative; it exemplifies and expounds a text; it bespeaks our notice for the telling feature; in so many words, it exhorts us: *Yea, verily . . . Lo, and behold!*

Hawthorne mastered the various gradations of prose, from journalistic hack-work to full-length romance. As between his sketches and his tales, the distinction is by no means clear-cut, although he is fairly explicit in tagging the latter with such labels as *parable, morality,* and *legend*—not to mention *fantasy* and *mystery*. To distinguish by broadly grammatical norms, the first person speaks more freely in the sketches—though "The Haunted Mind" is a pointed exception, which addresses us with second-person urgency. In the tales, the author is more impersonal; occasionally, he employs an intermediary; and he often exercises the rights of a commentator; but he remains detached from the characters; the alter ego has supplanted the ego. In the sketches, he may fancifully play with the situation; in the tales, his fancy is an immanent part of it. It is the difference between what might conceivably happen and what has apparently happened. But here again, we cannot be too categorical; the cameo is matched by the intaglio. Fiction, for Hawthorne, is always the working-out of an improbable hypothesis. What would happen if—? The notebooks abound in such *données*. What would happen, Franz Kafka must have asked himself, if a man were transformed into an insect? A sudden transformation, corresponding to an inner metamorphosis, is the principal event in Hawthorne's tales, as in his retelling of Greek myths; the characters of both are statuesque in their behavior, striking poses and waiting to be symbolically interpreted. Once the hypothesis has worked itself out, its interpretation is hedged with uncertainties. Was it a miracle? Or was it a delusion? Some believe . . . Others maintain . . . And what has been momentarily clarified is again bedimmed by a penumbra of doubtful alternatives.

Enough has been said of Hawthorne's approach to the problems of shorter fiction to indicate wherein he was idiosyncratic and wherein he was typical. It might be said that his idiosyncrasies strengthened his typicality, in that the Yankee and Puritan strains went so deep in him, enabling him to subsume much that went before and to lay the ground for much that came afterward. Among his first undertakings had been "Seven Tales of My Native Land"; but he was never a nationalist; he was a regionalist—and never more the wry New Englander than when he declared New England to be as large a lump of earth as his heart could hold. He made it his own terrain as Irving, a decade or so before, had used his sketch-book to annex the Hudson River Valley. It is a touching reminder of Hawthorne's indoor apprenticeship to encounter, among his jottings, the notation: "A lament for life's wasted sunshine." Nevertheless he spent many vacations traversing the country roads; he was personally acquainted with valleys and mountains, rivers and villages, natural landmarks and historical sites. Along with his impressions of them, he records a stranger's impression of him: that he is something of a hawk-eye. He has an eye for the moral picturesque, rather than for purely local color; when he is not using place-names, he is usually disavowing specific reference. But, though "The Threefold Destiny," is an overt allegory, it does not take place in the Orient or in fairyland. Rather, as he announces the formula, "a subdued tinge of the wild and wonderful is thrown over a sketch of New England personages and scenery." It was as if a Wordsworth and a Coleridge were collaborating in American prose.

It was inevitable that Hawthorne would perceive, in the landscape, those preoccupations which he brought to bear upon it. He is pleased to greet the whiteness of winter, with all its innocent connotations; yet, in "Snow-Flakes," it also signifies "dead nature in her shroud." But nature mourns nightly as well as seasonally; and then she puts on her black veil; then, as in "Night-Sketches," the sky seems "a black, impenetrable nothingness." The background is sunset, the foreground darkness, in Hawthorne's first published effort, "The Hollow of the Three Hills," where a witch conjures up the accusing phantoms that overwhelm the heroine. But he continues to be interested in the ordinary procession of daily events, as it passes down the road through "The Toll-Gatherer's Day." The road itself, which has been the major premise for so many novelists, for the novel itself, winds along with many a Hawthornesque twist. It is quite characteristic that, in "David Swann: A Fantasy," the youth of the title does not actually adventure upon it; he lies asleep at a crossroads while the author, in breathless present tense, apostrophizes the passing exponents of Wealth and Love and Death, and considers their hypothetical effect upon David's career.

The roadside meditation ends with the awakening of the recumbent hero, who stretches, yawns, and walks away. More enterprisingly, the peddler hero of "Mr. Higginbotham's Catastrophe" manages to overtake and foil the threat of murder. It is equally significant that a thrice-plotted crime hangs over this lighter tale and that it does not finally transpire.

Hawthorne—who confessed to having "sat down by the wayside of life," in dedicating *The Snow-Image and Other Twice-Told Tales* to his naval officer friend, Horatio Bridge—would baptise his last habitation "The Wayside." Not a few of his characters are wayfarers, who have abandoned their homes to set out on a pilgrimage, and who are welcomed and sent forth again in his tales. Some of his pilgrims are bound for a bleaker Canterbury than Chaucer's—the Shaker settlement in New Hampshire. Others pursue objectives of their own. In "The Great Carbuncle: A Mystery of the White Mountains"—a tale which invites a double-edged comparison with "The Diamond as Big as the Ritz" of F. Scott Fitzgerald—the blinding sight of the enormous jewel illuminates the private motives of its various seekers. Here the tinge of the wild and wonderful pre-existed in the scenery; what Hawthorne added was an ethical touchstone. Along parallel lines, he allegorized a familiar catastrophe in "The Ambitious Guest," where the mountain climber—seeking to make a name for himself—is namelessly buried under a landslide. Irony would yield to affirmation when Longfellow took up the same case in "Excelsior." Hawthorne, who was far removed from the naturalists, did not regard man as the victim or creature of his environment. Even a freak of nature, *lusus naturae,* might still be an act of God. It was man's adaptation to his environment which gave him the greatest opportunity for the cultivation of his character. The unassuming but ever-serious Ernest, in "The Great Stone Face," is morally superior to those other sons of his native valley who have left it to gain success in the outer worlds of business, warfare, politics, even poetry; it is Ernest whose noble countenance has been prefigured upon the hillside; and thus man rediscovers himself through topography.

Hawthorne's deep feeling for place was closely linked with his time-consciousness; no American region was so rich as his in history, and no other writer so possessed as he by the sense of the past. Half of his tales and sketches might be subtitled, as two of them were, "A Picture from the Past" and "An Imaginary Retrospect." Hawthorne had played the historian, in a small way, with his hack-writing for *Peter Parley's Universal History*, and later with his biographical series for children, *Grandfather's Chair*. Moreover, without stirring from his own chair or strolling beyond the old houses of Salem and Boston, he could embark upon a journey in time. In the four "Legends of the Province House," he found a setting and a framework at the former headquarters of the colonial governors, now drawing back from the bustle of Washington Street. To relieve the commonplace actuality of the bar on the ground floor, he summoned up the more colorful ghosts of the British regime, in "Howe's Masquerade." But legend, if it meant no more than a touch of romantic embellishment, another "tinge of the marvelous," was never enough; it had to be moralized legend. In "Edmund Randolph's Portrait," a favorite symbol, a "black, mysterious picture," enhances the other mysteries of the

Province House. In "Lady Eleanor's Mantle," the political issue between aristocracy and democracy is enacted as an emblematic tableau, where the proud lady tramples upon her over-ardent admirer; a set of charades is deliberately acted out, as she refuses the cup of communion with human sympathies, wraps the red mantle of pride around her, and suffers the poetic justice of the contagion it spreads.

The fourth and final legend of the Province House, "Old Esther Dudley," is the climactic episode that occurs when the Tories are swept out and the Yankees take possession. If that evacuation is incomplete, it is because the aged heroine insists upon staying and keeping the keys, until such time as she too becomes a ghost. In this respect, she sets a precedent for one of Melville's minor heroes, Bartleby. In another respect, she resembles another superannuated Bostonian, Peter Rugg. When she admits the newly elected people's Governor, John Hancock, he pauses for an instant to salute the loyalties she embodies. When he addresses her, it is the present addressing the past in a hail-and-farewell:

"Your life has been prolonged until the world has changed around you. You have treasured up all that time has rendered worthless—the principles, feelings, manners, modes of being and acting, which another generation has flung aside—and you are a symbol of the past. And I, and these around me— we represent a new race of men, living no longer in the past, scarcely in the present, but projecting our lives forward into the future. Ceasing to model ourselves on ancestral superstitions, it is our faith and principle to press onward, onward!"

These accents ring sincerely enough, in their break with
traditional bonds and their confidence in the new republic. They cry amen to Emerson's dictum that America has no past: "all has an onward and prospective
look." Yet "onward" could have another reverberation
for Hawthorne, which was less a rallying-cry than a self-
reproach; which measured his hesitations and anxieties
and inbred nostalgia against the rush of his contemporaries to get out and get ahead. The ambivalence is resolved, and resolved in favor of a staunch modernism,
in one of Hawthorne's most effective stories, "My Kinsman, Major Molineux." Here a lad from the country, a
clergyman's son, reaches town late at night and knocks
at many doors, in the hope of finding his prominent
uncle and being taken under his protection. Young
Robin meets many rebuffs, along with some blandish-
ments on the part of a woman in a red petticoat. He
likewise brushes up against a cryptic stranger with an
infernal visage: "the red of one cheek was an emblem
of fire and sword; the blackness of the other betokened
the mourning that attends them." This figure, as it
turns out, is the herald of a moonlight throng which,
to the smell of burning tar and the noise of harsh laugh-
ter, escorts Major Molineux out of town. His nephew
would like to dismiss it all as a dream or, at worst, a
nightmare. But it is real enough, and its reality is that
if Robin wants to rise in the world, he must rely upon
his own efforts and not upon family connections; that
an independent race of men must stand on its own feet,
rejecting the past while forging the future.

Diplomatic contact with England was to reinforce
Hawthorne's sturdy patriotism; but it is already strong
in his legendary resurrections of the Massachusetts Bay

Colony, where he unreservedly sympathizes with the colonists against the royalists. "The Gray Champion" is his tribute to the independence personified in "the type of New England's hereditary spirit," an indomitable if inexplicable spokesman for liberty, who emerges to announce the overthrow of the Stuarts and will reemerge in the darkest hours of the American Revolution. The conflict between the Puritans and the Cavaliers, as it is dramatized by the contrast between somber attire and parti-colored raiment, is not so one-sided in "The Maypole of Merrymount." Hawthorne draws upon English folklore and Elizabethan pageantry for his most gayly colorful depiction: a "lightsome couple," garbed as Lord and Lady of the May, and the semipagan ceremony by which they are to be married. The tale is darkened, suddenly and ineluctably, by the interruption of John Endicott—the stern iconoclast who tears down the red-cross banner in another tale—along with other "darksome figures" from the Puritan settlement. Darker still is the aspect of depravity they now cast on what before has seemed so naïvely attractive. The maypole is felled, the rebels are dispersed, and order is given that the bride and groom must exchange their rainbow garb for the sober garments of Puritanism. This is their initiation into the mystery that she has sensed—"earth's doom of care and sorrow." But since they must bear it together, they need not repine; their garlanded departure from carefree Merrymount is, like Adam's and Eve's from the garden, a transition from innocence into experience.

"The Maypole of Merrymount," as a literary performance, may well be a *Paradise Lost* in provincial miniature. But Hawthorne, whether through research or instinct, went much farther into the subliminal; he dared to center his graceful parable upon the most primitive archetype of sexuality. By surrounding the maypole with an orgiastic color-scheme, and opposing it with the gloomy denial of color, he balanced the rival claims of Eros and Thanatos, love and death in their universal phase. The compromise implied is an acceptance, specifically, of the institution of marriage, and generally, of the limitations of the human condition. This, despite a certain ambivalence, works to the advantage of the Puritan settlers as against the routed Anglicans. But when the problem is that of religious authority, and the opposition is between the Quaker conscience and the Puritan theocracy, in "The Gentle Boy" Hawthorne sides with the Quakers. Without pretending to share their inner light, he made it the unifying source of his imagery throughout this saint's legend of an infant martyr: "a domesticated sunbeam, brightening moody countenances, and chasing away the gloom from the dark corners . . ." The counter-effect is produced by "Young Goodman Brown," where the emphasis is on "the deep mystery of sin" rather than on the pathos of being sinned against. The pharisaical elders, "a grave and dark-clad company," meeting in "the benighted wilderness," are doing the devil's work while professing righteousness. The climax, the passage that incited Melville to his formulation of the power of blackness, is a crisis of faith and an agony of doubt.

Hawthorne is the most consistent of skeptics; and if he has reservations about orthodox religion, he is even more skeptical of religious liberalism. The show-piece of this two-faced skepticism is "The Celestial Railroad," a parody of *The Pilgrim's Progress* and a satire on Tran-

scendentalism. Hawthorne outdid his own allegorical
virtuosity in bringing Bunyan up to date, in facilitating
Christian's weary journey with all the latest improve-
ments and modernized comforts. The Valley of the
Shadow of Death is now illuminated—but by mephitic
gases from underground, which portend an ultimate
destination utterly remote from the Celestial City. The
fumes of hell are never far from the surface; intimations
of heaven are farther to seek. This is why retroactive
efforts to make a theologian out of Hawthorne are
doomed to failure; for his profound belief in original sin
is scarcely alleviated by any conviction of supernal
grace. The curse of Cain is on the heads of the genera-
tions of Adam. Their lot is ritualized in "Roger Malvin's Burial," wherein, under the stress of Indian warfare, Reuben Bourne has left his father-in-law dying
alone in the wilderness. His remorse is not purged until
he returns long afterward to the unhallowed spot, where
in a hunting accident—one of those coincidences that
seem to lay bare the design of the universe—he shoots
his son, the grandson of old Roger Malvin, whose
skeleton may now be buried in the same grave with the
youth. Innocent of the first death, Reuben Bourne is
inadvertently guilty of the second; yet his life is cru-
cially implicated in both; and the only expiation is
sacrifice. Such is the bourn that limits every man.

Taking a limited view of the potentialities of human
nature, Hawthorne remained a Calvinist in psychology,
if not in theology. In politics, he was a party man
through the least progressive epoch of the Democratic
Party; three times a political job-holder, he earned his
English consulship by a campaign biography of one of
Lincoln's most mediocre predecessors. To be a demo-

crat, in the broader sense, requires a considerable measure of "faith in the ideal," Hawthorne's interlocutor
tells him in "The Hall of Fantasy." That air-drawn con-
struction—like Milton's limbo—is the habitat of ideals
which have yet to become realities, reforms ahead of
their age, millennial prophecies, and other fantastic
projects, not excluding works of fiction. The gap between this cloudy realm and practical realization is hard
enough to bridge; and Hawthorne makes it virtually
unbridgeable in "The Snow-Image: A Childish Miracle," where the ambiguous figure, brought into the
house by the children, melts away. The response of the
sympathetic mother, who has a strain of poetry in her
temperament, is countered by the father, a hardware
merchant who is supported by a hard-headed moral:
that well-meaning philanthropists may do more harm
than good by intermeddling in other people's business.
But Hawthorne's most sweeping pronouncement on
the perfectibility of the species is "Earth's Holocaust,"
envisioned as a gigantic bonfire in which the worn-out
trappings and dubious influences that prevent mankind
from attaining perfection—titles, weapons, liquors, yes,
and books—are burned, while reformers fan the flames
with the repercussive shout: "Onward! onward!"

The blaze provides more light than heat, a wholly
characteristic illumination through which Hawthorne
peers for flickering truths. Though the accumulation of
follies goes up in smoke, there is no promise that any
great reformation will ensue. For, as a dark-visaged
stranger remarks with glee, the heart is still unpurged;
and from its cavernous depths the same old wrongs and
miseries will pour forth all over again. "That inward
sphere," for better or for worse the seat of passion, is the

ambivalent center of Hawthorne's values; and in the two tales published "from the *Allegories of the Heart*," it is exalted at the expense of the other faculties, particularly the brain. "The Christmas Banquet" belies its Dickensian title to develop the least convivial of cheerless subjects: an annual competition among the woebegone, whose very definition of existence is death-in-life. The most miserable of all proves to be a man blessed in every other regard, but cursed with the crowning misfortune of a cold heart, so that everything seems unreal to him. This tale is a sequel, related by the protagonist of "Egotism, or The Bosom Serpent," who has been rescued from a comparable state. The stock metaphor of that title is taken literally, though it is left conjectural whether the fancied snake is a physical ailment, a mental delusion, or a token of demonic possession. The egocentric sufferer contrives to project his mania, in some appropriate fashion, on everyone else. But the happy ending, the cure for his egocentricity, is consummated with the resumption of his broken marriage, and with his wife's admonition: "Forget yourself in the idea of another."

Hawthorne, practicing what he preached, had recently married when he penned that advice. Conjugal love, solitude *à deux* in the house and garden at Concord, was his means of coming to terms with society. Gradually he would be gravitating toward the more social domain of the novel; the bulk of his tales, those that carry the heaviest burdens of obsession, had been written during the hermit years of his bachelorhood; in the interim, his newly experienced happiness expressed itself through some of the more idyllic sketches, depicting the Old Manse as a paradise for a new Adam and Eve. In the long run, he was to become a devoted family man, as well as the most paternal of story-tellers; his shyness would be cushioned and his pent-up affections absorbed, by the satisfaction of his congenital urge for domesticity. Yet the tales are rife with matrimonial fears. "Mrs. Bullfrog" is the almost embarrassing narration of "a lady-like man" who is hen-pecked by a virago. An elderly couple marries much too late in "The Wedding Knell"; in "The Shaker Bridal," a youthful pair pledges the sexless troth of their sterile cult, chilled in their greenness by "the hoar-frost and the black-frost." More often than not, the relations between the sexes end in unkept trysts and wasted lives. "Edward Fane's Rosebud" is withered by a long-drawn-out widowhood; "The Wives of the Dead" dream vainly of their husbands' return; "The White Old Maid" awaits her dead lover in a winding sheet. Hawthorne's affirmations are double negatives, the author's repudiation of his characters' denials.

The fear of being immured—so powerful with Poe—is neutralized, with Hawthorne, by a desire to stay in the haunted chamber or to retreat to what it may symbolize. The revulsion from it is symbolized by the chilling metaphor, set down in his notebooks, "To have ice in one's blood." To insulate, to isolate, to intellectualize, to be utterly incapable of emotion—Hawthorne protests against that attitude so obsessively that he seems to damn himself. When he portrays the artist as a detached observer, "insulated from the mass of human kind," he seems clearly engaged in self-portraiture. The "penetrative eye," the diabolical insight of the painter in "The Prophetic Pictures," is dearly bought at the cost of an unfeeling heart. But it is morally justified by

its "pictorial fancy," which foresees the tragic fate in
store for the happy couple it contemplates. Hawthorne's
artists, in their estrangement from others, are akin to
those passive heroes of Thomas Mann, for whom the
artistic gift is such a dubious blessing. But the artisan of
"Drowne's Wooden Image" succeeds in transcending
his humble craft, Pygmalion-like, when he models a
ship's figurehead upon the woman he loves. More elabo-
rately, in "The Artist of the Beautiful," Hawthorne
limns his portrait of the unworldly perfectionist, to
hang beside Balzac's "Unknown Masterpiece" and
James's "Madonna of the Future." In this case, the
masterpiece is a hyperingenious work of mechanical
artifice, a butterfly presented as a belated wedding-gift
to the heroine, who has in the meanwhile married the
hero's rival, a hard-handed blacksmith; and it is the
child of this bourgeois match who grasps at the delicate
toy and crushes it.

But nothing is really lost; for the butterfly has tested
the sensibilities of those who have touched it; and since
it is merely a symbol after all, the artist who created it
may rest secure in his attainment of an ideal beauty.
So, at any rate, Hawthorne consoles his protagonist,
shifting characteristically from the picturesque to the
moral; whereas the less transcendental painters of Balzac and James, having been bereft of their living models,
must resign themselves to bedaubing a meaningless
canvas. What is redeeming in Hawthorne's protagonists
is the virtue of their defect, the idealism of their intellectuality. The scientist Aylmer is the prototype of
"every man of genius," in that "he handled physical
details as if there were nothing beyond them; yet spiritualized them all, and redeemed himself from material-

ism by his strong and eager aspiration toward the infinite." His story, "The Birthmark," focuses upon the single imperfection that mars the countenance of his beautiful wife, Georgiana, a mark in the shape of a small red hand against her pallid skin, "the symbol of his wife's liability to sin, sorrow, decay, and death." These are the very conditions of mortality; but Aylmer, aspiring to assert "man's ultimate control over Nature," ignores them. Amid the smoke and flash of his somber laboratory, with the mocking aid of the earthy Aminadab, he operates on the submissive Georgiana to eradicate the fatal flaw. Like the rainbow, it fades away altogether; her beauty now is perfect; but she is dead; and her monomaniac husband is confounded in his quest for perfection.

With a reference to the statue of Eve by the sculptor Hiram Powers, Hawthorne hints that his science-fiction retells the Biblical fable, letting the birthmark stand for original sin and replacing the tree of knowledge by the apparatus of the laboratory. But the roles are now reversed; for it is Adam who yields to curiosity, and it is Eve who plays the consenting victim. It may not be accidental that the Hawthornesque theme of the self-confounding egoist crosses the theme of marital union so poignantly in this tale, written soon after Hawthorne's marriage, and even more so in the ripe tale written shortly afterward, "Rappaccini's Daughter." Here the viewpoint is that of the wide-eyed student, Giovanni Guasconti, peeping down from his darkened window into the luxuriant garden next door. This miasmal Eden is cultivated experimentally by the black-garbed Dr. Rappaccini, a "scientific gardener" who "cares infinitely more for science than for mankind."

The fairest flower is his daughter, Beatrice, whom he has immunized to the poisonous vegetation around her, and whose rich allure is that of "Oriental sunshine"—that fascination of corrupted and corrupting purity which her namesake, Beatrice Cenci, exercised over Hawthorne and over Melville. Melville, in his copy of Hawthorne's *Mosses*, marked the account of Giovanni's mixed reaction: "Blessed are all simple emotions, be they dark or bright! It is the lurid intermixture of the two that produces the illuminating blaze of the infernal regions." It is illuminating, at all events, to penetrate that "gulf of blackness" which divides this single-minded Adam from his tainted Eve.

This time the onlooker does not remain at his peephole; he is decoyed into the serpentine enclosure below. Giovanni's love for Beatrice, exactly as her father has calculated, falls in with his scheme to provide her with a mate who will be suitably estranged from the norm. Giovanni finds himself being mithridated by the exhalations of the treacherous flowers. His antidote is Beatrice's poison, and her death is the upshot of Rappaccini's experiment. "It is a dream," Giovanni has tried to convince himself, "it is surely a dream." But the dream again cannot be shaken off, perhaps because its ambiguities do not depend on magic or on miracles, but on the vaguely plausible assumptions of pseudo-science, which pass among us with less questioning. Moreover, though the clusters of floral images may seem to be mainly decorative and conventionally innocuous, they are so heavily redolent with erotic suggestiveness that the allegory for once becomes an intimate experience, a dilemma of reluctant sexual entanglement. We should not overlook the fact that "Rappaccini's Daughter" is prefaced by a note of ironic self-evaluation: Hawthorne translates his own name into French and reviews the writings of M. de L'Aubépine, listing the translated titles of several tales as if they were heavy works in two or three tomes. He had done about as much as he could with his miniatures; indeed he had all but exhausted his fragile genre by loading it with the weightiest implications; and he had arrived at a point of maturity where his imagination was feeling its way toward a medium of ampler scope.

One of his handful of later tales, almost the last, "Ethan Brand," is purposefully subtitled "A Chapter from an Abortive Romance." It is obviously a final chapter; those chapters which should have led up to it have aborted. However, rather fully in this instance, Hawthorne's *American Notebooks* sketch out not only the moral conception, a quest for the Unpardonable Sin, but also the picturesque background, a New England village at the foot of Mount Greylock, through which Hawthorne had passed on a walking trip. His hawk-eye caught much of the local color, which—as in his romances—he contrasts with more portentous matters; the ordinary sinners of the tavern, where petty vice can be easily procured in a black bottle, constitute a drab and solid chorus for the confession of a greater sinner. If the child is an uncomprehending innocent, the dog's behavior seems strangely sympathetic; while the Dutchman, with his dark smile and his historical show-box, seems to reincarnate the Wandering Jew. The fate of the protagonist, as well as his former occupation, is signalized by his surname; for once again Ethan Brand stands before the lime-kiln that he tended eighteen years ago. The element of fire, which invariably fascinates Hawthorne and continually reminds him of Bunyan's side-gate to hell, flickers through the night of the story from sunset to sunrise. Its "lurid blaze," according to neighborly gossip, had sealed a pact with Satan. The brands that burn in this perpetual holocaust are not refined by the Dantesque flames of suffering and purgation.

There is poetic justice in the contrivance that applies this degree of heat to a psychological manifestation of coldness. This time the heart, too, is thrown into the bonfire—or rather, when Ethan Brand immolates himself, that organ retains its marble-like identity among his ashes, until it is raked away with the rest of the lime. "So much for the intellect!" Hawthorne moralizes.

> But where was the heart? That, indeed, had withered,—had contracted,—had hardened,—had perished! It had ceased to partake of the universal throb. He had lost his hold of the magnetic chain of humanity. He was no longer a brother man, opening the chambers or the dungeons of our common nature by the key of holy sympathy, which gave him a right to share in all its secrets; he was now a cold observer, looking on mankind as the subject of his experiment, and, at length, converting man and woman to be his puppets, and pulling the wires that moved them to such degrees of crime as were demanded for his study.

Here the writer obliquely betrays his hand, as the Dutch showman literally does when he manipulates the scenes in his box. So Hawthorne, running true to archetype, to that obsessive dark room which is always behind the focus of his vision, confesses himself an accomplice in the crimes he has ascribed to his puppet-characters. This is quite pardonable, since story-tellers must plot, and since Hawthorne—as a matter of fact—is tantalizingly unspecific about the misdeeds he attributes to his perverted alter ego. Ethan Brand is surrounded with innuendoes; but since these rely upon cross-reference to unwritten chapters of the abortive romance, much of the alleged malefaction is decontaminated for us. A muttered sentence alludes to a heroine, "the Esther of our tale," whom he seems to have coldly debauched by way of experiment; but that was, presumably, in another country. Hawthorne seems anxious to stress the "indistinct blackness" of such transgression, just as James refuses to specify the infantile misdemeanors of "The Turn of the Screw," preferring an appeal to "the reader's general vision of evil." We can hardly blame either Hawthorne or James for not having consorted with criminals, as Dostoevsky did, though their good conduct may have put them at a disadvantage when they attempted to probe into the motivation of crime.

But crime is incidental to sin, which is the single-minded motive of Ethan Brand—unlike Faust, who sins incidentally while pursuing illicit powers and pleasures. Unlike Orestes, hounded by Furies in consequence of his action, or Ibsen's Brand hounded by Trolls, Ethan Brand has acted in order that Furies or Trolls may hound him. Unlike Prometheus, he does not transgress with a purpose, humanitarian or utilitarian; what is unpardonable about the sin he investigates is that he wants to commit it for its own sake. That he discovers it within his own breast is not surprising, since it has been his fixed idea from the start. He need not have taken so much trouble to search for it, and Hawthorne has not troubled to follow the search. Instead, he has created a tragic hero without creating a tragedy, an agonist so completely cut off from "brotherhood with man and reverence for God" that his agony is a self-condemnation and his retribution is unrepentant. This exceeds the hybris of the Greeks; by the Christian calendar, it would seem to be the most excessive case of pride; and Hawthorne, ever strict in his casuistry, pushes his critique of the intellect to the verge of obscurantism. But is he being crotchety, or is he not prophetic, when he warns us against such dangers as may impend, with the triumph of cold-blooded experimentation over the sense of moral responsibility? And is it far-fetched to see, in Ethan Brand's lime-kiln, an adumbration of Los Alamos? Melville saw the immediate purport of Hawthorne's tale, which he praised with his usual generosity; for Melville, at its moment of publication, was completing the tragedy that Hawthorne could only adumbrate.

When William Butler Yeats sings of "the foul rag-and-bone shop of the heart," it is tempting to think of Hawthorne rummaging there, among the cobwebs, for curios which might acquire significance if rearranged in an appropriate context. Hawthorne himself had such a notion when he devised "A Virtuoso's Collection," an ingenious sketch which comprises a virtual catalogue for a museum of the time-worn symbols of myth and literature: notably the philosophers' stone, the Promethean fire, the burden of Christian; swords belonging to the illustrious heroes of romance; Nero's fiddle and Franklin's whistle, in the musical department; among the stuffed animals, Don Quixote's Rosinante and the wolf that suckled Romulus and Remus; Aladdin's lamp and Prospero's wand as instruments of imaginative evocation. Among Hawthorne's friends, it became a parlor-game to make contributions to this miscellaneous assortment of emblems and remarkables. We know that his wife adduced the congenial image of which he wrote: "My companion appeared to set great store upon some Egyptian darkness in a blacking jug." Appropriately, the door-keeper to the chimerical establishment is none other than our elusive friend, Peter Rugg; while the icily analytic virtuoso is another avatar of Ethan Brand's Dutch showman, the Wandering Jew. The item that takes his visitor's fancy most does not, at first, seem to be part of the exhibition:

> In the part of the hall which we had now reached I observed a curtain that descended from the ceiling to the floor in voluminous folds, of a depth, richness, and magnificence which I had never seen equalled. It was not to be doubted that this splendid though dark and solemn veil concealed a portion of the museum even richer in wonders than that through which I had already passed; but, on my attempting to grasp the edge of the curtain and draw it aside, it proved to be an illusive picture.

This, the virtuoso proudly explains, is the *trompe-l'oeil* painted by Parrhasius, which deluded Zeuxis in the classical anecdote, so that the visitor need not be greatly disturbed by the delusion. Nor is he, since he is used to being confined within four narrow walls, and since he is himself the consummate master of a two-dimensional art. Had his friend Melville visited the virtuoso's collection, we may surmise that he would have reacted differently. He would have banged his fist against the wall in Titanic rage, and clamored for a sight of what might lie beyond the curtain.

III

The Skeleton in the Closet

In his vignettes of the American scene, in his appraisals of historic tradition, in his anxiety over the self isolated individual, and in his curiosity to read the cosmic scheme of things, Hawthorne is truly the founding patriarch of our fiction, and sits upon its grandfather's chair with an air of authority. His position is so strategically taken, between the ethical and the esthetic spheres, that he retains his residence in both. As a moralist, he propounds an austere message; as an artist, he gracefully illustrates it. Although at times his premise may seem unduly fine-spun or fantastic, he manages to fill in the consequences with the utmost solidity—with that minuteness of touch which brings out a spiritual aspect in the commonest household articles, as painted by the Dutch masters. His apprenticeship as a writer of sketches makes itself felt in his later and longer fictions, where each of the neatly articulated chapters is a genre-painting, under a title which is usually pictorial and frequently symbolic. Sometimes, in the tales, a simple image becomes so fraught with an intricate idea that we have the impression of looking through a microscope at the Lord's Prayer engraved on the head of a pin. In the romances, conversely, it may seem that rather tenuous material is being richly elaborated, not to say heavily worked. When we compare the limited range of Hawthorne's dramatis personae with the innumerable beings that throng the pages of Balzac or Dickens or Tolstoy, the American novelist seems less humanly productive than his European contemporaries, albeit not so withdrawn and antisocial as some of his American characters.

But Hawthorne, who possessed the pioneer's skill at making virtues of necessities, not only made the most of his limitations by working within them; he transcended them by taking limitation as one of his principal themes. Not only did he cast a cold eye upon life; but, by the special damnation he meted out to his cold-hearted intellectuals, he made an oblique plea for companionship, and for the natural magnetism of society, which is quite as strong as the frank exhortations of Melville or Whitman. In coming to deal more directly and more searchingly with human relations, he had been coming toward the novel inevitably, yet fully aware that this developing medium would put increasing demands upon the experience of the author. Hence, with each of his books which might have passed for a novel, he was careful to claim the latitude of a romance. "I do not wish it to be a picture of life, but a romance, grim, grotesque, quaint," he writes in his notations for one of his last and most abortive romances, *The Ancestral Footstep.* In his published prefaces or introductory chapters, he warns his readers to expect a slight intermingling of the marvelous; and often, by way of contrast, he offers a matter-of-fact account of his personal circumstances. He even apologizes for this habit, in the preface to his final collection of tales, *The Snow-Image*:

> And, as for egotism, a person, who has been bur-
> rowing, to his utmost ability, into the depths of
> our common nature, for the purposes of psycho-
> logical romance,—and who pursues his researches
> in that dusky region, as he needs must, as well by
> the tact of sympathy as by the light of observation
> —will smile at incurring such an imputation in vir-
> tue of a little preliminary talk about his external
> habits, his abode, his casual associates, and other
> matters entirely upon the surface. These things hide
> the man, instead of displaying him. You must make
> quite another kind of inquest, and look through
> the whole range of his fictitious characters, good
> and evil, in order to detect any of his essential traits.

Here, at the very moment of deflecting attention from himself, Hawthorne invites a deeper scrutiny. He freely admits what we have been led to suspect: that his sources are internal, that—in his case, to a remarkably high degree—the act of creation is grounded in the process of introspection. If we say of him—as we do more readily of other novelists—that he creates a world of his own, it is *his own* that we should emphasize rather than *a world*. To consider his work as a whole is to watch the recurrence of certain thematic patterns so obsessive that, from another angle, they might well be regarded as complexes. Speaking of imagination in general, and in particular of the influence of the Maules over the dreams of the Pyncheons, Hawthorne predicts: "Modern psychology, it may be, will endeavor to reduce these alleged necromancies within a system, instead of rejecting them as altogether fabulous." Meanwhile the analytic approach of the psychologist is anticipated by the synthetic insight of the romancer; and it may be Hawthorne's inner conflict, his psychomachia, that stirs him to mythopoesis, that generates legends of his native land.

Insofar as we have been assuming that Hawthorne did not turn to romance-writing until his middle years, we have been overlooking his earliest published effort. He would undoubtedly have preferred us to do so; for *Fanshawe* is all too revealing in its thinness; our inquest is therefore all the more obliged to give it a glance. Written soon after Hawthorne's graduation from Bowdoin College, it is academic in every sense of the word. It may well head that inordinate list of first novels written out of college memories because the writer has so little else to write about. Most of them, in lieu of mature observation, draw upon sentimental fantasies or unappeased resentments. It might be said, to the slight advantage of *Fanshawe*, that it falls into the former category. A series of attempts to transfer the action from gown to town and beyond, stopping for refreshment at a laboriously jolly tavern on the edge of the campus, is foredoomed to bookishness. We never learn the first name of the titular character; but this trait of aloofness does as much as anything else to characterize him. High-minded and absent-minded, the pallid Fanshawe dreams of fame in his solitary study, while his fellow students, notably Edward Walcott, admire him from a distance. Occasionally, he goes for walks in the woods; and it is upon one such occasion that the single adventure of his career, and of the book, takes place; the heroine, Ellen Langton, is abducted by the villain, a swarthy angler; and, after a chase in the manner of Fenimore Cooper, who is it but Fanshawe that rescues her?

The manner in which that rescue is affected could not be attributed to anyone except Hawthorne himself. When Fanshawe overtakes the couple, he stands high above them upon a precipice. Seeking to climb it and grapple with him, the abductor nearly reaches the top; whereupon he slips and plunges dizzily to his death, overwhelmed not by the hand of Fanshawe but by his sheer inert moral superiority. Being too noble for this world, Fanshawe is much too noble for marriage; and the kiss with which Ellen rewards him is their first and last embrace. Since his friend Edward is also in love with her, a triangular situation is dimly adumbrated; but since this is neither *The Sorrows of Young Werther* nor *The Blithedale Romance*, the danger is averted without recourse to suicide for the third party. Fanshawe retires to his studies, and soon to a premature grave. The inscription on his tombstone is copied from that of Nathanael Mather: "The ashes of a hard student and a good scholar." But Mather's epitaph, though Hawthorne does not tell us so, also included the phrase "—and a great Christian." That last consolation is here withheld; and though there is a more or less happy ending, with Edward and Ellen married, Hawthorne rounds out their story by imparting the cheerless fact that they left no progeny. Twelve years afterward, in saying farewell to the little room where he wrote *Fanshawe* and so many subsequent tales, he recorded his conviction that nothing really existed, that all was "but the thinnest substance of a dream—till the heart be touched." Romance was still a blank page which awaited its boldest rubric, *The Scarlet Letter*.

Having first confronted that book as a classic of the schoolroom, we are cushioned against the shock we should properly feel: the realization that, at the midpoint of the nineteenth century, the primly subversive chronicler of the Puritans could base his first major work on an all but unmentionable subject. Not that this subject, the breach of the Seventh Commandment, is the theme of the book; rather it is the presupposition, the original sin from which everything follows. If there was any pleasure in it, any joy of the senses, that has been buried in the past, and Hawthorne has no intention of reanimating it. But its presence in the accusing shape of the majuscule, insisted on with every appearance of the heroine, lends the most vivid particularity to Hawthorne's general vision of evil, and motivates that unspecified remorse to which his characters are so habitually prone. A is for adultery—could any lesson be plainer than the stigma imposed by his title, "the general symbol at which the preacher and moralist might point?" But morality is not to be so arbitrarily spelled out; nor is it calculated, on this occasion, to warrant any confidence in preachers; and, as for symbols, they derive their ultimate meaning from the emotions with which men and women invest them. The letter A, on the bosom of Chaucer's Prioress, had signified the power of sacred rather than profane love: *Amor vincit omnia*. Hawthorne had even been tempted to ask himself whether another scarlet letter meant "adulteress" or

"admirable." By the final phrase of his book, the badge
of dishonor has become a heraldic escutcheon: "ON A
FIELD, SABLE, THE LETTER A, GULES."

The color-scheme is all the more arresting because the
spot of flaming red is set off against the usual background of somber blacks and Puritan grays. The initial
sentence introduces a chorus of elders clad in "sad-
colored garments," standing before "the black flower
of civilized society, a prison." The opening of the prison
door is "like a black shadow emerging into sunshine";
but the sunshine, as Hawthorne retrospectively sighed,
is conspicuous by its rarity. The dark-haired Hester
Prynne, emerging to mount the pillory, babe in arms,
is presented as a virtual madonna, despite the token of
self-denunciation which she has embroidered into her
attire. When the Reverend Mr. Dimmesdale is invited
to expostulate with her, "as touching the vileness and
blackness of your sin," the irony is precarious; for we
are not yet in a position to recognize him as her guilty
partner; nor is it until the next chapter that we witness
her recognition-scene with her long estranged and elderly husband, who conceals his identity under the
name of Chillingworth. The interrelationship between
open shame and secret guilt is dramatized by a tense
alternation of public tableaux and private interviews.
All men are potentially sinners, though they profess
themselves saints. Here in old Boston, as in the Salem
of "Young Goodman Brown," the Black Man does a
thriving traffic in witchcraft. If the letter is his mark,
as Hester tells her daughter, it must also be accepted as
the universal birthmark of mankind. Once, when she
tries to fling it away, it is borne back to her upon a

stream; thereafter she accepts it as her doom; she learns to live with it.

Therein she becomes innately superior to those fellow citizens who despise her, and whose trespasses are compounded by their hypocrisies. Their social ostracism may turn her into a "type of . . . moral solitude"; but it endows her with "a sympathetic knowledge of the hidden sin in other hearts," which ultimately leads to a kind of redemption, as it does with the virtuous prostitutes of Victor Hugo and Dostoevsky. The letter proves to be a talisman which establishes bonds of sympathy; whereas the proud mantle of Lady Eleanor cut her off from sympathetic involvements. Though Hester lives a life of saintly penance, she does not repent her unhallowed love. On the contrary, she shields her repentant lover, and tells him: "What we did has a consecration of its own." Since their lapse was natural, it is pardonable; it has a validity which her marriage with Chillingworth seems to have lacked. What is unnatural is the pharisaical role into which Dimmesdale is consequently forced. He cannot ease his conscience by wearing a black veil, like the minister of Hawthorne's parable; for he is not mourning the hidden sin of others; he is hiding his own, which is palpable enough. The pulpit and the pillory are the contrasting scenes of his triumph and his self-abasement. His internal anguish, projected against the sky in a gigantic A, is finally relieved when he bares his breast to reveal the counterpart of Hester's letter. Hawthorne is purposefully vague in reporting these phenomena and whether they happen by miracle, hallucination, or expressionistic device. His Dostoevskian point is that every happening must be an accusation to the sinner, who must end by testifying against himself.

Hawthorne rejects an alternative he ironically suggests, whereby the supposedly blameless pastor dies in the arms of the fallen woman in order to typify Christian humility. Nor is her rehabilitation achieved at the expense of the cleric's integrity, as it would be for Anatole France's *Thaïs*. Nor is he thoroughly corrupted, like an evangelical beachcomber out of Somerset Maugham. Arthur Dimmesdale is an unwilling hypocrite, who purges himself by means of open confession. Among the possible morals, the one that Hawthorne selects is: "Be true! Be true! Be true! Show freely to the world, if not your worst, yet some trait whereby the worst may be inferred." Hester is true; and so is Dimmesdale at last; but the third injunction rings hollow. These two have been a sinful pair, and he—by Hawthorne's standard—has been more sinful than she. But the most sinful member of the triangle is, most unnaturally, the injured party. Dimmesdale atones for his trespass by his death; Hester for hers by her life; but for Chillingworth, avenging their violation of his existence, there can be no atonement. "That old man's revenge has been blacker than my sin," exclaims Dimmesdale. "He has violated, in cold blood, the sanctity of a human heart. Thou and I, Hester, never did so." While their trespass has been sensual passion, Chillingworth's is intellectual pride. In short, it is the unpardonable sin of Ethan Brand, of Hawthorne's dehumanized experimentalists, and of that spiritualized Paul Pry whose vantage-point comes so uncomfortably close to the author's. Chillingworth, whose assumed name betrays his frigid nature, plays the role of the secret sharer, prying into his wife's illicit affair, spying upon her lover unawares, and pulling the strings of the psychological romance.

The drama centers less on the colloquies between husband and wife, or those between wife and lover, than on the relationship of lover and husband, each concealing something from the other. "The misshapen scholar" is a man of science, a doctor who treats the agonizing Dimmesdale as his patient. One day the latter inquires where he has gathered such strange dark herbs.

"Even in the graveyard here at hand," answered the physician, continuing his employment. "They are new to me. I found them growing on a grave, which bore no tombstone, nor other memorial of the dead man, save these ugly weeds, that have taken upon themselves to keep him in remembrance. They grew out of his heart, and typify, it may be, some hideous secret that was buried with him, and which he had done better to confess during his lifetime."

"Perchance," said Mr. Dimmesdale, "he earnestly desired it, but could not."

"And wherefore?" rejoined the physician. "Wherefore not; since all powers of nature call so earnestly for the confession of sin, that these black weeds have sprung up out of a buried heart, to make manifest an unspoken crime?"

"That, good sir, is but a fantasy of yours," replied the minister. "There can be, if I forebode aright, no power, short of the Divine mercy, to disclose, whether by uttered words, or by type or emblem, the secrets that may be buried with a human

heart. The heart, making itself guilty of such secrets, must perforce hold them, until the day when
all hidden things shall be revealed."

If the minister cannot shrive himself, the physician
has a disease he cannot cure. Yet it is his concentrated
malevolence, more than anything else, that implants the
idea of confessing in Dimmesdale's mind. Whether
Chillingworth may be his double or else a demon, the
spokesman for Dimmesdale's conscience or a devil's
emissary—these are possibilities which are raised but
scarcely probed. He himself concedes that he is per-
forming a fiend-like office, but considers this "a dark
necessity," the inevitable consequence of Hester's down-
fall, perhaps of Calvinistic predestination. "It is our
fate," he warns her. "Let the black flower blossom as
it may!" At the outset, when Esther was released from
the jail, it was compared to a black flower; and afterward, because Dimmesdale unburdens himself, black
weeds will not grow upon his grave. The color of the
lovers is red, which stands for blood, for life instead of
death; and their expiated sin is incarnate in the elfin
fairness of their innocent child, the black-eyed Pearl,
whose name betokens purity and whose radiance brings
a few sunny touches into the book. When we read, in
its concluding pages, that she grew up an heiress and
traveled abroad, we realize that we can pursue her further adventures through the novels of Henry James.

The Scarlet Letter, because it is set in the past, is the
only romance of Hawthorne's in which the past is not
a problem. He contrives a transition to the present
through that convention of the historical novel which
evokes the story from faded relics and fictitious docu-

ments. The extensive sketch that precedes the extended tale likewise gives him an opportunity, as an evicted job-holder, to make his sardonic farewell to the Custom House. "A better book than I shall ever write was there," he muses as he settles down again in his mirrored chamber, watches the moonlight fusing with the glow of coals at the hearth, and warms to the dream that will convert snow-images into the smouldering creatures of his fiction. Yet, from the midst of his next book, *The House of the Seven Gables*, he pauses to comment: "A romance on the plan of *Gil Blas*, adapted to American society and manners, would cease to be a romance." No, it would be sheer reality; the prospect America spread before the casual traveler, with its crude exertions and its flashy successes, was indeed the stuff of the picaresque novel. Turning home—with a vengeance—to contemporary Salem, Hawthorne was bound to connect it with "a bygone time," and to see that connection as the main issue. Nor could he fail to have been profoundly impressed by the details of a recent local crime—a wealthy householder murdered by his nephew—of which the state's attorney, Daniel Webster, had declared: "Its blackness is not illuminated by a single spark of contrition; not a ray of penitence falls upon it; it is all ink."

This coalesced with other hints and memorables: a curse laid on Hawthorne's witch-hanging ancestors, their half-forgotten claims to an estate, the misfortune of inheriting a large fortune, the impact of the dead upon the living, the caprice of a ray of sunlight falling upon a seated corpse in a darkened room. All these associations find their haven, and Hawthorne's sense of milieu finds its most substantial embodiment, in the rambling and weathered house itself, and in the pattern of years and lives it commemorates. Though it is not exactly "a gray feudal castle," it stimulates his talents for description, and accommodates itself to the machinery of Gothic romance. Moreover, it provides a theater —the metaphor is Hawthorne's—for the rehearsal of our social history in terms of the conflict between those well-known families, the patrician Haves and the plebeian Have-nots. Emile Zola would soon be tracing the emergence of modern France, in twenty volumes, through the entangled genealogies of the climbing Rougons and the proletarian Macquarts. Thomas Mann, at the end of the century, would chronicle the greatness and decline of a German burgher dynasty in his first novel, *Buddenbrooks.* There, as in *The House of the Seven Gables,* death is the earliest visitor to the proud mansion. For Hawthorne too, not less than for Zola, the family feud is a class struggle. The Maules have owned the land and built the house; the Pyncheons have been the exploiters, and are the possessors. The moral is "that the wrong-doing of one generation lives into the successive ones"; and the wrong, to be painfully specific, resides in "ill-gotten gold, or real estate."

Sins of fathers visited on children, love of money as the root of evil—such assumptions are of a Biblical orthodoxy. But, more immediately behind Hawthorne's book, there is also a decade of intensive radicalism, an international discussion of the question "What is property?", which the socialist Proudhon succinctly answered, "Theft." Hawthorne itemizes that sweeping indictment. All his misgivings over the dead hand of the past, in this context, register as protests against inherited ownership. He even entertains the hypothesis that the original sin may be capitalism. "What we call real estate—the solid ground to build a house on—is the broad foundation on which nearly all the guilt of this world rests," argues Clifford Pyncheon in hectic revulsion. Melville again put his sensitive finger upon the emotional mainspring when he praised the passage where Clifford, posted at his spectatorial window, feels momentarily impelled to plunge into the procession that marches by in the street below. "This long-buried man," imprisoned for a murder he did not commit, has been "summoned forth from his living tomb"; but the claustral atmosphere of the house prolongs the "black shadow" of his imprisonment. As "an abortive lover of the beautiful," he can do no more than blow soap-bubbles—"brilliant fantasies"—from his balcony; and when his sister Hepzibah persuades him to go to church, they are inhibited by the thought: "We are ghosts." The withered spinster, Hepzibah, is the incarnation of decayed gentility; and the little shop, to which her family pride is reduced, is her ineffectual way of opening an intercourse with the world.

Though she seems to have only one regular customer, the boy who keeps returning for confections, the tread of passing steps is intermittently varied by the tinkling of the shop-bell. An impression of movement outside, of currents eddying by, is conveyed to us by such indirect means; but everything seems to stand still within the house, where we share the limiting outlook of its few inhabitants, until the intrusion of the ruthless cousin who is its human counterpart. The smile of Judge Pyncheon, matched by the scowl of the timid old maid, should be a double warning against deceptive

appearances; for the Judge's visit, in quest of the family
secret, terminates in an apoplectic stroke; and the climactic chapter is a still life in the grimmest sense im-
aginable: *une nature morte*. Hawthorne had kept a
solitary vigil with the live figures of Dimmesdale and
Ethan Brand. Now his evocative fancy broods over
Judge Pyncheon's body, as the Judge's watch ticks off
the hours of what was to have been a busy day and
what will always remain a ghostly night. Dickens imi-
tated the morbid playfulness of this set-piece in *Bleak
House*; but there the painted allegory of Lincoln's Inn
points to a mystery which can be handled by detective
methods. Here we are present at a mock funeral, as it
were, where the round of appointments and commit-
tees, the bland self-interest and the professional bon-
homie of the politician are reduced to nothingness by
the gloating eulogy; where the ambition mocked at
by the heading, "Governor Pyncheon," is definitively
blacked out. "There is no window. There is no face!
An infinite, inscrutable blackness has annihilated sight!
Where is our universe?"

The prologue to this completely static episode is the
single dynamic chapter of the book, "The Flight of the
Two Owls." The catastrophe, like the Giant Despair in
pursuit of Bunyan's pilgrims, drives Clifford and Hepzibah out of the house and on to the train. The newly
constructed railroad is the vehicle of all that has passed
them by, of the progress that their conservatism has
previously rejected; and for Clifford it is strangely ex-
hilarating, stirring him to a valedictory harangue which
anticipates Ibsen's *Ghosts*. His denunciation of home
as a prison is also a rhapsody in praise of locomotion.
The journey is fated to break down in anticlimax; but

poetic justice plots with coincidence to deal kindly with brother and sister; it is disclosed that the original sinner, for whose guilt Clifford has suffered, was the late Judge. The residual happiness of the Pyncheons is supplemented by the betrothal of a younger couple, who have let fresh air into the musty abode. Phoebe, the country cousin, blends this freshness with a strain of practicality, "as if she were a verse of household poetry." Holgrave, the lodger, is the hopeful young American of his generation, self-made, self-taught, self-reliant. By profession he is a daguerreotypist, the practitioner of a technological art; or, as he more engagingly puts it, "I make pictures out of sunshine." By credo he is a socialist, a disciple of Fourier; and though marriage and middle age will temper his advanced views, he is Hawthorne's chief spokesman for the present and critic of "the moss-grown and rotten past." When Phoebe suspects him of being "a lawless person," Hepzibah replies that "he has a law of his own."

But, although Holgrave is thus a link with the outer world of the realistic novel, he has his romantic part to play. By revealing himself as a descendant of the downtrodden Maules, he completes the "long drama of wrong and retribution." The feud is over; the ghosts are exorcised; the sun shines; and the desiccated garden flowers into another of Hawthorne's domestic Edens, though the happy Maules and the surviving Pyncheons have wisely decided to begin their lives anew in a country house. In the anticipatory tale of "Peter Goldthwaite's Treasure," an old house was torn down through a futile search for its treasure; and the house-bound Peter Goldthwaite found release through that unintended gesture of iconoclasm. The Heartbreak House of Bernard Shaw is bombed; the spoils of James's Poynton go up in smoke; the cherry orchard gets chopped down in Chekhov's dramatic parable. But Hawthorne leaves the House of the Seven Gables to moulder, and in the long run to become a show-place for antiquarian nostalgia. Why should it be razed? So long as the heart survived the holocaust, he had prophesied, customs would not change greatly and institutions would be rebuilt along all-too-familiar lines. Expansionists could call for more stately mansions, equip them with the most modern conveniences, and lay out suburban real-estate developments. Hawthorne foresaw that, wherever there were closets, sooner or later a skeleton would be rattling. "Life is made up of marble and mud," he said, varying his tropes to fit his building materials. There is more idealism in Victor Hugo's formula, mud but soul—*la boue, mais de l'âme.* But if the house is like a human being, then the marble is a fitting domicile for the soul.

> Behold, therefore, a palace! Its splendid walls, and suites of spacious apartments, are floored with a mosaic-work of costly marbles; the most transparent windows of plate-glass; its high cornices are gilded, and its ceilings gorgeously painted; and a lofty dome—through which, from the central pavement, you may gaze up to the sky, as with no obstructing medium between—surmounts the whole. With what fairer and nobler emblem could any man desire to shadow forth his character? Ah! but in some low and obscure nook,—some narrow closet on the ground-floor, shut, locked and bolted, and the key flung away,—or beneath the marble pavement, in a stagnant water-puddle, with the richest pattern of

mosaic-work above,—may lie a corpse, half de-cayed, and still decaying, and diffusing its death-scent through the palace!

The Scarlet Letter and *The House of the Seven Ga-bles* constitute, with *The Blithedale Romance*, a New England trilogy, published successively in three fruitful years. Breaking away from an immersion in the historic setting, Hawthorne was free to pay his respects to the present, and even—like his Concord neighbors—to spec-ulate over the future. But since his emancipation was so hard-won, he was not likely to compromise it by unreservedly accepting the great American dream of Utopia. He had shared that ideal, to the extent of par-ticipating in the socialistic experiment at Brook Farm; and that participation was "certainly the most romantic episode of his own life,—essentially a day-dream, and yet a fact," as he acknowledged in the preface to *The Blithedale Romance* ten years later. In claiming the romancer's prerogative, he was astutely disclaiming any coincidental resemblance between his characters and the Transcendentalists; he was also hinting, by his title, that utopian colonies might be as fantastic as works of fic-tion. The proper name "Blithedale," a Hawthornesque modulation of "happy valley," takes on an additional overtone from the Owenite settlement at Hopedale. If this is a rural idyll, "a modern Arcadia," it is an uncom-fortably frosty one, where winter snowscapes and farm-ing chores make their comment on visionary aspirations toward "the better life." And if it is a community, as it professes to be, to the fullest degree of social coopera-tion, it is one where individualism still predominates, and individuals have the greatest trouble in understand-

ing one another. The cast, as in *The House of the
Seven Gables*, is restricted to about half-a-dozen persons—an artistic economy which, under the more con-
stricting conditions, begins to pinch.

Hawthorne for once deputes the telling of the story
to a character in it, the minor poet Miles Coverdale,
younger and more blithe but no less self-effacing than
Clifford Pyncheon. In his own words, Coverdale acts
as a chorus, "aloof from the possibility of personal con-
cernment." In order to keep in touch with the intimate
sentiments of the others, he must do a good deal of
eavesdropping; he "oversees" one scene while concealed
in a tree; and chance, or Hawthorne, stages another before a window just across from his own. His name,
which has an English literary flavor, in accordance with
Hawthorne's usage, conveys a hint of his function: he
covers the dale, or possibly is covered by it. If the suffix links him to Dimmesdale in *The Scarlet Letter*, then
Chillingworth should be linked with Hollingsworth in
The Blithedale Romance. In each case, there is attraction and repulsion between two opposing tempera-
ments, passive and active, sensitive and sinister, other
self and evil genius. The pair whose names have *worth*
as the terminal syllable are subjected to the severest
revaluation. The *donnée* for Hollingsworth, set down
in Hawthorne's notebooks, was the type of "a modern
reformer," whose fanatical eloquence would win many
converts for his crotchety doctrines, were he not suddenly to be discredited as an escaped lunatic. But Hawthorne did not go that far afield for his swarthy, black-
browed portrait of the philosophical blacksmith, the
self-educated lecturer, who is horrified at Coverdale's
explanation of Fourier's socialism:

"Let me hear no more of it!" cried he, in utter disgust. "I will never forgive this fellow! He has committed the unpardonable sin; for what more monstrous iniquity could the Devil himself contrive than to choose the selfish principle,—the principle of all human wrong, the very blackness of man's heart, the portion of ourselves which we shudder at, and which it is the whole aim of spiritual discipline to eradicate,—to choose it as the master-workman of his system?"

Hollingsworth's rival theory is based on the altruistic principle. He proposes to take control of Blithedale, and devote it to his philanthropical scheme for the reformation of criminals. Here again, since Hawthorne was not Dostoevsky, he had no way of testing this project, or of making it sound plausible; and, accordingly, the figure of Hollingsworth is diagnosed rather than characterized. What Coverdale recoils from is not madness, but "a great black ugliness of sin, which he proposed to collect out of a thousand human hearts, and that we should spend our lives in an experiment of transmuting it into virtue!" Worst of all, in overestimating this potential of goodness, Hollingsworth has overlooked the impurity of his own motivation, an egoism even less pardonable than Ethan Brand's since it poses as love of his fellow men.

Even more strikingly than with his heroes, Hawthorne tends to double his heroines, and to present them in a polar relationship which accords with all the romantic stereotypes of the delicate blonde and the spirited brunette, as well as with Hawthorne's inveterate symbolism of innocence and experience. In *The Blithedale Ro-*

mance, this differentiation starts with the heroine's names; Priscilla, so typically Puritan; Zenobia, so queenly and oriental. The waif-like seamstress Priscilla, the "shadowy snow-maiden," is manifestly the more conventional. The purses she continually knits are so finely meshed that they seem to have no aperture. If they are "a symbol of Priscilla's own mystery," as Coverdale surmises, her mystery might simply be virginity. The comparison with Zenobia could not be more strongly marked; for this "magnificent woman" carries with her the imputation of having "lived and loved." Her symbol is a single hot-house flower, brilliant, exotic, and costly, worn in her hair, which is glossy, dark, and of singular abundance. Her presence, like that of Beatrice Rappaccini, is perfumed with the aura of sexual danger. A chance remark about Eve, dropped in Zenobia's first conversation with the narrator, provokes his penetrating eye to undress her mentally. Appalled by his boldness, he apologizes to the reader by lamenting that physical womanliness has been almost refined away nowadays. But, for Coverdale, Zenobia is Lilith rather than Eve. Though she is very much of a woman, she does not think of him as much of a man; and in a later scene she tells him off for his constant espionage, his eavesdropper's attitude, his intellectualization of the emotions.

Yet the situation may be mysterious enough to warrant the spying and groping on his part. For Zenobia and Priscilla turn out to be daughters of one father, poor old Moodie, who has seen more respected days under the name of Fauntleroy—and perhaps at other times under other names, such as Blake's whimsical Nobodaddy. Furthermore, each half-sister has a curious

connection with the malign Professor Westervelt, whose
coal-black beard, grimacing false teeth, and snake-like
stick proclaim him a charlatan, if not the devil himself.
Priscilla, it surprisingly appears, is none other than the
famous Veiled Lady; and though her white veil is "sup-
posed to insulate her from the material world," she re-
sponds as a kind of medium to the mesmeric stimulus
of Westervelt. Hollingsworth frees her, after a hypnotic
battle of wills between the reformer and the mesmerist.
This unites Priscilla with Hollingsworth, in spite of the
jealousy of Zenobia, who has already betrayed her sister
and now can only betray herself. The manner of her suicide was determined by Hawthorne's poignant remembrance of a night when neighbors had summoned him
from the Old Manse to drag the Concord River for the
body of a distraught young woman. It was on first-hand
observation he drew, when he depicted Zenobia floating
down the "Black River of Death." In her mortality, as
in her sensuality, Zenobia personifies the flesh. By the
time her antithesis, the fragile Priscilla, emerges as the
one strong character in the parable, a consolation to
the penitent Hollingsworth, it should be clear that she
is the personification of spirit. As for the lonely bache-
lor, Coverdale, he concludes twelve years later by confessing his love for her; yet he has never penetrated beyond the transcendental veil.

The recent death by shipwreck of Margaret Fuller, so
vital an exponent of new womanhood and so nearly an
associate of Brook Farm, did not strengthen Hawthorne's protestations that he was merely romancing
after all. But though the intellectual environs of Boston
provided many targets for caricature, that was not Hawthorne's game, albeit it might occasionally be James's.

What is so telling about *The Blithedale Romance*, is
that, from the very hotbed of ultramodernism, it could
revert to a timeless Bunyanesque allegory, a medieval
debate between body and soul. But the train ran in both
directions for the author of "The Celestial Railroad."
He would not have been content for long in either of
Emerson's factions, "the party of hope" or "the party
of memory." Coverdale had backed away from Blithedale to talk with the "respectable old blockheads" of
Cambridge, and to renew his grip "on one or two ideas
which had not come into vogue since yesterday morning." In one of his last impressions of Zenobia, he fancies that she might resort to dagger or poison, were she
living in Italy rather than in New England. Hawthorne
was thus prepared for the climactic change that would
permit him to spend several years in Europe, and to set
against the Italian scene the latest and longest romance
he was to publish. In the preface to *The Marble Faun*,
he joins that band of traveling Americans who distinguish between the old and new worlds in terms of the
picturesque and the commonplace—or, in more Hawthornesque phraseology, shadow and sunlight respectively. He seems ready to write off the homeland for
romantic purposes, and to pay the old world the dubious
tribute of seeking among its ruins for crimes of passion.

He came late to European travel, so important a part
of education for most American writers and artists; but
he was not unresponsive; and his book is an educational,
a pedagogical novel, a *Bildungsroman* or novel of formation—its English edition pertinently entitled *Transformation*. A model for this broader enterprise, which he
mentions in passing, was Madame de Staël's *Corinne, or
Italy*, half-romance, half-guidebook, dominated by a

black-haired bluestocking who is the author's idealized self-portrait. Arriving at Rome as a tourist, if not as a pilgrim, Hawthorne must have been dazzled by the invitations it offered for word-painting; and, having tried so hard to look beyond the utilitarian surfaces of American life, he must have been embarrassed by the overplus of symbols which had virtually outlived their meanings. His *French and Italian Notebooks* reveal him as an earnest but imperceptive museum-goer, seriously troubled about the display of the nude. Perhaps the most puritanical paragraph in *The Marble Faun* is one suggesting that the damaged frescoes of Giotto and Cimabue be whitewashed over, in all charity. But the ethical comes to terms with the esthetic in the Miltonic conception of an unpainted masterpiece showing the fight between angels and smoke-blackened demons. On the opening page, which ushers in the four principals as they stroll through a gallery of sculpture, Hawthorne lingers over "a symbol (as apt at this moment as it was two thousand years ago) of the Human Soul with its choice of Innocence or Evil close at hand in the pretty figure of a child, clasping a dove to her bosom but assaulted by a snake."

Cross-reference to works of art is a technique of characterization in *The Marble Faun*, as it is with Proust. Since many of Hawthorne's characters seem to possess a sculptural quality it is not surprising that his protagonist should have been modeled on a Greek statue, the Faun of Praxiteles named for an Italian sculptor Donatello, and made to pose for a bust by Hawthorne's observer and commentator, the American sculptor Kenyon. But, since life is made up of mud as well as marble, this naïve child of nature who hates the dark, and whose ambiguous ears are vestiges of his animal origin, cannot be humanized without facing the problems that human beings are heir to. Sporting like a creature of pagan myth, on the wild Campagna or in the Arcadian grounds of the Villa Borghese, he seems to belong to "the Golden Age, before mankind was burdened with sin and sorrow, and before pleasure had been darkened with those shadows that bring it into high relief, and make it happiness." His companion, the artist Miriam, was suggested by the sight of an English Jewess at a banquet; the white marble of her complexion and the raven black of her hair had exercised a peculiar fascination over Hawthorne, which he had tried to catch in his notebook, and which is reflected in his delineation. Whatever the obscurities of Miriam's background, she is obviously related to Zenobia and Beatrice Rappaccini. She is the ripest of Hawthorne's dark ladies, and more aggressive than her victimized predecessors. The "warmth and passionateness" of her paintings are concentrated upon the vengeful spectacle of woman shedding man's blood: Jael and Sisera, Judith and Holofernes, Salome and John the Baptist.

These are the pictorial archetypes of Miriam's animus; but they do not express her plight as aptly as Guido Reni's portrait of Beatrice Cenci, the painting that Hawthorne seems to have most admired. What fascinated him was the idea of auburn-haired innocence caught in a net of corruption, from which the only escape was to suborn an accomplice into crime. Hilda, the fair young American girl in white, has taken a copy of this "fallen angel"; but the impassioned Miriam understands her as the inexperienced copyist could not.

Hilda's emblems are doves, which she feeds at the Virgin's shrine near the tower where she dwells. Miriam's emblem, at the other extreme, is the serpent's coil that metaphorically binds her to her accomplice. Whereas she feels an affinity with Kenyon's voluptuous statue of Cleopatra, Kenyon wishes to sculpture the ethereal Hilda as "maidenhood gathering a snowdrop." Hence the two heroines complement each other, like the half-sisters of *The Blithedale Romance*. The mysteries of the plot are as devious as the catacomb, "the labyrinth of darkness," through which it leads. The clue is the unspoken hold exerted over Miriam by the Shadow, agent of blackness and model for her man-hating portraiture, who reappears in other guises and disguises like the Wandering Jew, and—when he has been fully dispatched—is given the funeral of a Capuchin monk. A corpse was becoming as inevitable a feature of Hawthorne's romances as it is in a murder-mystery; and he had actually happened upon this funeral apparition during a Roman tour. The murder itself, along with other particulars, may have been inspired by Shelley's *Cenci,* where the location is also a precipice:

> At noonday here
> 'Tis twilight, and at sunset blackest night.

Miriam is morally responsible for the deed. She has been goaded to it, and Donatello has done it. Though she has been loth "to stain his joyous nature with the blackness of a woe like mine," he has voluntarily joined her in guilt. So, involuntarily, has Hilda, through the accident of having been a witness. She was an onlooker; but she is no longer a bystander, since guilty knowledge is accompanied by a recognition: "While there is a single guilty person in the universe, each innocent one must feel his innocence tortured by that guilt. Your deed, Miriam, has darkened the whole sky!" The contagion of evil from the dead man, which spread from Miriam to Donatello, has even attainted the virginal Hilda. All of them have been parties to, in the fullest sense, a mortal fall. Unwilling to expose her friend, yet unable to bear the unexpected burden of complicity, the perplexed Hilda gravitates toward Saint Peter's, and seeks to relieve her conscience at the confessional. Hawthorne's ambivalent interest in Catholicism reaches a culmination in this episode, which has an instructive parallel in Charlotte Brontë's *Villette*. Since Hilda— as she staunchly reaffirms—is a daughter of the Puritans, she cannot receive the sacrament; but it is her unabsolved confession that sets off the process of secular judgment. Meanwhile, the scene has shifted from the feverish capital to the fresher air of the countryside, where Kenyon abandons his artistic reserve to become the father-confessor of the fugitive lovers. The bond of their love, he counsels them, is intertwined with the black threads of their transgression. They will be doubly bound in their sufferings, not unlike Dante's Paolo and Francesca.

The latter half of the book is somewhat discursive, flagging and reviving to the rhythm of flight and return, and rather evasive in its treatment of Hilda's temporary disappearance. Hawthorne was prevailed upon to add a postscript tieing up the loose ends of his *dénouement*. Deliberately he winds up his story amid the confusion of the carnival season, letting his characters bedazzle and elude one another through the Roman streets: Donatello and Miriam masquerading in colorful peasant costumes with black visors, Hilda in a becoming white domino. Donatello has been briefly glimpsed in the white robe of a penitent, and he will eventually disappear into one of Rome's prisons; while Miriam is last seen at prayer in that least parochial of churches, the Pantheon. Their expiation and sacrifice bring the American couple together, and Kenyon proposes two or three morals to Hilda. One is the view which primitivists have held, from Rousseau to D. H. Lawrence, that creatures born for happiness are thwarted by the unhappy conditions of modern existence. It might be answered that man differs from the animals by being in Nietzsche's phrase, a sick animal; and that his sickness is the precondition of civilization. "In the black depths the Faun had found a soul, and was struggling with it towards the light of heaven." This is the transformation, the transfiguration that stimulates an alternative moral:

> "Here comes my perplexity," continued Kenyon. "Sin has educated Donatello, and elevated him. Is sin, then,—which we deem such a dreadful blackness in the universe,—is it, like sorrow, merely an element of human education, through which we struggle to a higher and purer state than we could otherwise have attained? Did Adam fall, that we might ultimately rise to a far loftier paradise than his?"

Such, at all events, is the Augustinian doctrine of *felix culpa*, the fortunate sin that endowed mankind with a conscience, the trial and error that taught him to discriminate between good and evil; and such is the resolution that Hawthorne attains, in the endless interplay between black and white. But Kenyon's theology is too

sophisticated for Hilda. Life will be simpler for them
when they have married, and returned to the prelap-
sarian paradise on the other side of the Atlantic.

Hawthorne waxes nostalgic in comparing the "bottled
sunshine" of Donatello's wine with New England cider.
Italy gave him more reason than Massachusetts to complain of the unwholesomeness of old houses. The villa
he rented became the seat of Donatello's faun-like ancestors; and though it is only an incidental locale, re-
named it dominated the subtitle of *The Marble Faun,
or The Romance of Monte Beni*. *The Old Manse, The
House of the Seven Gables, The Blithedale Romance,
Tanglewood Tales*—the homing instinct comes out in
Hawthorne's titles, and not least in his volume of English impressions, *Our Old Home*. The last of the many
mansions that stand by the wayside of his pilgrimage is
"that castle in the air," or more precisely "that visionary
hall in England, with its surrounding woods and fine
lawns, and beckoning shadows at the ancient windows,"
which haunted his subsiding imagination. Serving as
consul in—of all unromantic places—Liverpool, he became more and more attached to the notion of a young
American returning to the land of his ancestry and inheriting an estate. This is the theme on which Henry
James was to devise such resourceful variations, most explicitly in "The Sense of the Past." Mark Twain was to
treat it satirically in *The American Claimant*; and
Thackeray had approached it, from the other direction,
in *The Virginians*. This would be a homecoming for
the American cousin, as Hawthorne conceived him.
"O home, my home, my forefathers' home!" he would
exclaim, ". . . I have come back to thee!" But these
emotions would be mixed with others stemming from

Yankee independence, and voicing that democratic critique of feudal privilege which is so stalwart in Hawthorne's *English Notebooks* and *Our Old Home*.

On his tours of duty, where Hawthorne had indulged his predilection for ivy-encrusted manor houses, he had been struck by the legend of a bloody footstep imprinted on stone. Somehow this seemed to typify what repelled him in his quest for tradition. He planned to make the heir renounce his heritage, arguing that the past was a millstone around the neck of the mother country. The moral would be: "Let the past alone . . . Onward, onward, onward!" Yet that very adverb, as we have noticed, is Hawthorne's reiterated apology for looking backward. He could never leave the past alone, although—as he grew older—he grew more concerned with the prospect of a personal future, "the strange idea of undyingness." His posthumous fragments comprise four abortive romances, ranging in scale from rough outline to labored revision. Two are "transatlantic," *The Ancestral Footstep* and *Dr. Grimshawe's Secret*; two are "romances of immortality," *Septimius Felton, or The Elixir of Life* and *The Dolliver Romance*. They overlap considerably in their joint endeavor to transcend the barriers of space and time. Hawthorne had utilized an elixir of youth as a pretext for satire in his tale, "Dr. Heidegger's Experiment." *Septimius Felton* seems to be a reversion to Hawthorne's youth, insofar as it resembles *Fanshawe*. His half-Indian hero—a faun-like Paul Pry—is "only a spectator of life," though he seeks a potion to prolong it; though he cares more for the future than for the past, he sacrifices the present to his science. A pervasive feeling of weariness, of going through emotions meaninglessly, of having been there before, is self-evident: "As dramatists and novelists repeat their plots, so does man's life repeat itself, and at length grows stale."

Among his literary remains, *Dr. Grimshawe's Secret* seems to be Hawthorne's final undertaking, and the manuscript that has been most satisfactorily edited; but it is a saddening record of conscious decline. Dr. Grimshawe is a crabbed relative of Fanshawe; again the suffix is an identification, since *shaw* is an archaic word for thicket; our old friend, M. de l'Aubépine, is still playing on his name. For the last time he is playing the artist-scientist, specifically distilling balm from cobwebs, while congenially dwelling in a house by a churchyard. He is the presumable guardian of the boy who grows up and rediscovers England; but Hawthorne has his difficulties in joining these two remote themes, or in deciding what he wants to symbolize by the Gothic trappings that are so easily accumulated on the other side. What can he make of an ancient chest containing a handful of golden ringlets? Romance has faded because it is no longer animated by psychological acumen. "The story must not be founded at all on remorse or secret guilt—" Hawthorne advises himself, in one of his desperate asides, "all that Poe wore out." The question was not what Poe had written, but whether Hawthorne could write about anything else. Nothing but the grip of half-conscious compulsion could have brought his last unfinished work back to the scene of his constrained beginnings, the womb of his imaginative development. To think of that was, as he acutely knew, "like entering a deep recess of my own consciousness." Sooner or later, everything was comparable to a dream; but this dream was an unforgotten reality.

Looking into this chamber, in fancy, it is some time before we who come out of the broad sunny daylight of the world discover that it has an inmate. Yes, there is some one within, but where? We know it; but we do not precisely see him, only a presence is impressed upon us. It is in that corner; no, not there; only a heap of darkness and an old antique coffer, that, as we look closely at it, seems to be made of carved wood. Ah! he is in that other dim corner; and now that we steal close to him, we see him; a young man, pale, flung upon a sort of mattress-couch. He seems in alarm at something or other. He trembles, he listens, as if for voices. It must be a great peril, indeed, that can haunt him thus and make him feel afraid in such a seclusion as you feel this to be; but there he is, tremulous, and so pale that really his face is almost invisible in the gloomy twilight. How came he here? Who is he? What does he tremble at? In this duskiness we cannot tell.

Since he is not accompanied by a psychoanalyst, we need not label that dusky room the *id*, nor the voice he hears the *superego*, even though the young man can be no other than the ego, by any analysis. Let us not pry any further into his secret. Enough that he has one, and keeps it inviolable, in what he would prefer to call his conscience. Melville, who had discerned the source of Hawthorne's power, in reviewing *Mosses from an Old Manse*, had also sensed this predicament in a letter about *The House of the Seven Gables*. Reading that book, he wrote in congratulation, was like inhabiting a fine old chamber, comfortably furnished, its rich hangings embroidered with tragic scenes, where "finally, in one corner, there is a dark little black-letter volume with golden clasps, entitled *Hawthorne: A Problem.*" Melville, as an outdoor man, was intrigued by the indoor cast of Hawthorne's writing, by its interiors rather than its landscapes. Where openness, expansion, and a hankering after infinitude are characteristic of his contemporaries, Hawthorne sticks to his secretiveness, and to the atmosphere of enclosure, the awareness of things closing in. The journey ends in a house and within a locked room, with the rediscovery of another self for whom it has all been a dream; he has never left home. But this does not mean that he has never adventured; for there can be cosmic adventure in introspection, as much as in exploration. The shudder of solitude, the chill of empty space, which appalled Melville in the white whale, appalls Robert Frost in the whiteness of the snow. Hawthorne might well have agreed with his fellow New Englander:

> I have it in me so much nearer home
> To scare myself with my own desert places.

IV

Journey to the End of the Night

PASCAL, that patron saint of the obsessed, was troubled by the recurrent hallucination of a gulf which unclosed beside him. Hawthorne's obsession was his haunted chamber. Poe's, which has made him a bogeyman for schoolboys, was the grave. Not that it yawned for him more avidly than it has for many other men. His death-wish seems to have been much less intense than his morbid curiosity, his restless desire to penetrate the ultimate secret, which characteristically baffles him in the night-piece entitled "Spirits of the Dead":

> The breeze—the breath of God—is still,
> And the mist upon the hill,
> Shadowy—shadowy—yet unbroken,
> Is a symbol and a token—
> How it hangs upon the trees,
> A mystery of mysteries!

Tokens, however, were hardly enough for Edgar Allan Poe, whose admiration for Hawthorne was qualified by his own impatience with allegory. "There is no such thing as spirituality," he was to conclude in *Eureka*. "God is material." If this is so, it serves no purpose to look for transcendental correspondences; rather, the problem is to reduce the psychic to the physical. The consequence is Poe's unique absorption in atmosphere, his personal closeness to the material substance of his narration, where he is always in evidence as the narrator and frequently as the protagonist. Between his breathless evocations and Hawthorne's cool indications stands a diametrical contrast between involvement and detachment, between the arrested development of the elder writer and the younger's air of world-weary precocity. If Hawthorne is the man to whom nothing whatsoever has happened, Poe is the man to whom nearly everything happens, and who manages to tell us all about it, down to the instant of final catastrophe. While the reticent Hawthorne was so safely domiciled, the flamboyant Poe was homeless more often than not, eking out much of his forty-year existence as a free-lance "magazinist" in one city after another along the eastern seaboard. While his contemporaries were endeavoring to catch local colors and to limn familiar scenes, his imagination, pressing beyond immediate circumstance, projected a series of landscapes best described by his favorite Baconian maxim: "There is no excellent beauty that hath not some strangeness in the proportion."

Poe came by his own strangeness naturally. His loss of his actress-mother in infancy and of a beloved foster-mother later, his father's desertion and his foster-father's antipathy—this set of parallel facts may have doubled the symptoms of what can be all too easily diagnosed

as an Oedipus complex. We know that he constantly
sought maternal solace in one person or another, and
that his wife might more appropriately have been his
younger sister. To watch her die of consumption, as he
had earlier watched an epidemic of cholera, must have
seemed to warrant his lifelong preoccupation with
death and disease. His recourse to alcohol has its literary
hang-over in "The Angel of the Odd." His grievance at
having been disinherited, combining with the pride of a
displaced Southerner, has its intermittent wish-dream
of great houses and broad domains. The Bohemian actuality of his life, which left him a marginal figure
among his fellow Americans, turned him into a prototype for European symbolists: the poet as orphan, al-
ienated from his cruel step-parent, society, by its crass
philistinism. Poe himself expresses this opposition in
his satirical sketch, "The Business Man"; and it is the
theme of Mallarmé's commemorative sonnet, where a
fallen meteorite protects the poet's grave from the black
aspersions of the crowd. Although his style did all too
little "to purify the dialect of the tribe," it is possible
that the sound of his name tended to make it a byword,
and to make him an occupational hero, in France: *Poë,
poète, poésie.* According to his greatest apostle, Baudelaire, he was more of a cosmopolitan than a citizen of
his native country. If he was at home anywhere, perhaps it was in his "Dreamland":

> By a route obscure and lonely,
> Haunted by ill angels only,
> Where an Eidolon named NIGHT
> On a black throne reigns upright,
> I have reached these lands but newly

From an ultimate dim Thule—
From a wild weird clime that lieth, sublime,
Out of SPACE—out of TIME.

Whitman's assertion, that all of Poe's poems were "lurid dreams," is borne out by this oneiric stanza, which suggests not only the route of his journey to the end of the night, but also some of the phantoms that hounded him thither. "Alas," he wrote in a letter, "my whole existence has been the merest romance—in the sense of the most utter unworldliness." Yet he never escaped from the world of reality; as Dostoevsky pointed out in his preface to a Russian translation, Poe is a realist by comparison with a German idealist like E. T. A. Hoffmann; Poe's fantasies are strangely materialistic. "Even in his most unbounded imagining," Dostoevsky comments, "he betrays the true American." In "The Thousand-and-Second Tale of Scheherazade," that fabulous story-teller outdoes herself by instancing certain feats of western technology, such as the telegraph, the daguerreotype, and the bustle. Poe satirizes the present from the vantage-point of the future in "*Mellonta Tauta*"; and through the eyes of the ancient past, in "Some Words with a Mummy," he takes a sardonic view of progress, democracy, and the rule of the tyrant Mob. "The truth is, I am heartily sick of this life and of the nineteenth century in general. I am convinced that everything is going wrong." Yet he is never more the child of his century than when he is denouncing it or else, with all his mechanical ingenuity, busily devising the means to transcend it. The paradox is aptly stated by the stranger in "The Assignation": "To dream has been the business of my life." Three of Poe's sketches are timeless and placeless colloquies between disembodied spirits, who rejoice at having reached that plane of the ether which he likes to call Aidenn, a rarefied and sublimated Eden all his own. But their discourse is neither out of space nor out of time; it is earthbound on an astronomical scale, recapitulating the whole life-cycle from creation through decomposition to "blackness and corruption."

Poe's imagination was not incapable of upward flights, as on that notorious occasion when he hoaxed the readers of *The New York Sun* by describing, in the most factually journalistic tone, the crossing of the Atlantic by a balloon. What goes up must come down; and although "The Unparalleled Adventure of One Hans Pfaall" ascends to the orbit of the moon, it abruptly descends into the sphere of burlesque. The proper name, which suggests descent, has likewise suggested phallic significance to readers who are psychoanalytically predisposed; but we may be on a more solid terrain when we notice that Hans's adventure starts on April first, and that Pfaall stems from a root which means windbag or fool. His balloon, fashioned of dirty newspapers in the shape of a fool's cap, carries a further suggestion of hack-writing; furthermore he has been a bellows-mender, and has gone into debt because business was poor; so much hot air, we infer, is already in circulation. So much for the press, in other words, and for politics! The burghers of Rotterdam are caricatured, somewhat in the manner of Irving's Dutch New Yorkers; Hans is escaping from them, and particularly from his three creditors. Though his exploit gains plausibility through an assemblage of pseudo-scientific details, it is deflated into an escapade inspired by a "bottle conjurer"—or, to be more literal, the alcoholic revery of a debt-ridden hack-writer who finds it pleasant to envisage himself floating serenely away through the stratosphere from a harassing world which grows smaller and smaller in retrospect. A postscript, vaunting Hans's originality against other imaginary voyagers, brings Poe's defiance of the laws of gravity down to earth with a pedantic thud.

Poe's major explorations were not to be aeronautical —nor, for that matter, are they nautical, though several of them are conducted by sea. The earliest, and one of the most significant, is "Manuscript Found in a Bottle," a fragmentary tale of a ghost-ship and a polar catastrophe, which gathers immediacy by its use of the first person and the present tense. Dabbling absent-mindedly with a tar-brush, the narrator finds that he has spelled out the word *discovery* on a folded sail. But Poe had not the gift of serendipity, and his discoveries are never happy accidents; they are tantalizing glimpses into the structure of his luckless universe. "It is evident that we are hurrying to some exciting knowledge—some never-to-be-imparted secret, whose attainment is destruction." The same observation might be made with increased conviction today, but Poe's manuscript rushes on: "Perhaps this current leads us to the southern pole itself." The voyage, which leads through "the blackness of eternal night," terminates in a whirlpool; and the last words are "—going down!" A similar plight is more realistically described and more happily terminated in "A Descent into the Maelstrom," one of Poe's later tales in which the mind is enabled to exert control over matter. Here the yarn is recounted by the survivor, a Norwegian sailor who has coolly succeeded in breasting the vortex of "liquid ebony," though his raven-black hair has gone white in the course of the ordeal, and though he imparts to his eager listener a vivid sense of the terrors he has mastered: "the wild bewildering sense of *the novel* which confounds the beholder."

This eagerness to confront the unknown extends to the very brink of the abyss, and beyond it to that undiscovered country from whose bourn, though no traveler returns, he may send back desperate messages—manuscripts in bottles, as it were. Poe's French contemporary, Alfred de Vigny, elaborated the metaphor in his poem, *La Bouteille à la Mer*, where the anonymous navigator goes down confiding his message to the waves, no "black and mysterious elixir" but an imperishable idea. With Poe, the imaginary voyage becomes a catastrophic quest, a pursuit of exciting knowledge attained at the price of destruction. "Every man should confine himself to matters of experience," he remarks in "Loss of Breath." "Thus Mark Antony composed a treatise upon getting drunk." Despite his own qualifications for holding forth on that topic, Poe proceeds to reduce the cult of experience to absurdity by presenting a first-hand account of how it feels to be hanged and thrown into a charnel house. The attempt to push human awareness beyond the grave, crudely parodied in "Loss of Breath: A Tale Neither in Nor Out of *Blackwood's*," is accorded more speculative treatment in "The Colloquy of Monos and Una." Poe was fascinated by mesmerism because it produced a state of suspended animation, death-in-life; in one of his hoaxes, "The Facts in the Case of M. Valdemar," it prolongs the life of the black-haired, white-whiskered sleep-waker past the actual moment of death; and when the spell of hypnosis is broken, the body falls into an advanced stage of decay. Consciousness is extended by transmigration, in "A Tale of the Ragged Mountains," backward and eastward to a traumatic remembrance of black-barbed arrows from "dusky-visaged races."

"Sensations are the great things after all," advises the editor in "How to Write a *Blackwood* Article." "Should you ever be drowned or hung, be sure and make a note of your sensations—they will be worth to you ten guineas a sheet." This is Poe in his mood of strained facetiousness, which is often more dismal than his unchecked lugubriousness; but his editor mentions such serious examples as De Quincey's *Confessions of an English Opium-Eater*, along with tales of being buried alive and the once-famous *Blackwood* story of "The Man in the Bell," who was tolled into madness by a funeral. Poe's main contribution to fictional technique is his emphasis on the rendering of sensation, to the point where André Gide has credited him with the invention of the interior monologue. Though his subject-matter is often exotic, he is thoroughly American in his direct apprehension of violence. "I am the man, I suffered, I was there," he can say with Whitman. There is doubtless something immature in Poe's exaggerated sensibility, his childlike readiness to be terrified by the dark or to view unfamiliar things in a sinister light. But the characteristic point of view in American fiction may well be that of a boy, an adolescent initiated to manhood by the impact of his adventures, such as the heroes of Melville and Mark Twain, of Stephen Crane's *Red Badge of Courage*, William Faulkner's "Bear," and the stories of Ernest Hemingway. And it may not be sufficiently appreciated that all of these have their archetypal predecessor in Poe's single work of book-length, *The Narrative of Arthur Gordon Pym.*

The narrative of travel, a vehicle for the expression of the new world ever since the Elizabethan adventurers, has been a primary mode for the intermingling of fact and fiction since the days of Herodotus; and Poe knew how to make his marvels seem practical by relating them in that "plausible or verisimilar style" which he admired in *Robinson Crusoe*. He was well aware that the great age of exploration was not over; Arthur Gordon Pym reads himself to sleep with the memoirs of the Lewis and Clark Expedition. An enthusiastic reviewer of Irving's history of the fur trade, *Astoria*, Poe would imagine his own Northwestern exploration in "The Journal of Julius Rodman." Although he did not get beyond the Black Hills, he indulged Rodman's "love of . . . the unknown" by depicting landmarks of "solemn desolation," rocky bluffs along the Missouri River which seemed to be rather works of art than of nature. But Poe could never stay above ground for long; and when he took ship, as we shall see, he was unable to steer away from an underground destination. *The Narrative of Arthur Gordon Pym* owes its incidental solidity to Poe's astute reading in logbooks, geographical reports, and mariners' chronicles; but it derives its imaginative impetus from *An Address on the Subject of a Surveying and Exploring Expedition to the Pacific Ocean and the South Seas*, a project for discovering the South Pole and claiming the Antarctic continent on behalf of the United States. Here, maintained the projector, Jeremiah N. Reynolds, in a passage which caught Poe's eye, here was "a theater peculiarly our own from position and the course of human events.

Reynolds' proposal was addressed to the Congress in 1837, and helped to secure congressional support for what was to become the Wilkes expedition—from which, as Poe was quick to protest, the original proponent was "shamefully excluded." By an odd turn of events, the unwilling Hawthorne was invited to go along as Wilkes's chronicler. When we consider that Reynolds was also to influence Melville through his article, "Mocha Dick, or The White Whale of the Pacific," we cannot but be struck by the off-stage role he seems destined to have played in our literature. Poe acknowledged his indebtedness by a number of testimonials; indeed it remains an enigma for his biographers that he gasped out the name of Reynolds upon his deathbed. Whether or not he regarded that supreme emergency as another Antarctic misadventure, his *Narrative* could visit the promised land that Reynolds' *Address* could merely envision. The book, which was published in 1838, has a preface signed by A. G. Pym, explaining Poe's editorship of two installments that came out the previous year in *The Southern Literary Messenger*. They were presented "*under the garb of fiction*"; but readers had recognized "the *appearance* of . . . truth"; and now the presentation was being reversed. Poe, by this introductory sleight-of-hand, palms the fictitious off as the veracious; gradually, he moves from terra firma to the most distant outposts of credibility. If he does not speak in his own person, he has a perfect surrogate in his hero; and if their equivalence is not fully attested by the rhythmic equation between Edgar Allan Poe and Arthur Gordon Pym, it is underlined by Pym's family connection with the village of Edgartown.

Poe's protagonist is a native of the bleak New England island of Nantucket, which for Melville will symbolize man in self-isolation. Before Gordon can sail, he must cut himself off from his family; he must not only disguise himself, but actually disown his own grandfather. He must, he does, become the orphan ego: runaway, stowaway, castaway. In his schoolmate Augustus, the seagoing son of Captain Barnard, he encounters an alter ego who animates his wanderlust.

He had a manner of relating his stories of the ocean (more than one half of which I now suspect to have been sheer fabrications) well adapted to have weight with one of my enthusiastic temperament and somewhat gloomy although glowing imagination. It is strange, too, that he most strongly enlisted my feelings in behalf of the life of a seaman, when he depicted his more terrible moments of suffering and despair. For the bright side of the painting I had a limited sympathy. My visions were of shipwreck and famine; of death or captivity among barbarian hordes; of a lifetime dragged out in sorrow and tears, upon some grey and desolate rock, in an ocean unapproachable and unknown. Such visions or desires—for they amounted to desires—are common, I have since been assured, to the whole numerous race of the melancholy among men. At the time of which I speak I regarded them only as prophetic glimpses of a destiny which I felt myself in a measure bound to fulfil. Augustus thoroughly entered into my state of mind. It is probable, indeed, that our intimate communion had resulted in a partial interchange of character.

These two precocious shipmates will show us little of
seafaring life as Melville would learn to accept it; they
will find themselves more companionably embarked on
a search for calamities than on a hunt for whales; and
the story-teller will be overtaken all too soon by the circumstances he has been ardently striving to communicate. The opening chapter offers a prophetic glimpse
which is more or less autobiographical. The rash midnight cruise of the sailboat Ariel recalls one of Poe's
youthful escapades in Chesapeake Bay, while the intoxi-
cation of Augustus may be a reminiscence of Poe's endeavors to handle his drunken brother Henry. Augustus
takes the lead at the outset by smuggling his friend
aboard the whaler Grampus. But we do not accompany
him on deck; rather, we follow Gordon into the darkness of the hold; for even when Poe ventures across the
ocean, he cannot free himself from the suffocations of
claustrophobia; and the air is as close on shipboard as
in any of Hawthorne's houses. Gordon must enter a
coffin-like box and suffer a kind of living burial, for
three days and nights before the ship sails and for a
comparable period afterward, sinking into a semi-con-
scious condition from which he is uneasily aroused by
the odor of decay, the phosphorescence of a match, the
blankness of white paper, and the warning of blood—
"that word of all words—so rife at all times with mystery, and suffering, and terror."

After Gordon has told us, "My dreams were of the
most terrific description," we are less terrified when he
goes on to describe them. He describes a smothering
nightmare which exposes him to immense serpents,
limitless deserts, black morasses, and the onslaught of
fierce monsters. But it is "not all a dream"; for the

menacing animal is none other than Tiger, his faithful Newfoundland dog; and the peril of the situation is momentarily neutralized by this slight contact with security. What has really been happening all this while is relayed at second hand from Augustus, who has witnessed the mutiny and seen his deposed captain-father set adrift in an open boat. The son, too, will be a sacrificial victim; and his cadaver, blackened by putrefaction, will be torn to pieces by sharks. Yet, as in a picaresque novel, the hero is never without his traveling companion; and the place of Augustus is filled more and more by Dirk Peters, whose name bespeaks his nature, a sturdy combination of knife and rock. Dirk Peters, a half-breed from the Black Hills, employs the frontier gifts of a Leatherstocking to intervene in favor of anyone to whom his loyalty has attached itself. He rescues the boys from the hostile members of the crew and their leader, the black cook, "who in all respects was a perfect demon." Later on, in a suspenseful predicament, Peters saves Gordon, who is dizzied by a precipice and experiences "a *longing to fall*." Overcome by this vertiginous "crisis of fancy," he plunges, to be caught in Peters' dusky arms, and to feel himself "a new being" thereafter. Himself replacing the dead Augustus, who has lost a father through the rebellion, Gordon has found a father in Dirk Peters.

But Gordon, before he can take an active part, must come forth from his entombment below the decks; and he does so in the appropriate guise of a ghost, dressing in the garments of a dead sailor, and literally frightening the mate to death. We take a deep breath as we emerge with him from indoors to outdoors; but the next disaster, the shipwreck, follows hard upon the massacre of the rival mutineers. The Grampus itself is now half-submerged; the survivors dive into the cabins for water-logged provisions, notably a bottle of port; and drink once more becomes the agent of demoralization. Most ominous of all the portents that cross our track is the black death-ship, manned by a noisome crew of pesti-lential corpses. The "liver-like substance" of human flesh, gnawed by a sea-gull, has wider connotations which may be Promethean. The closest affinity of Arthur Gordon Pym is with the Ancient Mariner of Coleridge, that soul in agony who attains life-in-death, though not before his sin of killing the albatross has been expiated by blessing the water-snakes. But Poe's youthful mariner, who is to behold black albatross, could not drift past regions of snow and ice without landing to investigate them. No whales are sighted on his whaling trip; its climactic event, precipitated by apparent famine, is cannibalism—a gratuitous horror, as it turns out, since the ship's stores are subsequently available. Having seen men behave like sharks to their fellow men, we have seen the worst of society before we turn to nature; and we see the worst of nature before turning to the supernatural.

Though there are occasional inconsistencies, and at times the author seems as uncertain as the narrator of where he is going, his narration takes a form which is almost symmetrical. The first chapter, which centers upon the premonitory mishap in the Ariel, is followed by twelve chapters which cover the ill-starred cruise of the Grampus. The story is conveyed through twelve more—plus a postscript—by another vessel, the Jane Guy, and finally—when that English schooner is ex-ploded—by a primitive canoe. Pym and Peters, becalmed at the midpoint on the sinking Grampus, are picked up by the Jane. The new ship, despite the black ball on her foretopsail, is matter-of-factly engaged in "the southern traffic," which Poe sets forth in business-like detail: latitude, longitude, exports, rates of exchange, ports of call, one of the latter alluringly named Desolation Island. Pursuing "a constant tendency to the southward," Captain Guy is persuaded by Pym to enlarge his itinerary, in the hope of discovering an Antarctic continent and possibly the yet undiscovered South Pole. Curiosity is rewarded at the expense of plausibility when land is sighted beyond the ice floes, "a singular ledge of rock . . . bearing a strong resemblance to corded bales of cotton." But the Ultima Thule on which they eventually set foot has "no light-colored substances of any kind." Everything is black, the flora and fauna, the dwellings and artifacts, not only the skin but the teeth of the woolly-haired inhabitants. The very water is opaque and purplish. Whereas the shirts and sails of the visitors, the pages of their books and the shells of their eggs—everything white is taboo; and an untouchable white animal with red teeth is a sort of totem.

The mutual distrust, the latent repulsion, the inevitable antagonism between the natives and the newcomers seems to be deeply rooted in the nature of things. The black-skinned warriors exercise their command over natural objects by manipulating a cataclysmic landslide, thereby entombing the white-skinned mariners within a rocky fissure.

I firmly believed that no incident ever occurring in the course of human events is more adapted to in-

spire the supremeness of mental and bodily distress
than a case like our own, of living inhumation. The
blackness of darkness which envelops the victim,
the terrific oppression of lungs, the stifling fumes
from the damp earth, unite with the ghastly con-
siderations that we are beyond the remotest con-
fines of hope, and that such is the allotted portion
of the dead, to carry into the human heart a degree
of appalling awe and horror not to be tolerated—
never to be conceived.

So Pym declares, conceiving the inconceivable. Buried
again, he is saved again by Peters, the man of the rocks,
whose Indian resourcefulness guides them both through
a labyrinthine sequence of gorges and caverns, and who
thereupon completes his third rescue, when his companion falls from a cliff into his protective arms. They
are now "the only living white men upon the island."
They make their break from the howling savages by
entrusting themselves, in a fragile osier craft with a
wounded islander as hostage, to the Antarctic Ocean.
The last chapter consists in large part of day-by-day
notations, as the boat is hurried southward by a powerful current: the graying vapor in the air, the milkiness
of the water, the rain of "fine white powder, resembling
ashes," the flight of "many gigantic and pallidly white
birds," and the convulsive effect of these phenomena
upon the expiring black man. They seem to be rushing
toward an endless cataract, an ashy curtain suspended
between the dark sky and the glaring sea, beyond which
all forces seem to converge. Dick Peters cannot stand
below to ease this fatal plunge. As a chasm opens to
receive them, a shrouded figure, human yet "very far

larger in its proportions than any dweller among men," arises in their pathway. "And the hue of the skin of the figure was of the perfect whiteness of the snow."

The suspense of this concluding sentence is accentuated by its succession of prepositional phrases. The whiteness of the snow is suggestively that of the raiment of the angel, who announces that the sepulcher is empty in the gospel of Saint Mark. An editorial note, which is appended, explains the absence of two or three remaining chapters by the recent and accidental death of Mr. Pym. Presumably he had survived the polar catastrophe through that superhuman intervention which he allows to remain undescribed and indescribable. If Poe were more of an allegorist and less of a materialist, we should be tempted to interpret Pym's salvation in theological terms; but then we should be hard put to explain his subsequent fall from grace. Psychoanalysis has interpreted the god in this machine as a white goddess, identifying her with a radiant female who had appeared to the imprisoned Poe in an alcoholic hallucination; but, in another version of that anecdote, she is soon metamorphosed into an evil black bird who personifies the cholera. The lone survivor, at all events, is Dirk Peters; and the secret is reported to be missing with him, somewhere in Illinois. Poe was much too shrewd to go into particulars about the Pole, at a time when real explorers were setting out for it. It was for his energetic disciple, Jules Verne, in *The Sphinx of Ice*, to provide a naturalistic sequel, where the enigma is solved by magnetism. Poe devotes his appendix to philological interpretation. Those chasms of black granite, which Pym at least was able to diagram, viewed from a distance, would seem to be hieroglyphics. Scanning them, he discerns three cryptic words, meaning "to be shady" in Ethiopian, "to be white" in Arabic, and "the region of the south" in Egyptian. Philologists have not been able to confirm these findings; and any anthropological explanation of how such expressions got embedded in the earth, so much farther south than Africa, must continue to be a matter of wild surmise.

Poe invites further conjectures as to the designation of the island, Tsalal, and as to the cry of the affrighted Tsalalians in response to anything white: '*Tekeli-li!*' Simple English anagram could answer the invitation by transposing *Tsalal* into *as tall*, which might possibly connote an attitude of bitter rivalry on the part of an underdog. As for *Tekeli-li*, it should remind Bible-readers of the handwriting on the wall, *Mene, Tekel, Upharsin,* and of Daniel's translation: "God hath numbered thy kingdom, and finished it. Thou art weighed in the balances, and found wanting. Thy kingdom is divided, and given to the Medes and the Persians." But Poe, who is more of an oracle than a prophet, disappears at the end behind a pseudo-Biblical precept of his own: "I have graven it within the hills, and my vengeance upon the dust within the rock." Elsewhere he has literally inscribed his mood upon the landscape. The word *silence,* in the fable of that name, appears on a stone where graven characters have originally spelled out the word *desolation.* Poe's fascinated review of a book of travels in rocky Arabia (*Arabia Petraea*), written in the same year as "Silence: A Fable" and *The Narrative of Arthur Gordon Pym,* is a topographical link between them. "The Journal of Julius Rodman" pauses in awe before certain stratifications of rock, and wonders whether they were produced by geological upheaval or architectural design. On the other hand, Poe is compulsively lured by the maelstrom, or by the whirlpool out of which his "Manuscript found in a Bottle" purports to have been tossed. Arthur Gordon Pym navigates a hazardous course between Scylla and Charybdis, between living inhumation upon the rocky island and death by water at the swirling pole. But Dante's Ulysses weathered such obstacles, only to be shipwrecked against the Mount of Purgatory.

What took Pym so far and then confounded him, though it is only hinted in the text, may be inferred from other documents. Jeremiah Reynolds, who seems to have been the guide for Poe that Dirk Peters was for Pym, had embraced—along with his own Antarctic cause—a notion put forward in a circular of 1818, *The Symmes Theory of Concentric Spheres, demonstrating that the earth is hollow, habitable, and widely open about the poles.* This theory, which had been seriously expounded in memoranda and lectures by Captain J. C. Symmes, had also become a serio-comic byword; Thoreau refers to "Symmes's Hole" in *Walden.* For Poe, with his deep urge toward the subterranean, it was enough to justify the rigors of a calamitous ocean voyage. His fiction had a suggestive precedent in a utopian novel, *Symzonia: A Voyage of Discovery,* published in 1820 by a satirist who masked his identity under the waggish pseudonym, Captain Adam Seaborn. Here the direction is charted by an Ahab-like captain who, disregarding his semi-mutinous crew, presses southward past Worldsend Cape to confirm the hypotheses of "that profound philosopher," Captain Symmes. Once he has penetrated the tunnel extending from pole to pole through the center of the earth, his interest shifts to the inhabitants of this brave new world, which he christens Symzonia. He is impressed by "the strange rationality of the Symzonians," which reflects so unfavorably upon the irrationality of the North Americans, and supplies much opportunity for Swiftian satire. The most invidious of many comparisons is that between the skins of the so-called "internals" and of the "externals." The pigmentation of the narrator would ordinarily be considered fair; but, compared with the fairness of his hosts, he feels like the sootiest African.

This was not Poe's conception of the Antipodes, but it could hardly have failed to stimulate him. For sheer effect, as he noted in a letter, Monk Lewis had introduced black-skinned characters into a locale where they did not belong. The coloration of Poe's tales is predetermined by the eidolon named Night who reigns supreme over his poetry. Statistical investigation has shown what the common reader might expect: that blackness predominates, equaled—and slightly eclipsed —by whiteness, when the latter is taken together with grayness. Actual colors are not much in evidence, except for lurid yellow and various shades of red; "The Masque of the Red Death" is the polychromatic exception that proves the rule. And whereas, for Hawthorne, black and white more or less conventionally symbolize theological and moral values, for Poe, whose symbols claim to be actualities, they are charged with basic associations which are psychological and social. The "constant tendency to the south" in *The Narrative of Arthur Gordon Pym* takes on a special inflection, when we are mindful of the Southern self-consciousness of the author. His letters and articles reveal him as an unyielding upholder of slavery, and as no great admirer of the Negro. The

Negroes in his stories are comic stereotypes, among whom the servant Jupiter in "The Gold Bug" is a relatively favorable example. For Northerners who sympathized with the slaves, Poe's hatred was so intense that he could not review James Russell Lowell's poems without launching into a diatribe against Abolitionism. His bitterest complaint in his correspondence with his foster-father, John Allan, was: "You suffer me to be subjected to the whims and caprice, not only of your white family, but the complete authority of the blacks . . ."

In the troubled depths of Poe's unconscious, there must have been not only the fantasy of a lost heritage, but a resentment and a racial phobia. These impulsions seldom manifest themselves upon the surface of his writing; yet one of his humorous tales, "The System of Dr. Tarr and Professor Fether," has its subliminal revelations to disclose. Its scene is set in France, although not very convincingly, with frequent reminders that we are in one of the southernmost provinces. With the narrator we pay a visit to a dilapidated chateau, now converted into an insane asylum, and famed for its mild and sympathetic treatment of patients. This "system of soothing" has recently had to be changed for a more rigorous method, as we soon learn from the new superintendent, who seems to have a few crotchets of his own. Gradually, after some queer conversation with the staff and a dinner which is queerer, we become aware of what has happened. The pampered lunatics have revolted against their keepers, tarred and feathered them, locked them up, and crazily assumed their guardian functions. The *dénouement* occurs when the rightful guardians break out of their confinement, looking like an army of "chimpanzees, ourang-outangs, or big black baboons," and beat the rebellious inmates back into submission. Poe concludes by saying that he has vainly searched the libraries of Europe for the works of Dr. Tarr and Professor Fether. That is not surprising, since tar-and-feathers was an American system, the next thing to lynch law, the roughest and readiest way of disciplining colored persons and Northern abolitionists. It is as if Poe were asking the persistent question: What would happen if the slaves tired of slavery and dispossessed their masters?

The tables are turned the other way in "Hop-Frog," where a crippled jester revenges himself upon a vicious king and his heartless courtiers, who masquerade as ourang-outangs with the aid of tar and flax, and are burned into "a fetid, blackened, hideous, and indistinguishable mass." Similarly, a consciousness of guilt and a fear of retribution underlie *The Narrative of Arthur Gordon Pym*. The land, at first sight, looks like bales of cotton. The secret engraved within the rocks is a warning of vengeance. The labyrinths spell out, in Hamitic and other relevant languages, the verbs for being shady and being white and the noun for pointing southward. If we connect the language of the barbarians with the scriptural handwriting on the wall, we are warned against a divided kingdom, which stands in danger of being given over to dark-skinned interlopers. Poe's black men have a spontaneous antipathy for the white race— "from whose complexion, indeed, they appeared to recoil." They themselves, as Pym sums them up, "appeared to be the most wicked, hypocritical, vindictive, bloodthirsty, and altogether fiendish race of men upon the face of the globe"—a tribe decidedly not amenable to systematic kindness. The deepest-dyed ringleader of the mutiny on the Grampus is the black cook; the crew of the Jane Guy is massacred by the treachery of the Tsalalians. It is also worthy of note that the lone surviving character, sole bearer of the burden of the mystery, who has thrice delivered the hero, is a half-breed. However, the admixture of bloods, the fraternization of races, the demonstration that blackness and whiteness are not antithetical but complementary—that is another story, not Poe's but Melville's.

How much is artistry or how much is intuition, how much is allegory in spite of the author, remains an open question, like Poe's ending. If he shared those benighted sentiments of interracial hostility which have made the black man so tragic a victim of our history, then he deserves some credit for having concealed them under the strata of his symbolism. But at the farthest point south, it is whiteness in which Pym is all but engulfed; and his impending burial leads to a resurrection. Going down is as ambiguous a gesture for Poe as moving onward was for Hawthorne. Here we are again at the last extremity, *in articulo mortis*; but the milky water is more redolent of birth than of death; and the opening in the earth may seem to be a regression wombward. Psychoanalytic interpreters discern, in the gigantic protector, "clad all in white" like the Helen of Poe's verse, a mother-image. But Poe deliberately leaves the sexless image blank, and reverts to the problem of reading the earthwork inscriptions. The result is a *non sequitur*, as evaluated by Henry James in his preface to *The Altar of the Dead*; the climax fails, and all the imaginative effort is wasted. But James's evaluation is more generous, though his recollection is somewhat vague, when in *The Golden Bowl* he refracts Poe's book through the personality of Prince Amerigo, whose name proclaims him a European discoverer of America.

> He remembered to have read as a boy a wonderful tale by Allan Poe, his prospective wife's country-man—which was a thing to show, by the way, what imagination Americans *could* have: the story of the shipwrecked Gordon Pym, who, drifting in a small boat further toward the North Pole—or was it the South?—than any one had ever done, found at a given moment before him a thickness of white air that was like a dazzling curtain of light, concealing as darkness conceals, yet of the color of milk or of snow. There were moments when he felt his own boat move upon some such mystery. The state of mind of his new friends . . . had resemblance to a great white curtain. He had never known curtains but as purple even to blackness—but as producing where they hung a darkness intended and ominous. When they were so disposed as to shelter surprises, the surprises were apt to be shocks.

Black and white, in this context, fit into the usual Jamesian dialectic between old-world experience and new-world innocence. Yet more than that, the brightness signifies the challenge of novelty, the hazards of the unattempted, and the bedazzlement of the ultimate. It ends by drawing to itself many of the connotations of darkness, like Melville's white whale, and by bringing Pym's Antarctic shudder into a cushioned and carpeted drawing-room, a chill which is more of a shock than a surprise. Though we still may not be satisfied with the sudden termination of Poe's narrative, we may find the termination of our existence no less abrupt and unsatisfactory.

The snowy apparition, whatever it betokens, performs the function of balking further inquiry; and Poe's zeal for charting or changing the face of the globe must be diverted into other channels. In his most ambitious treatise he argues that "our propensity . . . for the symmetrical" is "the poetical essence of the universe." Consequently, he poetizes nature by imposing upon it a certain symmetricality. As a solitary wanderer, he contemplates patterns which seem to be inherent in the scenery, such as the glimmering shadows that eddy across the ebony rivulet, "making its blackness more black," in "The Island of the Fay"—an exemplification of that Miltonic conceit which held so obvious an attraction for Poe, "darkness visible." His mental horizons are heavily overcast: the dark tarn of Auber, the ghoul-haunted woodland of Weir, the sulphurous currents of the boreal pole, the night's Plutonian shore. One of his poems, "The Valley of Unrest," was originally entitled "The Valley Nis"—an inversion of *sin*. Other landmarks of Poe's geography, though less explicitly labeled, externalize his highly subjective outlook. Out of his more serene daydreams he created a happy valley, "The Domain of Arnheim, or The Landscape Garden"—and here the proper name is associated with German romance. The spokesman is another self named Ellison, lately deceased, describable in his own phrase as "a poet, having very unusual pecuniary resources." Since these resources are unlimited, and since his speculations are tinged with materialism, he has chosen the landscape as his poetic medium. Ellison's esthetic theories favor artifice as an improvement on nature. Spacious as his territories are, there is no room in them for withered leaves or stray pebbles. If the surface of the earth is no longer a garden because of man's fallen estate, he believes that its rocky outcroppings are "prognostic of death."

The topography of Arnheim, as Poe lays it out, seems comparable to that of Xanadu in all its "weird symmetry." The approach is by way of a watercourse which meanders through a luxuriant ravine toward a "chasm-like rift in the hills." To float down that river in a "light canoe of ivory, stained with arabesque devices in vivid scarlet"—is it a journey of the soul or the body, is its goal the womb or the tomb? It wafts us into some sort of a terrestrial paradise, a haven of what Ellison seeks most, seclusion. But we do not arrive until the final paragraph; and we scarcely begin to visualize Ellison's pleasure-dome; for the dream-like tracery of the architecture is mingled with the odors of the landscape in a single impression, "seeming the phantom handiwork, conjointly, of the Sylphs, of the Fairies, of the Genii, and of the Gnomes." Every touch adds to the evanescence of the vision, and to that feeling of tantalization which arrested the voyage of Arthur Gordon Pym. If this is earthly felicity, the prospect is quickly withdrawn. Yet Poe went on to compose what he subtitled "A Pendant to 'The Domain of Arnheim'" in "Landor's Cottage," his last published sketch. There the domain is Poe's own, the modest dwelling at Fordham outside of New York, where he found hours of refuge and repose during the closing years of his unsettled career. In that house his child-wife had died; and now it comforts him to imagine another woman, the married friend whom he so confidingly addressed as Annie, standing at the door and welcoming him. Eyeing her, and trying to capture in words the expression of her eyes, he confides to us: "*romance,* and *womanliness* seem to me convertible terms."

That this suburban idyll should have seemed so romantic to an arch-romancer is pathetic as well as paradoxical, since it implies that Poe's farther-ranging excursions were imaginative compensations for a commonplace domesticity which he had missed. The implication is strengthened by the cluttered gentility of Poe's taste in interior decoration, as delineated by his article, "Philosophy of Furniture." In his enthusiasm for the vista of coziness he has conjured up in "Landor's Cottage," he borrows a far-fetched epithet from the ultra-Gothic William Beckford: "*une architecture inconnue dans la terre.*" Beckford's architectural caprice, Fonthill Abbey, was out of this world, in the fantastic sense; Annie's cottage was out of this world in the pedestrian sense of being practically unattainable. Be it ever so humble, or ever so banal, there would seem to be simply no place like home; and there was not any reasonable facsimile of home for the nomad Poe. But homelessness, as we have recognized, was a precondition of his genius. It is what made him so poignant a voice from the depths, what makes him so percipient a witness to the cosmic gropings of modern man. It is what drives him to polar extremes, frees him to search for the absolute, and abandons him to the infinite. There are two modes of discussion, he maintained, ascent and descent. We can recognize the distinction as, in some measure, respectively corresponding with the manic and the depressive phases of his imagination. Predominantly, the phase is depressive; and then the

mode is descendent, a downward movement, a dying
fall. Yet there are occasions when the trend veers upward, and when the mood is exalted to the verge of
megalomania. No higher flight of fancy than Poe's
Eureka ever lost itself in the empyrean.

Eureka, Poe's testament, the synthesis of his analytic
ideas, offers itself as a treatise on nothing less than cos-
mology. Having begun as a scientific lecture, it winds
up as an apocalyptic revelation. If it is Poe's boldest
imagining, it is also his dullest piece of writing. In the
preface he qualifies it as an art-product, a romance or
a poem. But, though he addresses it "to the dreamers
and those who put faith in dreams as in the only realities," he also insists, "What I here propound is true."
It is dedicated to Alexander von Humboldt, perhaps
in acknowledgment of its borrowings from his *Kosmos*;
and it does not hesitate to take issue with so axiomatic
a theorist as Laplace. But, insofar as Poe's work is based
on the physics and astronomy of its period, its pretensions to exact truth are outmoded; while its artistic
beauty, as a prose-poem, is not enhanced by its airy
manipulation of more or less scientific jargon. On the
other hand, few laymen have even attempted to meet
the claims of science half-way, as Poe has done; while
scientists, in attempting to verbalize their methods and
results on a popular level, have rarely achieved his
degree of articulation. The force of gravity, as might be
expected, is central to his position. He senses the importance of electricity, though it was still unexploited
in his day. The major premise of this *Essay on the Material and Spiritual Universe* is that matter and spirit
are fundamentally one. The unity of time and space is
to be inferred, as well as the identification of the human

with the divine, through a creed of philosophical monism which does its best to piece together the fragments of a dismembered poet.

Eureka is more than a culminating hoax or a megalomaniacal rhapsody. It may be read as a rationalistic counterstatement to the metaphysics of Transcendentalism, or as a pioneering experiment in the embryonic genre of science-fiction. But it is also a distillation of themes which have concretely figured earlier. Poe interpolates a manuscript found in a bottle, floating upon a sea of shadows (*Mare Tenebrarum*) in an ocean fitly mapped by a Nubian geographer—a locus already cited in "Eleonora" and "A Descent into the Maelstrom." This tenebrous missive, echoing some of his futuristic satire, is a jocose attack upon the axioms of the philosophers. It is also a somewhat paranoid appeal to posterity, over the heads of uncomprehending contemporaries. The proposition that "there can be no antipodes," or that "darkness cannot proceed from light," Poe asserts, has been disproved. Indeed, the disproof of such propositions has been his life-work. In spite of an increasing tendency to identify himself with his subject-matter, he is willing to concede the difference between human and divine constructions. When works of fictitious literature are constructed, for example, their plots are predetermined by our reliance upon the limiting concept of causation; whereas the functioning of the universe, which Poe looks upon as "a plot of God," is free to achieve the perfection of indeterminacy. "The universe has no conceivable end." If an end were foreseeable, "creation would have affected us as an imperfect plot in a romance, where the *dénouement* is awkwardly brought about by interposed

incidents . . ." To break off *The Narrative of Arthur
Gordon Pym* was not only to avert the catastrophe; it
was to prove, by leaving matters indeterminate, that
there could be such things as antipodes, and that darkness could proceed from light.

Other writers, especially Flaubert and Joyce, have
likened the artist to a demiurge, and have stressed the
analogy between his work and material creation. For
Poe the relationship was no mere metaphor; it was a
personal apotheosis. *"Eureka!"* is his heart-cry. "I have
found it!" he breathlessly seems to announce. "The
secret of the universe, the burden of the mystery! Come,
sit down upon a cloud with me, and I shall explain it
all to you. Do you know who created the world? I did,
just now." In the last analysis, the condition to which
Poe aspires is not death but a state of "posthumous consciousness," as it has been formulated by Georges Poulet, in the American appendix to his penetrating study
of time in French literature. For the traveler who arrives at the end of the night, there must be some sort
of morning-land. And if Poe is ever serene, it is when
he looks down on—or back at—life across the light-years
from his poetic Mohammedan limbo, Al Aaraaf, or
from Aidenn, the interstellar region of his angelic dialogues. Out of space, out of time, "The Conversation
of Eiros and Charmion" discusses the planetary collision
that led to the end of the world. "In its impalpable
gaseous character we clearly perceived the consum-
mation of Fate." And Poe's flair for capturing sensations eclipses itself prophetically, as he renders the blinding flash and the gasping reaction. "Thus ended all."
Yet he cannot write *finis*; instead he goes back, through
"the night of time," to the very beginning of things;

and in "The Power of Words" he reasserts the creative principle of the *logos*. Every word is "an impulse on the air," a motion produced by thought, whereby dreams are created and world recreated. So Agathos, the good spirit, elucidates. But Oinos, the fledgling spirit, whose name suggests the befuddlement of wine, is still perplexed:

> But why, Agathos, do you weep—and why, oh why do your wings droop as we hover above this fair star—which is the greenest and yet most terrible of all we have encountered in our flight? Its brilliant flowers look like a fairy dream—but its fierce volcanoes like the passions of a turbulent heart.

And Agathos, hovering over the earth like the artist brooding upon his creation, like Poe reliving the pangs of lucubration, replies:

> They are! they are! This wild star—it is now three centuries since, with clasped hands, and with streaming eyes, at the feet of my beloved—I spoke it—with a few passionate sentences—into birth. Its brilliant flowers are the dearest of all unfulfilled dreams, and its raging volcanoes are the passions of the most turbulent and unhallowed of hearts.

V

Notes from Underground

Poe's sky-aspiring divagations come home, with a vengeance, to "the ultimate woe," the tragic fact of mortality. His aerial voyages, even as we try to follow them, take a terrestrial plunge. *The Narrative of Arthur Gordon Pym*, if it did nothing else, would prove that water is not his element. His imagination is of the earth earthy, to the most subterranean degree. He recognizes, yet is unreconciled to, the paradox contracted into the basic rhyme of *womb* and *tomb*: that the very matrix of all life should be its repository for death. But Pascal had learned to live with his private gulf; and Plato had envisioned the flickering shadows on the wall of a cave as the utmost knowledge to which mankind might aspire. Dostoevsky, under the heading "Notes from Underground," would set down insights painfully acquired through one of his case-histories in human degradation. More literally, and indeed more symbolically, Poe might have been justified in designating his tales as notes from underground. Actually, he used such designations as

Phantasy-Pieces or *Prose Romances,* and he considered other stratagems for presenting more or less unified collections. Working under pressure, he could not afford to become a devotee of the single precise word; instead, he seems to grope for several approximate synonyms, so that his writing smells of the thesaurus. Though his material is extremely concrete, his vocabulary tends to be abstract, so that his reader finds himself in the position of being instructed how he ought to react. For example, the adjective *terrific* is not a stimulus but a preconditioned response. Typography lends its questionable aid, with an excess of capitals, italics, dashes, and exclamation points. There are too many superlatives and intensitives and ineffables. There are also too many gallicisms like *outré, recherché,* and *bizarre,* repeated so loosely that Poe's French translator, Baudelaire, generally replaces them with a more elegant turn of phrase.

However, Poe seems to have hit his own mark when he called his first collection *Tales of the Grotesque and Arabesque,* utilizing a pair of romantic catchwords which he had probably encountered in Scott's essay "On the Supernatural in Fictitious Composition." The etymology of *grotesque,* deriving as it does from *grotto,* makes it particularly appropriate for his purposes. It means an artistic creation which is entirely imaginary, which has—in Milton's phrase—"no type in nature." It was paired against its classic antithesis, *sublime,* in the influential formula of Victor Hugo. *Arabesque,* on the other hand, is elusive by definition. It derives from the Arabic—or, rather, the Mohammedan—injunction against reproducing natural forms; hence its primary meaning pertains to geometrical design; and Poe's usage is strict as well as characteristic, in "Philosophy of Furniture," when he insists that "all upholstery . . . should be rigidly arabesque." The term had been extended to literary criticism by Friedrich Schlegel, who invoked it to formulate the interplay of contradictions and ironies in *Don Quixote*. Its broadest signification is the free play of fancy, a positive assertion of what is negatively implied by *grotesque*. Thus *arabesque* might aptly describe the art of Roderick Usher, who paints ideas in the form of "pure abstractions"; but Poe employs the catchword, more loosely, to characterize his hero's inhuman expression. Since both *arabesque* and *grotesque* mean much the same thing, in the sense of capricious or fanciful, efforts to subdivide Poe's tales between them are harder to support than Coleridge's problematic distinction between imagination and fancy. Yet gradations become important as we turn from Poe's outward and upward caprices to his more habitual direction, earthward.

His method, as enunciated in a well-known letter, was to intensify such differences of degree: "the ludicrous heightened into the grotesque, the fearful colored into the horrible, the witty exaggerated into the burlesque, the singular wrought out into the strange and mystical." The common denominator is Poe's extremism, which not infrequently sets up its tensions between the sublime and the ridiculous. A fierce sense of humor, defensive and offensive, not unconnected with the violence of his worldview and the intellectuality of his reaction against it, comes out most sharply in his wars with his fellow literati. Into his imaginative constructions, comedy enters by way of hysteria; his cultivation of strangeness in the proportion leads him now to beauty, again to caricature. As a child of theatrical parents, it was fitting that he should become a "literary *histrio*," and that his technique of narration should be enlivened by "dramatism." The role he plays is essentially that of a monologuist, addressing us in his own person so compellingly that we soon find ourselves enacting the Coleridgean role of the Wedding Guest. To be specific, he plays the hypnotist, continually bent upon effecting a transference of emotions or sensations. That is why the short story is peculiarly his medium, since its concentration helps him to cast a spell—or, in his own critical terms, to aim at unity of effect. "During the hour of perusal, the soul of the reader is under the writer's control." Small wonder, then, if Poe's style is comparable to the patter of a stage magician, adept at undermining our incredulity with a display of sham erudition, scientific pretensions, quotations from occult authorities, and misquotations from foreign languages.

In portraying the character he admires the most, his *raisonneur* Auguste Dupin, Poe toys with the notion of "the Bi-Part Soul . . . a double Dupin—the creative and the resolvent." This could be a description of Poe himself, an intuitive poet at one extreme and the most rationalistic of critics at the other, whose major work—his fiction—might be described as a collaboration between the creative and the resolvent faculties. Elsewhere, in "Eleonora," his interlocutor refers to the two stages of his existence as "lucid reason" and as "shadow and doubt." Though shadow and doubt are the essence of Poe's genius, they are also symptoms of potential madness in his narrators, to be counterbalanced by madman's cunning, if not by lucid reason. Paul Valéry has recaptured this state of mind with his usual succinctness, when he speaks of being possessed by a delirium

of lucidity. The sanity of Poe's characters is questioned
no less insistently than the righteousness of Hawthorne's. And if Poe's tales are beset with phobias of
persecution, *Eureka* is suffused with delusions of gran-
deur. The bi-part soul is both a creator and a resolver
of mysteries; the double mind spins yarns in order to
disentangle them. Poe is adept at making us feel the
inherent mystery of things, before which we can but
stand in awe. But the relationship has another side,
which is mystification, the aspect of Poe that manifests
itself in hoaxes, histrionics, masquerades, practical jokes,
and other impositions upon our will to believe. In a
jocular article on "the science of mystification," he illuminates his own psychology by describing "the habitual
mystific," who is "ever upon the lookout for the grotesque.

He liked to mystify; he did not like to be mystified.
If, with Dupin, he was "fond of enigmas, of conun-
drums, hieroglyphics," it was because he was confident
of his ability to solve them; and the act of solution was
a public performance. This has suggested, to T. S. Eliot,
the mentality of a clever adolescent, who is better at
puzzles than at the complications of life. It suggests,
too, the knowing professional competence of the practiced charlatan in debunking trickery—and not only
the tricks of the literary trade but financial chicanery,
"Diddling, Considered as One of the Exact Sciences."
For a time, through a weekly newspaper, Poe maintained a standing offer to read any cipher or break down
any system of cryptography. He matched wits with
Dickens by predicting how *Barnaby Rudge* would turn
out, while it was still appearing in monthly instalments.
His exposure of Maelzel's Chess-Player, which pur-

ported to be an automaton but really concealed a human operator, was an ironic triumph of intuition over the machine. His youthful sonnet "To Science" voices the stock objection of the romanticists: that the scientific attitude reduces everything to the most prosaic reality. Yet, in his prose, it proves to be a source of virtually poetic inspiration. It is not simply magical, as it may seem with Hawthorne's elixirs—or, for that matter, the conjurations of Hoffmann and Balzac. Rather, by believing in all the claims of all the sciences and pseudo-sciences, by expecting almost anything from nature, Poe can almost dispense with the supernatural. Like Brockden Brown, he is a rationalist, seeking to cast enlightenment on dark places. But the forces of the irrational have their revenge in jeopardizing the status of reason itself.

Poe is one of those authors whose works, diversified as they may seem, can be read as brief fragments from one long confession. If he ever attains the integration he strives for, it is by compulsively retelling a sequence of overlapping anecdotes. During a career of less than two decades, while he was energetically involved in many other journalistic activities, he wrote more than sixty tales. Though these register a technical advance from the eighteen-thirties into the 'forties, they keep reverting to a small number of themes; and though the variations are significant, the recurrences are even more so. Therefore it may be clarifying to consider them from a synoptic, rather than chronological, point of view. Formally, they range from newspaper articles to prose poems; from imitations of German romance, like "Metzengerstein," to experiments in detective fiction, like "The Murders in the Rue Morgue." Thematically, they might be classified according to Dupin's two states of mind. Those which create are, paradoxically, the ones that are most preoccupied with the theme of extinction; and they are our central and most dramatic examples. Whereas those which resolve, though they profess to convey truths stranger than fiction, are critical and expository in tone, not to say didactic. Another mode of classification, based upon the shifting emphases of the continuous monologue, would distinguish four successive types. The resolvent protagonist is a detached observer: scientist, explorer, or detective. The decisive shift is from spectator to actor, usually a malefactor confessing his misdeed. The next shift is from actor to sufferer, or agonist with whom we agonize. The terminal phase is the search of the solitary individual for a companion of the other sex, who eludes him.

The tales that proceed by detection are closely related to Poe's narratives of exploration; both are products of that restless curiosity which would not rest content without trying to answer the riddle of the universe. Aiming at a more limited objective in "The Gold Bug," he was rewarded—not, to be literal, by buried treasure estimated at more than a million and a half, but by a prize of a hundred dollars from a story-contest. In setting his scene at Fort Moultrie, South Carolina, where he had briefly served in the army, and where he imagined the landing of his "Balloon-Hoax," Poe must have been vicariously fulfilling an early daydream. He was to take a dim view of the California Gold Rush in the poem "Eldorado," and to argue that the success of alchemy would deflate the value of ore, in the hoax "Von Kempelen and His Discovery." Here he is less concerned with the trove of riches than with the devices whereby it is discovered, and mainly with his own skill in devising and deciphering a cryptogram. The discoverer, William Legrand, is eccentric enough to be suspected of insanity; while his manumitted slave Jupiter, though he provides invaluable assistance, threatens his master with flogging at one point. The symbolic title is somewhat misleading; the insect, which also figures misleadingly in "The Sphinx," is—as Poe and Legrand admit—"a sober bit of mystification." It has no connection with their chain of logic, but turns up by chance, and is pressed into service as a plummet to link the pirate skull with the hoard of Captain Kidd. The earth, for once, reveals itself a kindly mother; yet the burial place of the treasure-chest is likewise the grave of two skeletons, who retain their secret.

"The Gold Bug" is a *tour de force* of ratiocination; and we might infer, from Mr. Legrand's name, that his powers of reasoning are inherited. But the "perfect reasoner" had to be a native Frenchman, M. Dupin; and the cosmopolitan locale of his investigations had to be Paris, through which Poe was guided by Balzac, Vidocq, and Eugène Sue, and to which—though he had never seen it, and though the sinister-sounding Rue Morgue seems to be one of his imaginary place-names—he introduced Gaboriau and the detectives of the *roman policier*. Poe himself, attracted to his hero by "the rather fantastic gloom of our common temper," assumes the confidential part that Dr. Watson would take with Dupin's successor, Sherlock Holmes.

It was a freak of fancy in my friend (for what else shall I call it?) to be enamored of the night for her own sake; and into this *bizarrerie,* as into all his

others, I quietly fell, giving myself up to his wild
whims with a perfect *abandon*. The sable divinity
would not herself dwell with us always; but we
could counterfeit her presence. At the first dawn
of the morning we closed all the massy shutters of
our old building; lighted a couple of tapers which,
strongly perfumed, threw out only the ghastliest
and feeblest of rays. By the aid of these we then
busied our souls in dreams—reading, writing, or
conversing, until warned by the clock of the advent
of the true Darkness. Then we sallied forth into
the streets, arm in arm, continuing the topics of
the day, or roaming far and wide until a late hour,
seeking, amid the wild lights and shadows of the
populous city, that infinity of mental excitement
which quiet observation can afford.

It is for analysis to penetrate that nocturnal atmosphere
and bring hidden terrors to light. Dupin's analyses are
presented as inductive. As a matter of simple-minded
fact, they could hardly be more deductive, being de-
duced *a priori* from clues that Poe has already planted,
rather than following from genuinely empirical observations. Moreover, it is his emotion that has created
what is resolved by Dupin's intellect, as we vaguely
recognize in the victims of "The Murders in the Rue
Morgue," a mother and her daughter. But, though they
have been brutally murdered, no person is guilty; no
motive is discoverable, other than the grotesquerie of
subhuman agency. Through a hectic confusion of
tongues, by a logical process of elimination, M. Dupin
demonstrates that the murderer is an ourang-outang.
This victory for civilization is consequently a defeat,

since it subjects the orderly routine of the city to the purposeless malignity of untamed nature. And when we recall the ourang-outangs in "Hop-Frog" and "The System of Dr. Tarr and Professor Fether," possibly we catch another glimpse of an old Southern bugbear: the fear of exposing a mother or a sister to the suspected brutality of a darker race.

Poe completed a trilogy by giving M. Dupin two further opportunities for "the exercise of ingenuity in the detection of a mystery." There his ratiocinative talents are pitted against human opposition, in accordance with his theory of games or calculus of probabilities. One of the results is the mutual antipathy between the sharp "private eye" and the stupid policeman that is so rife in the "whodunit" today. But "The Murders in the Rue Morgue" has an impact which is conspicuously absent from its two sequels. "The Mystery of Marie Rogêt"—and the circumflex is the purest of Poe's arabesques—carries on a quarrel with the press as well as with the police. Fascinated as he invariably was by the death of a young woman, Poe offers a conjectural explanation for the actual murder of one Mary Rogers, Gallicizing the proper names and transposing the streets of New York to the banks of the Seine. His suspicions point to a crime of passion committed by a dark-complexioned sailor. It should be added that the mystery is still unsolved. "The Purloined Letter" reaches a plane of subtlety where the obvious is rediscovered. The torn white paper, with its black seal, quietly dominates the foreground and hints at an intrigue in the background, involving an unscrupulous statesman and compromising a royal lady. Questions remain, which M. Dupin is much too discreet to raise: what was written in that letter? by whom to whom? and how did its temporary disappearance affect the writer and the recipent? But these would form a subject for a novelist rather than a romancer, the sort of subject Balzac had just been treating in A *Shadowy Affair.*

Poe's tales of ratiocination, because of their detachment, occupy a special category. No doubt they protest too much that the situation is under control; the author makes so self-conscious an exhibit of rationality that we feel he has been challenged on that score. His spokesman is an imperturbable master of ceremonies, who says in effect, "Please observe, I have nothing up my sleeve." In most of his other tales, the speaker is a maniacal stranger who says, "Don't look now, but we're being followed." A typical figure is William Wilson, who apostrophizes himself as "outcast of all outcasts most abandoned," and asks himself whether he has not been living in a dream. Yet "William Wilson," like *The Narrative of Arthur Gordon Pym*, has certain roots in autobiographical reminiscence. The narrator tells us he will not sully the fair page with his real appellation, but will call himself by "a fictitious title not very dissimilar to the real." William Wilson is not altogether dissimilar to Edgar Allan; for Poe went under the surname of his hated foster-father during the period of schooling he spent in England, which he vividly recollects in the story. In the disgrace that terminates Wilson's sojourn at Oxford, there is a recollection of the gambling and drinking that led to Poe's withdrawal from the University of Virginia. Self-portraiture may be emotionally exaggerated when Wilson reproaches himself with a record of "unspeakable misery and unpardonable crime." But the whispering voice of the other Wilson—namesake and schoolmate, best friend and worst enemy—is even more intimately to be identified with Poe himself; for, as the epigraph warns us, this is the specter of conscience.

Among the many and varied appearances of the alter ego in our literature, this is the most explicit. It is not a psychological case of split personality, like that of Dr. Jekyll and Mr. Hyde, who are really two personages struggling within one schizophrenic person. Rather, it is the mythical archetype known as the *Doppelgänger*, a spiritual emanation of the self as it ought to be, and hence a standing rebuke to the ego, like *The Double* of Dostoevsky or Wilde's *Picture of Dorian Gray*. That intensive bond runs parallel to the vicarious kinship between writer and reader, which Baudelaire so poignantly evokes: *"—Hypocrite lecteur,—mon semblable—mon frère!"* When Poe brings the two William Wilsons together for the last time, during a Roman carnival, they are masquerading in identical costumes; and when the narrator stabs his black-masked double, his bloody apparition in a mirror informs him that he has committed moral suicide. Thus William Wilson is at once the accuser and the accused, with the better of the two selves tracking down the crimes that the worser perpetrates. When Poe's point of view pivots from the detective to the criminal, and to the grisly business of perpetration, he produces a series of confessions in which the narrator accuses himself. The impulse to confess is the "nightmare of the soul" that animates "The Imp of the Perverse." The details of self-incrimination, in this mordant sketch, are incidental to Poe's generalizations regarding the motive of perversity and the need for release. These are illustrated by a harrowing metaphor, through which we share not only his mood but his danger. "We stand upon the brink of a precipice. We peer into the abyss—we grow sick and dizzy." Despite the urge to draw back, we are transfixed by a shapeless feeling which becomes a nameless thought. What can it be?

> It is merely the idea of what would be our sensations during the sweeping precipitancy of a fall from such a height. And this fall—this rushing annihilation—for the very reason that it involves that one most ghastly and loathsome of all the most ghastly and loathsome images of death and suffering which have ever presented themselves to our imagination—for this very cause we now the most vividly desire it. And because our reason violently deters us from the brink, *therefore* do we the most impetuously approach it. There is no passion in nature so demoniacally impatient, as that of him who, shuddering upon the edge of a precipice, thus meditates a plunge.

This must be the longing to fall that suddenly overtook Arthur Gordon Pym at the most vertiginous stage of his misadventures. Poe's insight has focused upon that apparent lack of motivation which has nonetheless eventuated in the most desperate deeds, and which has been given its latter-day formulation in André Gide's concept of the *acte gratuit*, the lawless code of so many modern heroes. Poe, indeed, may have put his finger on the animus that Hawthorne failed to specify in the unpardonable sin of Ethan Brand. The spirit of perverseness, in capital letters, motivates "The Black Cat"; but here it is abetted by alcoholism, "the fiend Intem-

perance," and personified by the titular animal, a demonic familiar who is also an agent of retribution. The
splash of white upon its breast is a portent which differentiates it from its wholly black predecessor, and
makes its hideous shriek a denunciation no less pointed
than the accusing conscience of William Wilson. The
blackness of the other cat, Pluto, has externalized the
pointless cruelty of its master; and after he has hanged
it, the gruesome catastrophe is portended by the im-
press of its body on the white plaster, an accident caused
by the burning of the house. Since the story is recounted
as a chronicle of "mere household events," it may be
relevant to think of Poe's own domestic surroundings:
his wife, dying of consumption, and her pet, a tortoise-
shell cat. In his tale the cat has a larger part than the
wife; and her assassination is the outcome of the hatred
the cat incites; but the two are exhumed together at
the climax, when the narrator perversely betrays himself by boasting of his well-constructed house. Even in
Landor's cottage, as in the house of Usher, there may
be a corpse immured.

The same last-minute compulsion, the gesture of
hybris that serves as an invitation to nemesis, rounds
out the highly concentrated recital of "The Tell-Tale
Heart." Here the task of reducing the phantasm to the
commonplace, which Poe enjoins on the readers of
"The Black Cat," is simplified by internalizing the action. Again the interlocutor is the murderer; but his
antagonism seems so unmotivated, and he is so terribly
anxious to fend off the suspicion of insanity, that he
establishes himself in our minds as a monomaniac. Two
kinds of blackness, madness and murder, seem to coin-
cide. In the pitch-black room we see little of the victim,

the old man whose baleful eye is refracted through the deranged mentality of our informant—or is this Poe's way of retrospectively dealing with the surveillance of John Allan? What we seem to be hearing, the heartbeat of the dead man, is the subjective impression of the man who has killed him, and who awaits his own doom in a state of pulsating suspense. The heart was a conventional symbol, an allegorical virtue, a tell-tale in another sense for Hawthorne. For Poe, to whom the tick of a watch could be ominous, the cardiac rhythm marks the expiring flow of time itself. As a professed materialist, he prefers to dwell upon the psychology of crime rather than upon the ethics of guilt. The psychological twist that makes his criminals more effectual than his lovers is hinted in an embittered sentence from his correspondence: "It was my crime to have no one on earth who cared for me or loved me." Crime, in the absence of love, becomes a test of values; and murder, the transgression of ultimate law, becomes a moral equivalent for original sin. Hence it has been argued by a German philosopher, Max Bense, that the murder-mystery is a *Mordepik*, the epic of our time.

Through adroit use of compression and allusion, Poe's favored medium, the soliloquy, reaches its fullest development in "The Cask of Amontillado." This is because so much of the attention centers upon the antagonist, who is ironically named Fortunato, and who is tricked out for the carnival season in the descriptive motley of a fool. By an unspecified insult he has provoked the protagonist, less conspicuously garbed in black cape and mask, to plot a revenge which leads through the catacombs. The revenger bears the proud name of Montresor (*mon trésor*); and his boasted treasure, the cask with which he appeals to the connoisseur-ship of his bibulous enemy, is buried in the family wine-cellar. But the dank vaults, whitened by niter, are littered with skulls and bones as well as bottles; for the underground destination is also a family crypt. There, in the torchlight, Montresor deliberately condemns the drunken Fortunato to living burial, and literally im-mures him with his masonic trowel. The final words are *"In pace requiescat."* Of course, the ghost will not rest in peace; he will continue to haunt the author; yet for once it would seem that the murderer goes free, while the reproving voice of his victim is securely in-terred. The cold-blooded ending of "The Cask of Amon-tillado" has a close counterpart in Balzac's story, "La Grande Bretèche," where a jealous husband walls up his wife's lover. There is an instructive contrast between that French triangle and Poe's preoccupation with the double, two devoted enemies with no heroine standing between them. For Poe the lure is not sex but drink; the wine is the instrument of poetic justice; and the venge-ance, on a moralistic level, almost invites us to read the story as a temperance tract.

At a more subliminal level, Poe seems to be punishing himself for his dipsomania. Under its confounding in-fluence, his criminals become victims, more passive than active, masochistic rather than sadistic. "The Man of the Crowd" is a lonely drunkard, whom Poe tracks to nis lair, a gin-palace. In "Thou Art the Man," which forcibly combines the humorous and the detective vein, a corpse, concealed in a wine-case and delivered as a present, is empowered by ventriloquism to lodge the accusation against its murderer. Along with drink, food exerts its attractions—the more so, perhaps, because Poe

could never quite take it for granted—in such hungry
sketches as "Bon-Bon" and "The Duc de l'Omelette."
His references to opium are frequent and fascinated.
If the phantasmagoria of Coleridge and De Quincey
were inspired by drugs, then it might be said—in the
equivocal sense—that Poe's manuscripts were found in
bottles. Yet if he makes nothing else clear, in "The
Angel of the Odd," he shows his awareness that intoxi-
cation is a treacherous source of inspiration. Rather, it
may be a foretaste of death. The connection between
the two is explicit in "Shadow: A Parable," where the
interlocutor is the Greek Oinos, whose name would
mean wine to his compatriots, and the epigraph is from
the Twenty-Third Psalm. In a black-draped chamber,
around a table of ebony, a company of seven carouses
at the bier of a shrouded youth who has just died of the
plague:

> There were things around us and about of which I
> can render no distinct account—things material
> and spiritual—heaviness in the atmosphere—a sense
> of suffocation—anxiety—and, above all, that terrible
> state of existence which the nervous experience
> when the senses are keenly living and awake, and
> meanwhile the powers of thought lie dormant. A
> dead weight hung upon us.

This is the stifling air that Poe's neurasthenic characters
habitually breathe, the aura of dread that envelops all
he touches. Now it presages an unfamiliar visitant who,
upon challenge, announces himself to be Shadow. The
reverberation of this announcement, through a closing
sentence, is curiously similar to the last cadence of
Joyce's story, "The Dead," where it is the whiteness of

snow that symbolizes all those who have preceded the living into the Valley of the Shadow.

> And then did we, the seven, start from our seats in horror, and stand trembling, and shuddering, and aghast, for the tones in the voice of the shadow were not the tones of any one being, but of a multitude of beings, and varying in their cadences from syllable to syllable, fell duskly upon our ears in the well-remembered and familiar accents of many thousand departed friends.

The themes of drink, disease, and death are closely interwoven in "King Pest," which unwontedly describes itself as "A Tale Containing an Allegory," and seems much too slight for so heavy a burden. Two fuddled sailors, looking for a tavern, stumble into an undertaker's shop in a plague-ridden area. The funereal creatures they encounter, in the full panoply of black palls and sable plumes, seem to be allegorical cartoons of the reigning monarch, Andrew Jackson, and other political figures of the day. The dubious point of the hostile joke seems to hinge on the word *pestilential,* a term of condemnation which functioned as a genteel euphemism for *damned.* But pestilence was a grim reality for Poe, who had lived through an epidemic of cholera, and who generalizes the experience in his most pictorial composition, "The Masque of the Red Death." As a "decorist," he stages his revels in an imperial suite, which he expressly compares to the *décor* of Victor Hugo's archromantic spectacle, *Hernani,* consisting of seven rooms, six of them lavishly colored, the seventh furnished with sable draperies and lit by scarlet-paned windows. Always fond of fancy-dress, he attires his characters as masquers, both grotesque and arbesque, so that the entrance of Death itself seems a part of the masquerade. This quickly turns into a *danse macabre*, which re-enacts its medieval object-lesson by striking down Prince Prospero in his prosperity, after a pursuit through the seven rooms. Through the implications of the number, the spatial arrangement becomes a temporal sequence; and time itself stops with the midnight stroke of the ebony clock. The closing note, echoed from the pseudo-Miltonic last line of Pope's *Dunciad*, predicates a reduction of cosmos to chaos: "And Darkness and Decay and the Red Death held illimitable dominion over all."

The true darkness, as Dupin's friend calls it, is non-existence. And, since "the valley of the shadow of death" is one of Poe's thematic phrases, it is worth observing that the Psalmist's image has been more literally translated—by the revisers of the Authorized Version—as "the deep darkness." The color-scheme of red and black is a manifest configuration of disease and death. But "the redness and the horror of blood" must have been especially painful for Poe because of an intimate association; we know that disease had first stricken his wife, even while she was singing, with a hemorrhage. Many of his characters seem to have pathological defects, as well as neurotic peculiarities. "The Man That Was Used Up" is a cruel joke about an old Indian-fighter, so badly maimed that he hardly exists apart from his artificial limbs and synthetic organs. The character whose physical endowment is most extravagantly praised, the social lion of "Lionizing," is chiefly remarkable for the size of his nose—though it does not have the autonomy of Gogol's "Nose." Not all of Poe's protagonists suffer from so absolute a deficiency as Mr.

Lackobreath in "Loss of Breath"; but something vital seems, more often than not, to be lacking. Poe's interest in suspended animation, in exactly determining "the boundaries which divide Life from Death," is the other side of his phobia against living inhumation, "the most terrific of . . . extremes which has ever fallen to the lot of mere mortality." Imagination goes into the grave alive, in "The Premature Burial," and experiences the rush of subsiding thoughts and last feelings:

> The unendurable oppression of the lungs—the stifling fumes of the damp earth—the clinging of the death garments—the rigid embrace of the narrow house—the blackness of the absolute Night—the silence like a sea that overwhelms—the unseen but palpable presence of the Conqueror Worm—these things, with the thoughts of the air and grass above, with memory of dear friends who would fly to save us if but informed of our fate, and with consciousness that of this fate they can *never* be informed— that our hopeless portion is that of the really dead —these considerations, I say, carry into the heart, which still palpitates, a degree of appalling and intolerable horror from which the most daring imagination must recoil.

Yet Poe does not recoil. On the contrary, his charnel fancy lingers over "the one sepulchral Idea," rehearsing horrendous anecdotes, shuddering enthusiastically over ghoulish circumstantial details, and ranging the lore of entombment from Young's *Night-Thoughts* to the Black Hole of Calcutta. After this rhapsodic and essayistic introduction, the tale itself comes as an anticlimax, an exorcism calculated to release us from the spell of such terrors, a rescue from the clutches of earth via the elements of water and air. The cataleptic narrator is a Poe-like inventor who, against such a mortal emergency, has contrived some ingenious modes of escape. But, alas, he has no chance to utilize them. The premature burial, it appears, is a hoax which his obsession plays upon him. Instead of having awakened in his coffin, he gradually realizes that he is in the cabined berth of an anchored boat, a somewhat healthier and happier place of confinement; and, though it scarcely proved so for Arthur Gordon Pym, here the realization is a catharsis.

"The Pit and the Pendulum" moves toward a similar outcome, a deliverance from forces of darkness; but, unlike Poe's other tales, it is framed by historical circumstance. The narrator is a prisoner of the Spanish Inquisition; and he is delivered, in the final paragraph, by the armies of the French Revolution. His narrative begins, "I was sick—sick unto death with that long agony . . ." And the rest of the staccato paragraph is his confused remembrance of the trial, the sentence, the grotesque white lips of the black-robed judges, and finally "the blackness of darkness" itself. With him we sink through deepening states of unconsciousness—the swoon, the dream, delirium, madness—toward the definitive blackout. For a short while he fears the worst of Poe's deaths, premature burial. Physical torture adds to mental torment, as the dungeon becomes discernible and the stage-machinery comes into play. If the pit is "typical of hell," the pendulum is arranged and decorated to resemble the scythe of time. This menacing device of execution was foreshadowed in a tale published as "The Scythe of Time," and republished as "A Predicament," which is Poe's burlesque of the *Blackwood* thriller, "The

Man in the Bell." That predicament was decapitation by the hand of a clock; and Poe's earlier victim is a bluestocking, who stands upon the back of a Negro servant and looks out through an aperture in a clock-tower. In the more serious "Colloquy of Monos and Una," recording the transition from time to eternity by way of death, Poe terms it "a mental pendulous pulsation." Time is the pendulum, the sword of Damocles, that hangs over every man, while space is the pit to which a smouldering and ever-contracting existence condemns him.

So suggestive is the elaborate contrivance which Poe has brought to bear upon his suffering protagonist that it has encouraged interpretation at numerous levels. At the most unblushingly Freudian, the pit and the pendulum are the respective symbols of feminine and masculine sexuality; and the author is, as it were, the witness of his own conception. We may well prefer, more objectively, to connect Poe's allusions with history, reading his tale as a memoir of the imprisoned revolutionary, who was an archetypal hero for the romanticists, and as an unanticipated triumph for the spirit of enlightenment over the bugbears of superstition and bigotry. The hero is not less heroic because he suffers rather than acts; nor is he less contemporary in an epoch which has so vastly multiplied the sentence of political imprisonment, and which has visualized the ordeal of life itself—through the apprehensive eyes of Franz Kafka—as an arbitrary trial, an unjust imprisonment, and an unjustified condemnation. For Poe the will is constrained to choose between evils which, upon confrontation, seem worse than their alternatives: the pit or the pendulum, the frying-pan versus the fire. If his version

seems prophetic of Kafka's penal colony, it is likewise
reminiscent of Plato's cave; and he is consistently drawn
toward the cavernous and the tenebrous because, as
D. H. Lawrence has memorably put it, "He was an adventurer into vaults and cellars and horrible underground passages of the human soul." His climactic adventure, "The Pit and the Pendulum," abandons him
to the existential dilemma: the agony of the prostrate
individual, isolated and immobilized, surrounded by
watchful rats, threatened by an encroaching mechanism,
and impelled toward a gaping abyss.

Poe's dramatism tends toward monodrama, in which
the sole actor is acted upon by chimeras, like Flaubert's
Saint Anthony. Faced with such isolation, Hawthorne's
egoists had been urged to forget themselves in the idea
of another, in love and marriage and domesticity. But
that idea was foredoomed, with Poe, to throw him back
upon himself. "I was a child and she was a child"—he
might have been lyrically celebrating his own marriage
in "Annabel Lee." In his child-wife's illness, and in their
common immaturity, both were dependent upon her
mother, to whom Poe addresses one of his most fervent
sonnets. Motherly or sisterly types predominate, in his
limited gallery of heroines. Characteristically, the poet
walks with Psyche, his sister, his soul, while lamenting
the lost Ulalume; in one of his extravaganzas, "The
Spectacles," the myopic narrator is nearly tricked into
marrying his great-great-grandmother. Poe's verse is an
echo-chamber through which the names of his heroines
ullulate, none more plangently than that of Lenore,
which he borrowed from the raven-haired maiden of
Bürger's romantic ballad. In the whole range of his

tales, Baudelaire has observed, there is not a single love-story. This sweeping observation is reinforced by the handful of exceptions to it: a series of love-stories in which the heroine dies, or is dead, or is temporarily recalled from the grave. Two discarded lines from an early poem, "Romance," are disarmingly candid in their avowal of necrophilia:

> I could not love, except where Death
> Was mingling his with Beauty's breath.

Poe's couplet echoes the meter and the matter of a poem upon which he modeled two or three others, Bishop King's "Exequy" on the death of his wife, with its metaphysical conceit of the tryst in the tomb. A quotation from "The Exequy" is the key to Poe's overwrought tale, "The Assignation," in which suicide dictates the terms whereby the lovers are united. A tale originally titled "Life in Death," and subsequently "The Oval Portrait," is Poe's variation on the theme of "The Artist of the Beautiful" or "The Unknown Masterpiece." Poe's treatment contrasts with Hawthorne's and with Balzac's by enabling the artist to capture the beauty of his model at the expense of her life. "The Oblong Box" could only be what we suspect, a coffin enshrining a dead heroine. Poe varies the usual design by transporting that object on a sea-voyage in the manner of Pym's narrative, and by detecting an imposture as in the tales of ratiocination; nevertheless the maid, who travels in the place of her deceased mistress, conforms to Poe's habit of substituting one woman for another.

The most persistent motif of his prose, as of his poetry, is what might—all too etymologically—be termed the posthumous heroine. Under four different names, she dominates a sequence of analogous tales, among which the earliest is "Berenice." The focus of "Berenice" is still on the narrator, the visionary heir of gloomy halls, who pursues daydreams and mystical studies in a library, where he was born and where his mother died. "The realities of the world affected me as visions, and as visions only," he confesses, "while the wild ideas of the land of dreams became, in turn, not the material of my every-day existence, but in very deed that existence utterly and solely in itself." This is the crazed perspective through which we glimpse his cousin Berenice, passing the raven-winged hours in the domain of Arnheim. For her, he admits, his passion has not been of the heart but of the mind. She has become subject to trances, and thus to the hazards of living inhumation; it is her apparent death that prevents their hesitant nuptials. That she must have been buried alive is revealed along with the even more horrible revelation that he, in a fit of monomania, has visited her tomb and extracted her teeth. Since he is so demonstrably mad, we are skeptical of his explanation, and even of his testimony: did she really die, or did he kill her? Groping to explain his fetishism, he adapts a sentiment from the French: *"Tous ses dents étaient des idées."* Unquestionably, her teeth constitute an *idée fixe* for the narrator; and yet, in fixing upon this particular fetish, he seems to have accorded expression to fears and antipathies located deep within the author's unconscious, and vulgarly adumbrated in sexual folklore.

Now there is factual evidence of premature burial, enough to furnish a basis for legends of vampirism, though the occurrence can hardly have been as universal as Poe would have us believe. Nearly everything in "Berenice," even the transformation of her ringlets from jet to yellow, could be accounted for on naturalistic— if not altogether normal—grounds. When she has died at last, presumably, she will not be heard from again. But some of the other tales press beyond the grave and into the legendary sphere, replacing the absent heroine by a female alter ego. Like so many of his contemporaries, Poe had been beguiled by the enchantments of *Undine,* the romanticized folktale of the Baron de la Motte-Fouqué. In the waverings of the German knight between the earthly princess to whom he is plighted and the naiad of the fountain who claims him, there is ample precedent for the weird dilemmas of Poe's lovers, torn as they are between two loves, one of them in this world and the other out of it. Thus "Morella" is the name of both mother and daughter; and it may be that the mutual relation between these two is more significant than their relations with the narrator of their tale. The senior Morella is mystical, erudite, and somewhat pedagogical, as befits the graduate of a German university. Her husband tells us frankly that he abhors her in life and adores her in death. The junior Morella so completely takes her mother's place that, if we do not believe in reincarnation, we must perforce suspect incest. The crucial scene enacts a ceremonial, as the narrator carries his dead daughter from her baptismal font to her mother's empty tomb. The epigraph, cited to stress the persistence of identity, is from Plato's argu-

ment that lovers are halves seeking wholeness: "Itself,
by itself solely, ONE everlastingly, and single."

"Morella" was a rehearsal for "Ligeia," which Poe regarded as his most imaginative tale. Here again the
arithmetical formula is the coalescence of two into
singleness; but Poe enlarges it by making the heroine's
double her polar opposite and by dramatizing, with his
eeriest stage-effects, the substitution of the one for the
other. It is not for nothing that *Ligeia* rhymes with
idea in "Al Aaraaf." In her own story, she is the most
brilliant of Poe's dark ladies, another learned paragon
from a decaying city near the Rhine. After her death,
the narrator takes up his abode at an old abbey in England, where he finds solace in opium, if not in Ligeia's
rival, "the fair-haired, the blue-eyed Lady Rowena Tre-
vanion of Tremaine." That name is all but a cross-
reference to *Ivanhoe,* and to the polarity between the
blonde Rowena and the brunette Rebecca; but Poe's
taste differed utterly from Scott's. Understandably, the
Lady Rowena languishes amid the embellishments of
her bridal chamber: the ebony couch with its pall-like
canopy, the cloth-of-gold tapestry with its jetty arabesques, the five Egyptian sarcophagi of black granite.
Little by little her decorator-husband realizes that a
vampire has taken possession of her. Her hair is no
longer fair: *"it was blacker than the raven wings of
midnight!"* Her eyes are not blue: "these are the full,
and the black, and the wild eyes—of my lost love—of
the Lady—of the LADY LIGEIA." Since Poe could go no
farther in this direction, a pendant, "Eleonora," seeks its
new thrill by means of a happy ending. The wraith of
the first wife, Eleonora, absolves her cousin-widower of

his vow to her memory, and blesses his union with her successor, Ermengarde.

The pattern is most spectacularly embodied in "The Fall of the House of Usher," where it has been visualized through the impressionable sensibilities of a spectator, and relayed to us "with an utter depression of soul which [he] can compare to no earthly sensation more properly than to the after-dream of the reveller upon opium." Poe is therewith afforded his best opportunity for an atmospheric presentation, in which scenic detail is artfully confounded with emotional reaction. The house of Usher is, ambiguously, "both the family and the family mansion," the stately gloom of the building itself presaging the decadence of its inhabitants. The pallid and cadaverous Roderick Usher and his twin sister, the Lady Madeline, happen to be the last of their ancient and inbred race. "Sympathies of a scarcely intelligible nature had always existed between them," we are told, with Byronic innuendo. Roderick, languidly poring over his esoteric books, is a Hamlet whose artistic gifts have been introverted by "the grim phantasm Fear." The most describable of his abstract paintings brightly depicts an inaccessible tunnel. Of the dirges he wildly improvises, to the accompaniment of his rhapsodic guitar, Poe reprints one, the poem he elsewhere printed as "The Haunted Palace." By a similar transposition, "The Conqueror Worm" is reintroduced as a poetic commentary upon "Ligeia." Another poem, "Israfel," is linked with "The Fall of the House of Usher" through the quoted metaphor comparing the heart to a lute. Roderick's heartstrings vibrate to the decline, the catalepsy, and the interment of Madeline. Heralded by a reading from a romance, she emerges from the vault in her bloody shroud, and brother and sister share their death-agonies.

Shakespeare's image for the gates of the sepulcher, "ponderous and marble jaws," is significantly modified by Poe, who replaces "marble" with "ebony." The symbolism of his interpolated stanzas—eclipsing the downright melodrama of Thomas Hood's stanzas on "The Haunted House"—rests upon the analogy between the façade of a palace and the face of a man, between the house and the brain. In Poe's theoretical phraseology, Roderick's *morale* is influenced by the *physique* of his dwelling, from which for years he has not ventured forth. Its "vacant eye-like windows," which strike the approaching observer, foreshadow the mental condition of its occupant. The final collapse of its ruins into the tarn, while the retreating narrator looks back through the moonlit storm at the desolated landscape, projects an apocalypse of the mind. So much is explicit in the verse and prose of the tale; more is implicit if we look ahead, or if we relocate Poe's Gothic terrors within a regional perspective. Much that seems forced, in William Faulkner's work, becomes second nature when we think of him as Poe's inheritor. We think of Caddy and Quentin, those two doomed siblings of the house of Compson, or of Emily Grierson, that old maid who clings to the corpse of her lover. In retrospect, Poe's work acquires a sociological meaning when it is linked with the culture of the plantation in its feudal pride and its foreboding of doom. But there is still another sense in which Roderick Usher with all his idiosyncrasies, awaiting his own death and hastening that of his sister, prefigures a larger and nearer situation: the accomplished heir of all the ages, the hypersensitive end-product of civilization itself, driven underground by the pressure of fear.

Poe never exorcised his posthumous heroine. Her ghost reappears and vanishes again; and when she is gone, she leaves some ghastly memento. The teeth of Berenice glimmer in the dusk like the disembodied grin of the Cheshire Cat. It is not surprising that the death of a beautiful woman should be the theme of Poe's most remembered poem, or that he should have considered it "emblematical of mournful and never-ending remembrance." It is harder to believe that he arrived at this theme by a process of sheer ratiocination, or that "The Raven" was so deliberate an exercise in euphony as he makes out in his essay, "The Philosophy of Composition." Poets, from Sir Philip Sidney to T. S. Eliot, have rationalized their practice by writing criticism; and Poe was peculiarly eager, as we have seen, to convince the world of his self-mastery. Yet his very phrase for obtaining a concentrated effect, "a close circumscription of space," harks back obsessively to his dread of confinement. The poem itself, with its echolalia, with its repeated sounds predominating over redundant meanings, is most satisfactorily read as an incantation. The bird of ill omen, even more than Poe's cat, seems to be an official emissary from the powers of blackness. Ravens had served as literary companions from the days of Elijah to those of Barnaby Rudge. What distinguishes this one is not the faculty of speech, but the specialized ability to utter no more than one word, which is the echo of the poet's hopelessness. Each reiteration of the

compound adverb sounds the note of finality with *never*;
whereupon, with *more*, it prolongs the suspense; whereupon the subsequent stanza revives the interrogation
and repeats the deadening negation.

Poe too, like Hawthorne, has his haunted chamber.
The pallid bust of Pallas over the door may indeed
be emblematic of those middle-aged bluestockings to
whom he looked for motherly consolation. But it is
quite overbalanced by the bird—or devil—who, like the
vulture preying on the liver of Prometheus, finally sinks
its beak in the poet's heart. His questioning has elicited
a refrain which, upon repetition, becomes as meaningless as the blank result of Captain Ahab's explorations
of the ultimate mystery. The scholar ends by sitting
alone in his Faustian study; everything else in his world,
including the expectation of an afterlife, is lost with
Lenore. He can envision other illusory mates, as he does
in "The Colloquy of Monos and Una." But, after all,
Una is merely the Latin feminine for the pronoun signified by Monos in the Greek masculine: one. Again the
dialogue is reduced to a monologue. All of Poe's dramatis personae scale down, sooner or later, to the singular and single-minded person of their creator. He was
much impressed by Bulwer-Lytton's "Monos and Dai-
monos: A Legend," where the fugitive vainly searches
for solitude in the wilderness, and learns—like William
Wilson—that he cannot shake off his demon. Poe also
liked to quote La Bruyère (or was it Pascal?) to the
effect that most of our ills spring from our inability to
be alone with ourselves—a maxim which "The Man
of the Crowd" exemplifies, and which *The Lonely
Crowd* has latterly confirmed. The dread of loneliness,
the terrors of the night, the anguish of being isolated

with one's demon—or raven—the prospect at which other men blench, Poe made it his business to contemplate. The "tendency to one," which reduces his tales to monologues, and his monologuists to solipsists, is reformulated in *Eureka* as the principle of creation itself.

"Everything in Poe is dead," Allen Tate has remarked. This does not controvert the tribute of Baudelaire, who ascribes Poe's special illumination to the phosphorescence of decay. The premise of knowledge is that all men are mortal, and the insights of tragedy culminate in the posture of dying. If Tolstoy's outlook could be summed up in his infantile effort to break through his swaddling bands, then it would be Poe's self-revealing gesture to assume the shroud. More than once he reminds us that Tertullian's credo, "I believe because it is absurd," was inspired by the doctrine of resurrection. And though Poe's resurrections prove ineffectual or woefully incomplete, we are reminded by the Existentialists that the basis of man's plight is absurdity. Poe's cult of blackness is not horripilation for horripilation's sake; it is a bold attempt to face the true darkness in its most tangible manifestations. If life is a dream, then death is an awakening. The dreamer coexists with another self, who may be his accuser or his victim, or his all too evanescent bride. His house may be a Gothic ruin or a home-like cottage; but any sojourn must be temporary; and the journey thence, though it ranges outward and upward, leads downward toward the very closest circumscription of space, the grave. Place and time, to sum them up in Poe's symbols, are his pit and his pendulum; the narrowing yet bottomless abyss that underlies the human condition, the ticking and tolling that measure and limit the heartbeat. Character, though it wears many masks, does not escape detection: it is the cowering spirit of underground man. Yet plot threads a lucid course through delirious labyrinths of grief and disaster, a mind encompassed by shadows, reason in madness.

VI

The Avenging Dream

HERMAN MELVILLE seems, at first glance, simpler: not so haunted by memories as Hawthorne, not so driven to extremes as Poe. As the boy who really went to sea, the man of action relating his adventures, impulsive rather than compulsive, self-taught and extroverted, Melville seems to live up to the pioneering ideals of the American character. "We are the pioneers of the world, the advance-guard, sent on through the wilderness of untried things, to break a path in the New World that is ours," he declares in *White-Jacket*. That it should have been he who discerned and attested the power of blackness is our strongest evidence of its importance in our literature. His literary success, while it lasted, was based upon other and easier qualities: on our national preference for writings which have been lived, on the perennial fascination of the exotic or the adventurous, and on his vivid talent for communicating what he had experienced or observed. But he was not content to remain, like so many of our successful writers, a reporter exploiting the extrinsic interest of his material. He wanted, as he asserted in a poem, "To wrestle with the angel, Art." He was a born story-teller who, with much effort and little appreciation, made himself into an artist. The sailor-reader in *White-Jacket* boasts of men of letters who have once been sailors; and Melville interrupts his chronicle to express the enthusiastic wish that his fine countryman, Hawthorne of Salem, might have served on a man-of-war. This is not an inviting thought to pursue; and Hawthorne did not respond to the theme that Melville later pressed upon him, a grim anecdote about a sailor's homecoming. No, it was Melville who gravitated in Hawthorne's direction, toward the introspective and the speculative. Melville's career was a gradual introversion, overshadowed with a special melancholy of his own, unfolding a latent complexity which makes the elder writer look simplistic in retrospect.

"From my twenty-fifth year," he wrote to Hawthorne, "I date my life." This is to reckon Melville's development from the beginning of his authorship, not including four previous years of intensive South Sea voyaging or the brief maiden voyage before, out of which his earliest and most popular books would be drawn. During the twelve years that followed, which witnessed his marriage and the birth of his children, he wrote and published ten volumes of imaginative prose. To call them works of fiction would be begging a moot question: the interaction between his autobiography and his artistry. To use his simplest terms, he begins with narrative, with first-hand accounts of his own experiences, and proceeds toward romance in the Hawthornesque definition, overshooting the mark for better and worse. But though he could work wonders with a set of facts, though he could exaggerate like a backwoods humorist, invention did not come to Melville naturally; the factual anecdotes he had passed along to his readers so casually seemed much more wonderful to them than his desperate efforts to symbolize deeper and stranger truths; and after he had used up his personal repertory, he found his characteristic subject-matter in documents about fellow adventurers. To complete the paradox, his single book that might with any precision be called a novel, *Pierre, or The Ambiguities*, the book that comes closest to home in its domesticity, is the most sensational in its violence. It is also Melville's most explicit depiction of the literary life as he knew it, an existence far less comfortable than maritime service. Not the least of those ambiguities is the self-portrait of the young author at his desk composing his masterpiece. "Two books are being writ"—not successively, as some of Melville's interpreters would have it, but simultaneously. One, a work of observation, addresses itself to the public; the other, a work of imagination, stays with the author.

Every man has two saddles, according to *Pierre*, one for the land and the other for the sea. Pierre Glendinning, as it were in the saddle, rides forth in quest of truth from his ancestral estate, Saddle Meadows, all too heavily saddled by those Titanic burdens which he sees prefigured in Mount Saddleback. He stands, among Melville's heroes, uniquely landbound. Yet, just as Melville's seascapes are metaphorical landscapes, just as the Pacific becomes a prairie, so *Pierre* shifts from equestrian to nautical imagery:

Weary with the invariable earth, the restless sailor
breaks from every enfolding arm, and puts to sea
in height of tempest that blows off shore. But in
the long night-watches at the antipodes, how
heavily that ocean gloom lies in vast bales upon the
deck; thinking that that very moment in his de-
serted hamlet-home the household sun is high, and
many a sun-eyed maiden meridian as the sun. He
curses Fate; himself he curses; his senseless madness, which is himself. For whoso once has known
this sweet knowledge, and then fled with it; in
absence, to him the avenging dream will come.

That dream is nostalgia, the idyll of security, the penalty
we pay for our aspirations, the bliss of the commonplace which Thomas Mann would so poignantly regret.
Its revenge is to overtake the seafarer, who has defied
it in Bulkington's belief "that all deep, earnest thinking is but the intrepid effort of the soul to keep the
open independence of her sea; while the wildest waves
of heaven and earth conspire to cast her on the treacherous, slavish shore." But *Moby-Dick* also warns us expressly against pushing off from the gentle earth into
the devilish ocean that surrounds it. "Yonder, to wind-
ward, all is blackness of doom; but to leeward, homeward—" and Starbuck is interrupted by a flash of lightning. The intellectual voyager, like the youth Redburn
at the moment of sailing, may well wish that the ship
were a dream and that his home were the actuality. A
youthful sketch, one of Melville's first publications,
"The Death Craft," conjures up a Poe-like vision of
horror which reappears in *Redburn* and is transmuted
in "Benito Cereno." But here the spectral apparition

turns out to be merely a nightmare, and the sailor-narra-
tor awakens in the arms of his bride. The situation is
reversed in *Moby-Dick*, when Ishmael wakes up in the
bed he shares with Queequeg and remembers a circumstance of his childhood—whether a reality or a
dream he cannot say. He recollects that his stepmother
sent him to bed in the daytime as a punishment for attempting to climb up the chimney like a sweep. Dozing
off at last, he did not regain his consciousness until the
sunlit room was enveloped "in outer darkness." Then,
with an appalling shock, he seemed to feel that a nameless phantom was sitting at his bedside, and that "a
supernatural hand" was clasped in his.

Though the mystery still puzzles Ishmael, Melville
sheds some light by recurring to it at this point—a
point of transition between the land and the sea. He
looks backward through time and homeward through
space to a childish prank which, were it not for maternal intervention, would have had the effect of black-
ening Ishmael. The area he wanted to explore, the most
vital part of the house, figures in the later sketch, "I
and my Chimney," as a symbol of the narrator's inner-
most integrity. From Ishmael's day of enforced seclusion Melville, unlike the centripetal Hawthorne, will
break out and range far into the night; the journey
from this house, and from this room, is centrifugal. The
wanderer, in his loneliness, may seek companionship;
and, to his own surprise, he may find such another self
as the black man now sleeping at Ishmael's side. But
his wanderlust has an ulterior objective, which is nothing less than to come to grips with the supernatural, as
it has been obscurely apprehended in Ishmael's dream.
And if that object eludes his philosophical curiosity,

at the social level he continues to reach out a fraternal hand. Hence Melville, lured by cosmic enigmas and hounded by mundane worries, has sea-dreams at home and land-dreams on shipboard. The familiar and the strange change places, just as night and day reverse themselves in the antipodes. The realities of seafaring, such as he recounts them, were the stuff of dreams for a man like Poe; while the realities of other men, which seemed so unreal to the dreamy Hawthorne, reappear to Melville in vengeful shapes. *Mardi*, his largest venture into fantasy, intersperses its oceanic vistas with oneiric rhapsodies in the manner of De Quincey ("All seemed a dream"), merges the private reveries of the narrator with the collective unconscious ("Many souls are in me"), and projects his narration through the range of geography into the dimension of history ("I was there").

That a sailor should be at liberty to enlarge upon his own yarn, of course, was a well-established convention long before Sinbad. Melville could also claim the timely license of the pioneer, extending the frontier beyond the western coast, and commemorating that exploit with tall tales. The presupposition was not strict veracity, but the impression of authenticity conveyed by hearing the story from a man who had been there. To enter into direct relations with his audience, on the basis of an informality which soon becomes an intimacy, is Melville's arresting gift as a *raconteur*. Often his opening sentence is an abrupt exclamation, and always it sets a conversational tone. Moving at ease from the anecdotal to the hortatory, he repeatedly moves from the first person into the second. "Yes, reader . . ." "Judge, then . . ." In his search for further themes

and new viewpoints, after *Moby-Dick*, he decisively
shifted from the first to the third person. This meant
giving up the strategic role he had played in his narratives; and Melville was tired, he complained to Hawthorne, of being stereotyped as "a man who lived among
the cannibals." However, he did not fit happily—few
of our best writers do—into the part of a professional
man of letters. The motives that led him to withdraw
from it, during the latter half of his life, are tersely summarized in Ishmael's heartcry: "Oh, Time! Strength!
Cash! and Patience!" To restore his physical and mental
health, he traveled abroad. He lectured about his travels,
but his hearers were as unreceptive as his readers. In
the gnomic style he had evolved for himself, he kept
on writing verse. He read and reflected comprehensively.
By means of a routine job in the New York Custom
House, he barely managed to support his family. Out
of these years of silence he added one posthumous volume, *Billy Budd*, to his collected works.

Thus he has left us eleven volumes of prose, plus
a handful of uncollected sketches which might well be
comprised among his *Piazza Tales*. Viewing them
chronologically, we note that *Moby-Dick* occupies the
appropriate central position; five books lead up to it
and five more lead away from it. Taking for granted
this predominance, to which we shall be returning, we
may find it suggestive to consider the others in brief
succession, tracing the thread of blackness that inter-
twines with the given pattern in each case. Our starting
point, then, is the *roman vécu* of earthly paradise. Melville does not start with an account of his whaling
voyage; he saves that for *Moby-Dick*. Rather, he dis-
embarks—jumps ship, to be exact—at "pantheistic

ports"—so he would term them in a later poem—"authentic Edens in a pagan sea." In his wintry season he
would satirize the easy acclaim that Pierre first won
with a sonnet, "The Tropical Summer." But Melville
was no Robert Louis Stevenson, no Pierre Loti, no
purveyor of balmy exoticism or languid escapism. Amid
the coral reefs and breadfruit trees, amid the dalliance
and luxuriance, the note that prevails is cannibalism,
stressed by the title of his first book, *Typee: A Peep at
Polynesian Life*, where the title-word signifies a lover
of human flesh. Whether the natives are actually man-
eaters or noble savages, enemies or friends, is a doubt
sustained to the very end. At all events, they are the
most "humane, gentlemanly, and amiable set of epi-
cures" that the narrator has ever encountered. He is
welcomed by mermaids with jet-black tresses, feasted
and cured of his wound, and allowed to go canoeing
with Fayaway, a less remote enchantress than her name
suggests. But danger looms behind felicity; ambiguous
forbodings, epicurean but inhumane, reverberate from
the heathen idols in the taboo groves; and the narrator
escapes to a ship, as he had escaped from another one
at the outset.

In the mean while, he has tasted the happiness of
the pastoral state. He has enjoyed the primitive condition, as it had been idealized by Rousseau: a respite
from cares and anxieties, from guilt and shame, from all
that will be cursed by Redburn's shipmate for "bein'
snivelized." Such dubious blessings of civilization as
money, "that root of all evil," do not encumber these
islanders. As for clothes, they wear little more than
"the garb of Eden"; and Melville, whose attitude toward nakedness contrasts healthily with Hawthorne's

prurience, is tempted to moralize over how unbecoming the same costume might look on the civilized. Where Poe's black men were repulsive creatures, Melville is esthetically entranced by the passionate dances of the Polynesians; and his racial consciousness begins to undergo a radical transposition when he envisions them as pieces of "dusky statuary." On the whole, he believes, "the penalty of the fall presses very lightly upon the valley of Typee." Long afterward, in his Mediterranean journal, he is to draw an invidious comparison between the isles of Greece and the Polynesian archipelago. "The former have lost their virginity. The latter are fresh as at their first creation." If there is any serpent in the Marquesan garden, it is the contaminating contact of the white men. If the children of nature are losing their innocence, that is to be blamed upon their would-be civilizers. And if there is to be any evangelizing, Melville would make the suggestion that Marquesans be sent as missionaries to the United States. His views accord closely with the analysis of Diderot's *Supplement to the Voyage of Bougainville,* where the Tahitian tribesmen denounce their European corrupters, singling out the French priest as the veritable black man (*"cet homme noir"*).

Tahiti is the principal scene of Melville's immediate sequel, *Omoo: A Narrative of Adventures in the South Seas.* Advancing in self-dramatization, the narrator styles himself *omoo,* a rover; he resumes his interrupted tale after his rescue from the Typees by a vessel designated the Julia and commanded by Captain Guy—a pair of names which reecho from *The Narrative of Arthur Gordon Pym.* Omoo, whose misadventures can be documented by Melville's at this stage, joins a crew which is on the verge of mutiny, participates in their protest, and shares their punishment: they are taken ashore in irons and imprisoned. The island itself, so much exploited as a colonial outpost, has become a corrupting limbo between two worlds, both of which shore their cultural debris at the slatternly court of the barefoot queen. At the other extreme, which is not far away, there is the Calabooza Beretanee, that most disarming of prison camps; and Melville dwells upon its sorts and conditions of damaged humanity as fondly as Dostoevsky upon the inmates of his Siberian *House of the Dead*, or E. E. Cummings on some derelicts of the First World War in his comparable *Enormous Room*. The polemic against Protestant missions goes on, with the bibulous Father Murphy upholding the decencies. Shady Europeans, jailbirds and beachcombers, are concretely measured and found wanting by native standards of beauty. "A dark complexion. . . in a man is highly esteemed, as indicating strength of both body and soul." *Omoo*, for circumstantial reasons, may make less of an impact than *Typee*; but it marks an advance in control over more complicated materials; it presents the satiric edge of the pastoral; it concerns itself with character rather than race, with society rather than scenery.

Melville might easily have continued to hold his readers with breezy memoirs of travel, had he not veered away from the "romance of real life" to try his hand at "a real romance." *Typee* and *Omoo*, to be sure, had aroused a certain amount of incredulity; but that was an incentive to larger designs. Since fact has been received in some quarters as fiction, he argues through the preface to *Mardi: and a Voyage Thither*, why not fabricate something and pass it off as a verity? Such has invariably been the aim of the novelist. But Melville's concern was not with what contemporaneous critics, in spite of their self-conscious Americanism, liked to label *vraisemblance*. The encyclopedic subject of this large-scale exploration is what he referred to, in a letter to Hawthorne, as that "great allegory, the world." Under the guise of a South Sea archipelago, Mardi stands for the world, verbalized in the fictitious language that Melville invented along with the chartless geography of his imaginary voyage. His microcosm is neither an ideal commonwealth like Utopia nor yet an antipodal looking-glass kingdom like Erewhon; nor does it, like the countries of *Gulliver's Travels*, cast back the reflection of irony. Melville's recent reading, avid but unassimilated, provided a ballast which well nigh sank his ambitious undertaking. The result is not continuously readable, though it abounds in episodes and insights which would be the making of a lesser writer, and at least deserve to be canonized as purple passages. The difficulty is that, once he leaves the literal plane, Melville is caught between an allegory which is too narrowly topical in its allusiveness and a symbolism so transcendental that it bodies forth no more than a "spirit's phantom's phantom." Inevitably, "the mystery of mysteries is still a mystery."

If *Mardi* does not reach its symbolic Ultimate, it faces an allegorical Penultimate, surveying the nations in critical panorama and directing its sharpest criticisms at Melville's own nation, Vivenza. Through a series of political cartoons and editorial comments, he demonstrates that freedom is not the same in theory as in practice. His observations on equality might be summed up by rephrasing George Orwell: some men are less

equal than others. Those exceptions belong to the tribe
of Hamo; and on the issue of Negro slavery Melville
is an outspoken and bitter critic. "These South Savan-
nahs may yet prove battlefields," he prophesies in 1849.
But the social commentary is recklessly outdistanced
by the philosophical inquiry. King Media and his at-
tendants, philosopher, historian, and poet, seem to
stand for the mind and its traditional faculties, reason,
memory, and imagination. All their travels seem to
convey them "from dark to dark." Their guide, at one
juncture, is a blind man who tells them: "I brood and
grope in blackness." Again, the poet Yoomy takes his
perplexities to the cave of an oracular hermit.

At last, the silence was broken.

"What see you, mortal?"

"Chiefly darkness," said Yoomy, wondering at
the audacity of the question.

"I dwell in it. But what else see you, mortal?"

"The dim glimming of thy gorget."

"But that is not me. What else dost thou see?"

"Nothing."

"Then thou has found me out, and seen all.
Descend."

An imposture and an undeception, simply this and
nothing more, is an answer which will not satisfy Melville for long. For the time being, he sails onward, con-
ceding that the itinerary is endless, but pausing to emphasize two incidental relationships which will lend it
a pattern by their recurrence. The first is his version of
that eternally feminine polarity which seems to magnet-
ize all three of our authors, suspending their heroes
between those counterattractions which Henry Adams

would hail as the Virgin and Venus. Greeted as a sun-god by the Mardians, his spokesman Taji pursues the Albino beauty Yillah, she of "the snow-white skin, blue firmament eyes, and Golconda locks." He in turn is pursued by the dark vampire Hautia, heralded by three hooded damsels, "deep brunettes," avengers. "Yillah I sought; Hautia sought me." Taji's metaphysical quest becomes a domestic flight; Yillah, the fair heroine, eludes him and fades away; while the menacing Hautia, in her snaky bower, all but immolates him.

The second theme is even more recurrent; and though it is not as conspicuous in *Mardi* as elsewhere, it is fully articulated in the chapter describing Taji's favorite companion, the Viking Jarl. Melville describes their relationship as "a Fidus-Achateship" or, to put it more familiarly, "chummying." Each of Melville's sailor heroes has a bosom friend or alter ego, a room-mate approached through connubial metaphors. The first of them, the boyish Toby, who disappears from *Typee*, actually turned up to corroborate Melville's book. His place is taken, in *Omoo*, by a more weathered figure, the bookish and independent Dr. Long Ghost. There too the native, Poky, in accordance with Polynesian custom, woos the somewhat unwilling narrator. The culminating friendship, celebrated as if it were a marriage, is between Ishmael and Queequeg; and there the theme of brotherhood converges with the embodiment of blackness. A similar convergence, in *Israel Potter*, brings the young hero together with John Paul Jones, who recalls having had an African from the Congo as his hammock-mate. Melville, like Joseph Conrad, acknowledged "the bond of the sea," regarding all men who loved the sea as his brothers. He linked himself with Richard

Henry Dana, as he linked Ishmael with Queequeg, by
the metaphor of Siamese Twins. Dana had pioneered in
Two Years Before the Mast, not as a chronicler of navi-
gation but as a sincere and sympathetic witness to the
sailor's way of life, "a voice from the forecastle" expressing the vantage-point of the crew. Melville warmly
praised that contribution, and noted how much it had
done to substitute matter-of-fact details for romantic
preconceptions about the sea. His own books had thus
far been preoccupied more with life ashore than with
life afloat. But the marvelous realms of *Mardi* held so
little charm for readers and critics that he was now willing to recreate his own years before the mast, turning
back from *roman* to *récit*.

Consequently, *Redburn: His First Voyage* harks back
from the Pacific to the Atlantic Ocean, and to Melville's
nautical initiation aboard a merchantman. With the
self-amused detachment of a decade's experience, he re-
assumes the naiveté of the greenhorn, Wellingborough
Redburn. "Such is boyhood." On the way across, Wellingborough is shunned and scorned by veteran seamen
as "a gentleman with white hands." On the way back,
he is already a seasoned mariner; and the scapegoat is
his Fidus Achates, the Englishman Harry Bolton, who
is treated as the "sort of Ishmael" his friend has been.
A further, and no less crucial, initiation takes place when
Wellingborough is introduced to the old world. Liverpool must have been its least auspicious port of entry;
it was to be rather a place of exile than an old home
for Hawthorne; and Henry James would be careful to ignore it in *The Ambassadors*, bringing Lambert Strether
as quickly as possible to medieval Chester a few miles

away. For Henry Adams, the vista of English industrialism, "the Black District was a practical education."
Wellingborough's expectations have been nourished by
a guidebook inherited from his dead father—like Melville's, "a broken-down importer of French silks." The
hotel where his father stayed, he discovers, is no longer
there; wherefore he learns the lesson that "this . . .
is a moving world," that "every age makes its own guidebooks"—the lesson of modernity that Hawthorne's
Robin learned in "My Kinsman, Major Molineux." In
the flush of disappointment, he asks himself, "And this
is England?" Washington Irving's *Sketch-Book* was no
preparation for this. Where are all the abbeys and may-
poles then, the coronations and Derby races that Wellingborough has read about—the absence of which from
the American scene would occasion James's most elegiac
lament? He has not expected every house to be a Stras-
burg Cathedral or a Leaning Tower of Pisa; but he is
hardly prepared to be greeted by rows of dingy warehouses, all too reminiscent of New York.

For a New York boy educated up-state, this encounter with the wants and woes of metropolitan poverty is
the most abysmal revelation. This is "snivelization"
with a vengeance, a nightmare to avenge the South Sea
daydream. The elemental blackness of soot and grime
heightens a sequence of Dickensian scenes, which proceed through "Sodom-like" slums to a climactic glimpse
of a woman and child in an underground vault, literally
dying of starvation. The abashed recoil seems to give
new urgency to Melville's fellow feeling for the seagoing
underdog, and to that hatred of commissioned authority
which had manifested itself in *Omoo*. "Miserable dog's

life is this of the sea!" Wellingborough exclaims, "commanded like a slave, . . . brutal men lording it over
me, as if I were an African in Alabama." Wellingborough's commander, Captain Riga, despite his Russian antecedents, will seem a petty despot when compared with that absolute czar, Captain Ahab. A likelier
predecessor is the darkly picturesque castaway, Jackson,
who wears so malevolent an expression that he might
have posed for the blasted figurehead of a doomed ship
in a lurid seascape by Salvator Rosa. But, though Jackson is characterized as diabolic, Satanic, "a Cain afloat,"
he does little else except pose, to the very instant of
melodramatic retribution, when he falls headlong to
his death from the mast. He is indeed a personification
of evil; but Melville has yet to show evil in action or in
emotion. Nonetheless Jackson's presence is one of the
signs that *Redburn* has profited from *Mardi*; that it has
a symbolic burden to relay through *White-Jacket*; and
that both books are more than autobiographical reportage. Melville could step back to jump farther, but
he would never head in another direction. Along with
Pierre Glendinning, he could immaturely attempt a
mature book; but, along with Wellingborough Redburn
sighting his first ship at sea, he could never suppress "a
feeling of wild romance."

Reverting to the cycle of *Typee* and *Omoo*, he
rounded it out by using his homeward journey from
Hawaii on the frigate United States as the framework
for *White-Jacket: The World in a Man-of-War*. Hawthorne of Salem, though he had never served on a man-
of-war, had edited the *Journal of an African Cruiser*
for his friend, Horatio Bridge; and therein Melville

may have found his *donnée*: ". . . the private history
of a man-of-war's crew, if truly told, would be full of
high romance, varied with stirring incident, and too
often darkened with deep and deadly crime." The official name of Melville's warship—which he rechristened
the Neversink—may have suggested the analogue that
the subtitle underscores, and that the closing verses
amplify: "Life is a voyage that's homeward bound."
Melville has discovered the potentialities of the ship as
a self-contained Mardi, a working model of society not
unlike Hobbes's Leviathan, and a microcosm of this
world-frigate's voyage through the universe. He has also
discovered, indignantly, that naval discipline is not entirely compatible with democratic ideology; it would
be better suited, he frankly maintains, to the repressive
institutions of Russia; as against the Articles of War,
he appeals to the Sermon on the Mount. He had balked
at hierarchical tryanny within the merchant marine, and
was soon to embody his critique of authoritarianism in
the person of a whaling captain. The navy, with its
ranks and regulations, was the most obvious target of
all; and he seconded Dana and others in the campaign
that led to the congressional abolition of corporal punishment. Melville's chapters on flogging are less powerful and more overtly propagandistic than the account
in *Two Years Before the Mast*. But when his narrator
is almost flogged, significantly the real victim is a mu-
latto. The conflict between the officers and "the people," as Melville observes it, is a class struggle more unrelenting than that between the Pyncheons and the
Maules. Though his quick humanitarian sympathies
take sides upon every occasion, he understands his mess-

mates too well to sentimentalize them. They are an assortment of unfortunates, sons of adversity, children of
calamity: "Bankrupt brokers, bootblacks, blacklegs, and
blacksmiths." Any endeavor to whitewash their characters would be misapplied.

But Melville's idealism expands with his recollection
of the most heroic of chums, the "sailor's sailor," the
blond British captain of the maintop, Jack Chase.
"Wherever you may be now rolling over the blue bil-
lows, dear Jack! take my best love along with you; and
God bless you, wherever you go!" Jack, who had gone
ashore to strike a blow for the rights of man in the
Peruvian Revolution, is the very incarnation of masculine vitality; whereas the ship's surgeon, Cadwallader
Cuticle, whose patient dies under the knife, and whose
own body constitutes "a patchwork of life and death,"
is a study in morbid anatomy. The symbol that controls
the book and nicknames the narrator is announced by
the title and particularized at the start. That white
jacket is a makeshift garment devised by its unlucky
wearer. It has a ghostly aspect; it looks like, and nearly
proves to be, a shroud; and White-Jacket, at the yard-
arm, is taken for an albatross. He longs to paint it
black; he tries to auction it off; but in vain. Its clumsi-
ness seems to confirm his greenhorn's status: thirteenth
at mess, defended by Jack Chase but avoided by the
others, and stigmatized as a Jonah. The climax, which
rids White-Jacket of his encumbrance, is a dizzying
plunge from the mast overboard—an interpolation borrowed from the published recollections of another mariner, and vividly adapted to Melville's symbolic purposes.
These would seem to recapitulate the fall of Adam, as

every man does in his fashion—as Hawthorne's innocent did in *The Marble Faun*. But Melville's innocent,
rather more like Poe's, seems to be motivated by that
imp of the perverse, the longing to fall. If the whiteness
of the jacket connotes innocence, it likewise has the
connotation of faith. The loss of one or the other or
both, after the sensation of drowning, is the precondition of survival.

The survivor, initiated into the guilty knowledge of
good and evil, has completed his passage from the
happy islands of the Pacific home to the corrupted
cities of the Occident. After the open space and fresh
air, the confined and cabined mode of living below the
decks has seemed to White-Jacket a "black world," a
breeding-place for pent-up vices "so direful that they
will hardly bear so much as an allusion." Yet Melville
does allude:

> The sins for which the cities of the plain were over-
> thrown still linger in some of these wooden-walled
> Gomorrahs of the deep. More than once com-
> plaints were made at the mast in the Neversink,
> from which the deck officer would turn away with
> loathing, refuse to hear them, and command the
> complainant out of his sight. There are evils in
> men-of-war which, like the suppressed domestic
> drama of Horace Walpole, will neither bear repre-
> senting nor reading, and will hardly bear thinking
> of. The landsman who has neither read Walpole's
> *Mysterious Mother*, nor Sophocles' *Oedipus Tyran-
> nus*, nor the Roman story of Count Cenci drama-
> tized by Shelley, let that landsman guardedly re-

main in his ignorance of even worse horrors than
these, and forever abstain from seeking to draw
aside this veil.

Assuming—as we certainly should—that Melville was
no hypocrite, this shocked paragraph should make it
clear that he could not consciously reconcile his idealization of male friendship with the erotic fulfilment
Walt Whitman would soon be celebrating in "Cala-
mus." On the contrary, Melville's sensibilities must
have intensified his anxieties in this regard. The taboo
intervenes when, after hinting at homosexuality, he
specifies three classic examples of incest—one vice which
could scarcely taint a man-of-war. *Pierre*, which threatens to tear aside all veils and "see the hidden things,"
glances at *Oedipus* in its mother and son, at Walpole's
tangled closet-drama in its brother and sister, and at
The Cenci in its blonde heroine, "double-hooded . . .
by . . . the black crape" of an unspeakable situation.
Meanwhile, between *White-Jacket* and *Pierre*, Melville
attained his apogee; and *Moby-Dick* succeeded in per-
fectly fusing his practical observation with his speculative imagination. Blackness was counterbalanced there
by whiteness in such dazzling radiance that its successor was bound to be an anticlimax. "Blackness advances
her banner," in *Pierre*, beyond all previous limits; the
Black Knight of Woe, materialized and challenged,
rides triumphant. Pierre, the landsman, is metaphorically drowned. Literally, in withdrawing from his habitual element, Melville was braving shipweck at the
lee shore. Properly handled, his conception might have
become a psychological novel. His bookish endeavors
to eke out his characterization, with Dantesque maledic-

tions and Shakespearean soliloquies, widened the gap
he was earnestly striving to bridge. Not surprisingly,
"one is apt to look black while writing Infernoes."

Pierre derives from intimate circumstances: the fatherless young writer seeking his fortune, the genteel
background of the Glendinnings reflecting the family
of Melville's mother, the Gansevoorts. But Pierre Glendinning sees his plight universalized in the mountain
to which Melville has dedicated the novel—the mountain that broods over Hawthorne's "Ethan Brand"—and
in the myth that Pierre attaches to it: it imprisons the
mutilated giant Enceladus, child of the incestuous mat-
ing between Earth and Titan, who has defied the gods
and stormed the heavens. So it is with the ambitions
and the encumbrances of our hero, who discovers—like
other children of Adam—that his patrimony is a liability. Pierre is given the somewhat Hamlet-like opportunity to compare two portraits of his late father,
one more "blackly significant" than the other. One is
the official memory, in which Pierre was brought up by
his dowager mother. The other is a testimonial to his
father's unknown trespass, inasmuch as it belongs to his
illegitimate daughter. She is Pierre's "dark angel," Isabel Banford, whose funereal hair, olive cheeks, and
Nubian eyes betoken "mysteries interpierced with mysteries, and mysteries eluding mysteries." The spell they
cast upon him, he avows, would turn white marble into
mother's milk. To right the paternal wrong and offer
the protection of the family name to his half-sister, he
pretends to marry her—a gesture of perverted chivalry
which creates more ambiguities than it resolves. The
most acute of these concerns Lucy Tartan, the "nun-
like cousin" to whom he has been engaged, and the

purest type of blue-eyed, golden-haired, fair-skinned femininity. This is a reversal of the double pursuit in *Mardi*, where the hero sought the blonde heroine and fled from the brunette. And it is a far cry from a sailor's existence to Pierre's *ménage à trois* with his two heroines, neither of whom he is in a position to love.

His nightmarish transference from the greensward of his mother's domain to the pavements of the bleak city has been a shift from "Paradisiac beauty" to "Tartarean misery." His lodging is symbolically located in an abandoned church, still appropriately known as "The Apostles," since it houses Bohemian writers, messianic philosophers, and other preachers of latter-day gospel. He pursues his ill-fated labors ("I will gospelize the world anew") under the chilling eye of Plotinus Plinlimmon, an Emersonian optimist who expounds a relativistic ethic, a philosophy of the conditional, in a lecture entitled *Ei*, or "if." On the analogy of time, which is relative or "horological" in most of this world, though it may be absolute or "chronometrical" at Greenwich or in heaven, Plinlimmon counsels the worldly wisdom of the watchmaker, Bacon. In contradistinction, Christ is a moral chronometer who, as *Mardi* predicted, might be recrucified if he returned. Pierre will not compromise nor become a time-server; if he is unable to square his surroundings with the dictates of his heart, he is determined to play the fool of truth. But to probe the heart is an endless descent by a spiral stair down a black shaft. The more straightforward his conduct, the more ambiguous its consequences. If there is "a certain fictitiousness" in every marriage, there is an incredible amount of it in Pierre's. The fiction that he is writing, his new apocalypse, has its in-

spiration and its obstacle in his marital obligations—
or rather, in the unhallowed family ties that they mask.
"This vulnerable god, this self-upbraiding sailor, this
dreamer of the avenging dream," roused at last to melodramatic reality, precipitates a triple catastrophe. The
final cadence binds him in death to the agent of his
tragedy: ". . . and her long hair ran over him, and
arbored him in ebon vines."

Pierre, though it did not exhaust Melville's "black
vein," exhausted his decreasing audience; as a novelist,
he was—in a word which came more and more fittingly
to his pen—whelmed. Essaying next the field of magazine fiction, in two or three years he produced some
fifteen stories and sketches, half a dozen of which were
collected in *The Piazza Tales.* The earliest of these,
which might be read as a muted epilogue to the sound
and fury of *Pierre,* was originally published as "Bartleby
the Scrivener: A Tale of Wall Street." Wall, in this
context, can be taken at its literal meaning; for the
law-office, the constricted locale of the unadventurous
tale, looks out upon a dead wall; and that is suggestive
of the predicament Melville had arrived at in his literary
career. Bartleby can be taken as his double, the copyist
who mildly but stubbornly asserts his individuality by
refusing either to copy or to leave. He sits there like
the Raven, croaking a negative answer to all requests
and queries; he says *no* to the devil, not in thunder, but
in the quietest sort of desperation. "I would prefer not
to." What protagonist has ever voiced a more diffident
non serviam, a more laconic *gran rifiuto?* After removal
to the old New York prison, the Tombs, where he appropriately dies, it is revealed that the half-crazed Bartleby had been a clerk in the Dead Letter Office. Mel-

ville himself, though not yet thirty-five, seems to be contemplating his own retreat from the profession of letters. Three of his tales are compassionate studies of has-beens: the unsuccessful inventor in "The Happy Failure," the man-about-town reduced to shabby gentility in "Jimmy Rose," and the former genius adjusted to cheerful mediocrity in "The Fiddler."

Melville tends to detach his narrator more and more from his other characters as, after Ishmael, he modulates into a minor key. "Bartleby," to be sure, is narrated by the legal employer, an affable foil for his antisocial employee. The genial surface of "Cock-a-Doodle-Doo" blandly conceals the bitterest of pronouncements on the optimism of Emerson—and on our wishful tendency to keep smiling, to ignore the tragic, to be affirmative at any cost. The flamboyant rooster, whose crowing makes things seem less black, is an ironic compensation for the abject misery in which a poor woodman's family lives and dies. A trick of juxtaposition, pairing off contrasts of wealth and poverty, American and English customs, man's lot and woman's, is utilized by some of the sketches—most suggestively by "The Paradise of Bachelors and the Tartarus of Maids," the latter a guided tour through a paper mill situated beyond the Black Notch, which can manufacture a sheet of blank paper in nine minutes by a process minutely parallel to that of child-bearing. Some of the more informal pieces center on houses, in the mood of Hawthorne: "The Lightning-Rod Man," with its covert defiance of professional religionists; "I and My Chimney," with its defensive insight into the hidden recesses of personality. But the prospect is outward from "The Piazza," where "truth comes in with the darkness." And when Melville revisits the South Seas in a last reminiscence, his chastened fancy dwells no longer upon the lost paradise of the lush Marquesas; rather, it seeks a natural habitat in the volcanic wastelands of Galapagos. "The Encantadas," for all the enchantment they promise, are disenchanting islands as he depicts them, bleak settings for unavoidable tragedies of human erosion. "In no world but a fallen one could such lands exist."

But his most forthright confrontation of blackness occurs in the richest and ripest of *The Piazza Tales*, "Benito Cereno." This has its origin in the record cited, the deposition of a New England sea-captain, Amasa Delano. Melville portrays him as a typically innocent American who, like the witnesses in *The Marble Faun* or in the novels of James, finds himself inadvertently drawn into the evils of the old world. Proceeding by indirection, through his naïve point of view, we board the drifting Spanish craft, a slave-ship which resembles a whitewashed monastery or a dilapidated chateau. The pallid and languishing captain, Benito Cereno, makes a sinister impression at first. When his Negro servant Babo shaves him, it is as if a Nubian sculptor were chiseling a marble statue. More ominously, the black is compared to a headsman, and the white to a man at the block. For as it transpires, with the retarded impact of a "rush from darkness to light," the slaves have revolted and slaughtered the crew; and Babo, who is the ringleader of the revolt, by keeping the razor at his master's throat, keeps him from undeceiving Captain Delano. The figurehead of Columbus at the prow has been replaced by a skeleton with the chalked inscription: *"Seguid vuestro jefe"* (follow your leader). The implication, for the new world, is a change of course: from discovery to corruption. Though Don Benito is saved and sustained, he guiltily pines away. When Captain Delano asks him, "What has cast such a shadow upon you?," his response is "The Negro." Perhaps the most significant commentary on "Benito Cereno" is one of Melville's epigraphs to "The Bell-Tower," his Frankenstein parable of a mechanism which destroys its inventor: "Like Negroes, these powers own men sullenly; mindful of their higher master; while serving, plot revenge."

That higher master can be no other than nature itself, which, outraged by slavery, authorizes the vengeance of the enslaved. Yet Captain Delano, with simple-minded reluctance, is compelled to recognize the interracial antagonism that confronted Arthur Gordon Pym; and Melville, the exponent of brotherhood among races, seems ready to concede that life is a blood-feud: "Shadows present, foreshadowing deeper shadows to come . . ." The book that relieved his present state of mind, *Israel Potter: His Fifty Years of Exile*, borrowed its substance from a forgotten chapbook about a private in the American Revolution. Melville would be paying tribute to such men in the ranks, veterans of the fore-castle or of the Civil War, unknown soldiers who had outlived their heroic days, in the poems of his otherwise silent years. His dedication of *Israel Potter* to the Bunker Hill Monument, following his dedication of *Pierre* to Mount Greylock, was a confession of the extent to which he felt himself isolated from appreciative friends. "In desperation of friendliness," his sympathies go out to the wild heart of John Paul Jones or to the rugged spirit of Ethan Allen, a "Samson among the Philistines"; whereas he recoils from Benjamin Franklin

as from a model of successful philistinism. Israel, the
tired old ex-hero, fulfils the scriptural allusion of his
name; he wanders abroad in the wilderness more than
forty years before coming back to die in the promised
homeland; his brick-making sojourn in England has
been an Egyptian bondage. For a short episode, he is
buried alive in a Hawthornesque chamber of a country
house. But it is the industrialized metropolis that is
cramping to his soul:

> The black vistas of streets were as the galleries in
> coal mines; the flagging, as flat tombstones minus
> the consecration of moss, and worn heavily down
> by sorrowful tramping, as the vitreous rocks in the
> cursed Galapagos over which the convict tortoises
> crawl.

The vista of desolation, which disclosed itself to Redburn in Liverpool, now extends all the way from London to the Encantadas—and to the Black Hole of Calcutta, a few pages later. Pierre, while reading Dante,
had found New York a city of woe. Israel Potter, watching pedestrians throng across London Bridge as if they
were damned souls entering the underworld, anticipates
the despondent outlook of a later American expatriate,
T. S. Eliot in *The Waste Land*. Dickens, whose *Hard
Times* is contemporary with *Israel Potter*, could trace
the blight of the city through myriads of lives. Melville,
coming to it from a distance and out of the open air,
with an overwhelming accumulation of similes, can only
voice the apocalyptic reaction of the traveler who has
descended to hell.

> As in eclipses, the sun was hidden; the air dark-
> ened; the whole dull, dismayed aspect of things, as

if some neighboring volcano, belching its premonitory smoke, were about to whelm the great town, as
Herculaneum and Pompeii, or the Cities of the
Plain. And as they had been upturned in terror towards the mountain, all faces were more or less
snowed or spotted with soot. Nor marble, nor flesh,
nor the sad spirit of man, may in this cindery City
of Dis abide white.

The sad spirit of man, finding it cannot exist without being sullied, is prone to lapse into misanthropy.
And if the misanthrope is likewise a writer, he may
evolve a technique of denigration, applying blackness
to blackness "like stove luster on a stove—black, brightening seriously." Such was the deliberately baffling experiment that Melville now undertook in *The Confidence-Man: His Masquerade.* Never a social realist,
he sought to convey "more reality than real life can
show" by means of a morality—or rather, an immorality.
His disclaimer of satire and irony is merely a sign that
he was wielding those weapons more freely than ever,
pushing past Bartleby's negation to nihilism. His micro-
cosmic vessel is now a river-boat, traversing the length
of mid-America, though gaining a dimmer view of life
on the Mississippi than we see when we take Mark
Twain as our pilot. "Speeds the daedal boat as a
dream." It is a ship of knaves if not of fools, bound on
a picaresque pilgrimage together, mutually suspicious
yet endlessly capable of swindling one another. They
transact their business through a sequence of varied and
animated conversations, a medium combining Lucian's
Dialogues of the Dead with the olio of a minstrel show.
The continuity that interlinks these episodic encounters

is our surmise that the protagonist has a different role to play in each of them. Thus the notion of a masquerade, which Poe and Hawthorne employed to diversify their somber tonalities, is an integrating concept for Melville. In a notable pair of disquisitions on the art of fiction, and on what constitutes true originality, he defends the presentation of character through its conflicts and inconsistencies. The protean masks, the successive guises and disguises of the confidence-man, are all we know about him. But dare we claim anything more for our acquaintance with the characters of Proust?

Melville's versatile operator makes his appearance—shortly after a mysterious impostor is reported from the East—as a mute, lamb-like stranger, inscribing a message of charity on a slate. This modest Messiah is quickly succeeded by a Negro cripple, begging for alms and accused of being "a white masquerading as a black." There is a salesman who offers infernal stock in the Black Rapids Coal Company, but seems equally involved in a land development advertised as New Jerusalem. Patent medicines are peddled, such as the Omni-Balsamic Reinvigorator; then an up-to-date philosophy, which approximates Emersonianism; all the suspected devices of quackery and chicanery. "Faith! Faith!," the despairing cry of Hawthorne's young Goodman Brown, carried a reverberation of doubt; somewhat less ambivalently, Melville's confidence-man is a disseminator of non-confidence, religious and metaphysical, scientific and humane. Though the steamboat is ironically baptised the Fidèle, its faithless credo is succinctly formulated in its barber's sign, "No Trust." Yet the barber himself is taken in by a self-proclaimed philanthropist,

a skeptic from Missouri named Pitch, whose association with boys has convinced him of man's innate depravity. From the Rousseauistic trust in natural goodness fostered by his Polynesian interlude, Melville
sounds the depths of revulsion in four corrosive chapters on the metaphysics of Indian-hating: the undying
vendetta of the harassed backwoodsman, hunting down
the redskins who have wronged him, forced to become
a wolf to his fellow men. "In new countries, when the
wolves are killed off the foxes take over"—and savagery
yields to barbarism. A cheerless drinking scene culmi-
nates in a philosophical dialogue between two "hypothetical friends" who refute that hypothesis; who, by
their inability to negotiate a friendly loan, test Melville's cherished principle of comradeship and expose
it as another flimflam.

The Confidence-Man, which marks the nadir of his
confidence in society and nature, and in himself as
well, is the terminus of authorship for Melville. His
additional narrative, *Billy Budd*, which would be begun
a full generation later and not quite finished at his
death, should therefore stand apart from the main body
of his work. Its deferred publication in our time, together with its sentimental appeal to some critics, may
have disproportionately affected our understanding of
Melville in his totality. Though it adds an impressive
last word to many of his longstanding preoccupations,
it is unevenly written, and would seem to be more of a
postscript than a testament. Its point of departure is a
retrospective dedication to Jack Chase, the ideal British
shipmate of *White-Jacket*. But if he is more youthfully
reincarnate in the blond and blue-eyed Billy Budd,
the angle of vision has changed; the writer is not a bud-

ding seaman looking up to an elder comrade, but an old man who has lost both his sons, one of them apparently by suicide. On the other hand, after the arbitrary despotism of Melville's earlier captains, the commanding officer under whom his protagonist now serves, "starry Vere," treats him with fatherly—not to say godly—consideration. The story takes its politico-historical bearings from certain mutinies in the British Navy during the epoch of the French Revolution; it also echoes a nearer controversy in the United States Navy, where one of Melville's cousins sat on the court-martial. But Melville broadens, even more than usual, the parable of naval discipline. His "inside story" of the boyish civilian, impressed from the merchantman, the Rights of Man, to the man-of-war, H. M. S. Indomitable, is a *mysterium iniquitatis,* another inquiry into the problem of evil, as charted against the intersecting lines of free will and necessity.

On the assumption that "the physical make" is in keeping with "the moral nature," a fair exterior is again conventionally equated with goodness, and it is assumed that "the Handsome Sailor" will behave handsomely. But Melville instances the birthmark in Hawthorne's tale to indicate the flaw that so pointedly qualifies Billy's perfection: a stammer, a hesitation of speech, a mental articulation which lags behind his muscular reflexes. Toward him the jet-curled Claggart, master-at-arms, feels an antipathy which might have been sympathy, an animus which is clearly attributable to a frustrated homosexual impulse, though it is set forth as an ethical contrast rather than as a psychological motive. When the angelic Billy is traduced by his diabolical foe, he cannot speak; he is unable to comprehend the malevolence that could bear false witness against him. In his bewilderment, he strikes out, and Claggart is struck dead. If this act is not physically improbable, it it is morally indefensible; yet Melville lays it down as the condition of his dilemma. Billy has been "a sort of upright barbarian," like Hawthorne's Donatello; he has shown the primitivistic simplicity of "a period prior to Cain's city and citified man," not unlike Melville's South Sea islanders. He is a specimen of mankind, Melville tells us, "who in the nude might have posed for a statue of young Adam before the fall." If we follow the parallel, we infer that the original sin was to strike back in revenge against dire provocation; hence Billy too, no less than the Negro slaves rebelling against Benito Cereno, no less than the Indian-hater resorting to force in *The Confidence-Man*, is a revenger. And the good man, as Pierre learned from *Hamlet*, has no retaliation which will keep his goodness intact; he cannot fight the world's evils without becoming entrammeled in them himself; whether he resists or suffers them, he is overwhelmed.

This may help to explain the paradox that Hawthorne's protagonists come to grief when they ignore the heart, while Melville's do when they make it their sole guide. The heart, with its feminine sensibilities, will always be on Billy's side, as Captain Vere acknowledges in his compunctious summation of the case; and so will nature, whose primeval element is the ocean. But manhood, on joining the navy, submits itself to the King's law; and whether we take that as the naval code or the divine order, its decree is that "the angel must hang." Here, at last, there is no ambiguity between the celestial and the terrestrial. Ishmael may waver between Plato's

Phaedo and Bowditch's *Practical Navigator*; but Socrates himself, when he was condemned by the Athenians, bowed to their condemnation. More concerned with the apologue than the psychology, Melville draws a curtain over the farewell interview between Billy and Captain Vere; their relation has been prefigured in that of Isaac and Abraham, and commented upon in Kierkegaard's *Fear and Trembling*; yet the filial sacrifice, averted in the Old Testament, must be consummated here. The accident of White-Jacket's fall from the mast becomes a ritual with Billy's execution—and Melville purifies it by carefully affirming that it is not accompanied, as hangings usually are, with a sexual spasm. Jumping from the yard-arm with the shout, "God bless Captain Vere!", Billy accepts the justice of the sentence. Does Melville? He could not have gone on existing for so long unless, with Margaret Fuller's sweeping concession, he had accepted the universe. But that acceptance, whole-hearted at the beginning, was subjected increasingly to re-examination. The alternative of rejection has its emphatic counterstatement in *The Confidence-Man*; and, though it may be finally neutralized in *Billy Budd*, the outcome seems at best to be a truce. It would still be a state of suspense, by Eliot's reckoning:

> Wavering between the profit and the loss
> In this brief transit where the dreams cross.

It should be noted that the paternalistic Captain Vere dies soon afterward, more grieved than wounded —even as Benito Cereno retires to die in a monastery significantly placed on Mount Agonia. Their resignation contrasts with the catastrophes that end the lives of Ahab and Pierre; whereas the bulk of Melville's narratives break off abruptly, as if to imply that life is a continued tale, and that the narrator—like Bulkington —will soon be embarking upon a more distant and dangerous voyage. "The countless tribes of common novels laboriously spin veils of mystery, only to complacently clear them up at last." But Pierre, in coming to realize the difference between fiction and truth, has come to distrust the happy ending. The booming hope that all is for the best, the Emersonian doctrine of compensation, is grimly answered by Melville's cult of revenge, his vote of non-confidence in those material forces which—to the great majority of his countrymen— seemed the agents of a favoring destiny. "Neither pessimist nor optimist," he professed to an English correspondent that he relished pessimism "as a counterpoise to the exorbitant hopefulness, juvenile and shallow, that makes such a bluster in these days." Perhaps his most balanced statement occurs when, in viewing the bleakness of the Encantadas, he raises the question whether existence is wholly sackcloth and ashes. To this he replies, after the fashion of a bestiary, by instancing the two sides of the specter-tortoise.

> Moreover, everyone knows that tortoises as well as turtles are of such a make, that if you but put them on their backs you thereby expose their bright sides without the possibility of their recovering themselves and turning into view the other. But after you have done this, and because you have done this, you should not swear that the tortoise has no dark side. Enjoy the bright, keep it turned up perpetually if you can; but be honest, and don't deny the

black. Neither should he, who cannot turn the tortoise from its natural position so as to hide the darker and expose his livelier aspect, like a great October pumpkin in the sun, declare the creature to be one total inky blot. The tortoise is both black and bright.

A mature perception, then, frankly presupposes the coexistence of blackness and brightness. Melville, in his quest for such an attitude, directed his pilgrimage to the Holy Land, the source of our distinctions between good and evil. The poetic consequence, *Clarel*, is neither the new gospel that Pierre hoped for nor the old guidebook that Redburn discarded. Again pursuing his habitual train of speculations, through its travelogues and dialogues, Melville does not overtake the absolute; but he does achieve the perspective of relativity:

> Degrees we know, unknown in days before;
> The light is greater, hence the shadow more.

The last words ascribed to Goethe, who is momentarily glimpsed upon his deathbed in *Moby-Dick*, would seem to affirm that knowledge is an infinite progression. "More light"—and, with it, Pierre discerns "the gloom of that light," obscurantism encroaching upon enlightenment. Conversely, "more gloom" brings with it "the light of that gloom," the special illumination of painful experience. Melville's protagonists stray, in the wake of Faust, because they strive; their explorations are zigzags of trial and error; and their errors, like that of *The Marble Faun*, are educational. Brilliant sunlight interpenetrates with leafy shadows, as it shuttles across a whale's skeleton, overgrown with verdure,

on the isle of Tranque in the Arsacides: "Life folded
Death; Death trellised Life." The white whale itself
is finally sighted on the mildest of days; the sky is smiling, the air caresses Ahab, and "the step-mother world,
so long cruel," embraces him. Leaning over the side of
the Pequod, gazing down at his shadow in the water,
striving to pierce its profundity, the sternest of captains
drops a remorseful tear. To the mate, Starbuck, he
fitfully speaks of home, of "the green land," of "the
bright hearthstone." He thinks of the boy there awakening from a nap, to be told by his mother about his
cannibal father, "abroad upon the deep." And, since
Ishmael is our ambivalent witness, we cannot help thinking of his childhood dream: going to bed in daylight at
the behest of a stepmother, waking up in darkness to
feel the handclasp of an apparition. Which is the reality,
which the dream? Who is the dreamer, Ishmael or the
egoistic commander who projects into him such "a
wild, mystical, sympathetical feeling?" Where are we,
safe at home or on an unfathomable sea? And whither
the journey, toward happy discoveries or shipwrecked
hopes?

VII

The Jonah Complex

"**R**OUND the world! There is much in that sound to inspire proud feelings; but whereto does all that circumnavigation conduct?" Ishmael stops to ask himself, and answers: "Only through numberless perils to the very point whence we started, where those that we left behind secure, were all the time before us." The cycle is bound to lead homeward; the tired adventurer will manage to live down his exploits and to live out an ordinary career. Yet, from terra firma, his seaward glance will keep roving toward terra incognita. And Ishmael continues:

> Were this world an endless plain, and by sailing eastward we could for ever reach new distances, and discover sights more sweet and strange than any Cyclades or Islands of King Solomon, then there were promise in the voyage. But in pursuit of those far mysteries we dream of, or in tormented chase of that demon phantom that, some time or other,

swims before all human hearts; while chasing such
over this round globe, they either lead us on in
barren mazes or midway leave us whelmed.

It may not be altogether fortuitous that Melville's
tale of being whelmed by the phantom should come
midway in the sequence of his books, or that his mas-
terwork should take the form of a catastrophic quest,
as it had been adumbrated by *The Narrative of Arthur
Gordon Pym*—as it would be refined upon in Conrad's
Heart of Darkness. Melville's subsequent endeavors
might well be regarded as mazes, leading on to barren
silences and terminating in what he could have called
an "uncatastrophied fifth act." After all, there were no
bigger fish than Moby-Dick. The pains of its composition and the disappointments of its reception are set
down in his next volume, *Pierre*, under the heading of
"Young America in Literature." Reviewers, calling for
the great American novel, continued to do so; and indeed they still do, just as if Melville had never supplied
that desideratum with such overwhelming adequacy.
The fact that the great book might be something less
and something more than a novel had been foreseen by
Hawthorne, in that very parable which fostered Melville's awareness of his own mission. The long-awaited
work that would mark the emergence of a truly indigenous literature, hewn from the unexploited granite of
our intellectual quarries, might be "modelled in the
form of an epic poem or assuming a guise altogether
new." But Hawthorne also foresaw that the Master
Genius, when he arrived at last, would pass unrecog-
nized.

Hawthorne's *Mosses* provided examples for Melville,

as well as a harbinger, through their demonstration that tragic power lay within the grasp of native authorship. Melville's recognition, in its turn, may have influenced Hawthorne toward a more conscious emphasis on blackness. Melville, not content to spin seafaring yarns, had been steadily tacking in the direction of allegory. Now, in reviving his most treasured memories of whaling, he could utilize practical details as poetic symbols—even though, as he admitted to Dana, it was hard to get poetry out of blubber. In choosing the largest of all living creatures and pursuing its unchartable zigzags around the world, he found a theme commensurate with the enlarging scope of America itself. "Are the green fields gone?" If the frontier had been pushed across the continent, then the open spaces of the Pacific were waiting to be explored. "Columbus ended earth's romance," Melville would lament in a later couplet. "No new world to mankind remains." Yet in the South Seas he had rediscovered romance; and though the search for Moby-Dick moves eastward, skirting the old worlds of Africa and Asia, it reaches its object and its catastrophe somewhere in the midst of the westward ocean. In setting forth the infinite lure of the sea, along with the Ulyssean curiosity that impels men to venture upon it, Ishmael formulates his motivation as "an everlasting itch for things remote"—and here Melville's prose, as so often when charged with excitement, falls into blank verse. This wanderlust has its martyr in Bulkington, who is to Melville's epic what the dropped pilot, Palinurus, was to Vergil's *Aeneid*. "In landlessness alone resides the highest truth, shoreless, indefinite as God." The underlying rhythm oscillates nostalgically between the sea and the land, the respective extremes of inscrutable danger and docile security, the ebb and flow of the exotic and the familiar.

Moving from the known to the unknown, proceeding as we must from light toward dark, and into the wild and watery, the untried and unshored, it is noteworthy that we start on Christmas Day. After warmly particularizing the villages on the Massachusetts seacoast, the journey proceeds with a shudder into the cold, damp night-breeze of the Atlantic. Yet the farther it goes, and the vaster the region it penetrates, the more imagination reverts to local reminiscence. The ship carries its America in its hold: sand from Nantucket soundings, fresh water from New England springs, tonics neatly tucked away by Aunt Charity for a decorous Fourth of July in the tropics. Ishmael betrays his homesickness for green fields when he speaks of homestead land selling for a dollar an inch on the plains of Illinois and Missouri. Yet the ocean itself resembles a prairie; the waves are its hills and valleys; the particles of brit are its fields of wheat. A lone whale is compared to Daniel Boone; a herd of them might be a stampede of buffaloes. The ultimate quarry, as he is described in a progressive series of topographical metaphors, has traits which connect him with landmarks in several regions of the United States: his hump is like Mount Monadnock, his mouth like a wigwam on Mackinac Island, his stomach like the Mammoth Cave of Kentucky, his body like the Natural Bridge of Virginia. Wherefore the task of harpooning him is comparable to that of the pioneer in taming the wilderness. When the boats are first lowered, one long-drawn-out sentence registers the impact of perils directly confronted:

The vast swells of the omnipotent sea; the surging, hollow roar they made, as they rolled about the eight gunwhales, like gigantic bowls in a boundless bowling-green; the brief suspended agony of the boat, as it would tip for an instant on the knife-like edge of the sharper waves, that almost seemed threatening to cut it in two; the sudden profound dip into the watery glens and hollows; the keen spurrings and goadings to gain the top of the opposite hill; the headlong, sled-like slide down its other side;—all these, with the cries of the headsmen and harpooneers, and the shuddering gasps of the oarsmen, with the wondrous sight of the ivory Pequod bearing down upon her boats with outstretched sails, like a wild hen after her screaming brood;—all this was thrilling.

Melville has caught that thrill in the up-and-down movement of sight and sound, in the play of alliteration and assonance, and in the substitution of terrestrial for aquatic imagery. From phrase to suspended phrase, we participate in the actions and sensations of the rowers; but it is as if we now were driving a horse uphill, and again were coasting downhill on a sled; while the final image, suddenly returning from the high seas to a farmyard, lends the utmost immediacy to a remote situation.

Redburn, making a more traditional pilgrimage, had announced Melville's personal discovery that every age must write guidebooks for itself. The logbook of the Pequod is scarcely a guidebook, except perhaps in the cautionary sense that it charts the course of disaster.

That its place should be everywhere and nowhere, leaving the homeland so far behind, accords with Melville's concept of the ship as a melting-pot and with his ideal of a democratic cosmopolitanism. All of our most characteristic writers, from Whitman to Hemingway, have been internationalists. Melville constantly glances back to the old world and to the past, in spite of his commitment to the present. He is so fully involved in his time that, in "The Fountain" chapter, he specifies the actual minute of writing—postdated, in the American edition, to a month after the book's publication in November 1851. Yet the subject is timeless; the shroud of the sea, at the close, rolls on as it has rolled for five thousand years. The titular figure is envisaged as a prehistoric monster, antediluvian, nay, pre-Adamite, who once swam through the waters that covered both hemispheres, when primeval nature reigned where man has since built cities and palaces. But Melville is likewise concerned to embellish his human material with the patina of historic tradition. To that end he draws upon his reading, especially upon certain discursive old English favorites from the seventeenth century and upon the emphatic Carlyle, for literary devices and bookish references. The pallid usher, thumbing his lexicon at the outset, ought to remind us that Melville himself taught school before he went to sea. The sub-sub-librarian, with his introductory compilation of extracts from whale-lore, Biblical, classical, antiquarian, scientific, encyclopedic—these touches of pedantry whet our apprehension of the first-hand encounters that lie ahead.

Meanwhile whales are classified, according to a bibliographical system, as folios, octavos, and duodecimos.

Conversely the book, in all its massive ramification, is very like a whale. Though there is much opportunity to expatiate, there is no need to magnify the animal itself; it is on behalf of the pursuit, for "The Honor and Glory of Whaling," that the narrator frankly plays the advocate. His glorified whaleman is a culture-hero, a dragon-slayer and therefore a liberator, a crusader under the patronage of Saint George, a demigod claiming descent from Perseus. Furthermore, those heroic prototypes should be honored by the comparison with their modern counterparts; Melville, reversing the obvious simile, refers to Hercules as "that antique Crockett or Kit Carson." The vessel on which his argonauts sail bears little resemblance to the brand-new Acushnet, on which he had acquired his whaling experience. The Pequod, named for an extinct Indian tribe, is "a ship of the old school," weather-beaten, seasoned with misadventure, and hoary with antiquity. Its hull is as dark as the tanned complexion of a French grenadier; its whalebone decorations are likened to an ivory necklace on a barbaric Ethiopian emperor. But, though it is "a cannibal of a craft," its masts are "like the spines of the three old kings of Cologne," and its decks are "like the pilgrim-worshiped flagstone in Canterbury Cathedral where Beckett bled." In short, it is an appropriate stage for tragedy. From the playbill inserted at the beginning to the epilogue ("The drama's done!"), Melville projects his narration by making deliberate use of dramatic techniques: stage-directions and soliloquies, the gloomy-jolly chorus in the forecastle, the captain's harangues on the quarterdeck, the pledges of the crew, the baptism of the harpoon. Strange mummeries, as Ishmael is the first to acknowledge, yet "not unmeaningly blended with the black tragedy of the melancholy ship."

His mock-epic, with its Homeric catalogues and its Miltonic horizons, consciously darkens as Melville accepts his own challenge and elevates his characters to the stature of Shakespearean dramatis personae. In transforming his "poor old whale-hunter" into "a mighty pageant creature, formed for tragedies," his first concern has been to endow this personage with "a bold and nervous lofty language." Since Captain Ahab is a Quaker, albeit of the swearing denomination, he naturally employs the archaic *thee* and *thou*. In addition, he has a self-conscious habit of echoing Shakespeare's heroes: he addresses himself to the head of a whale in the manner of Hamlet apostrophizing the skull. The cosmic forces ranged against him operate like the melodramatic tricks of witchcraft in *Macbeth*: the equivocal prophecies of the hearse and the rope closely parallel the riddling auguries of the wood and the babe. But he himself has been most aptly paralleled with Lear in his patriarchal isolation, companioned by the little Negro Pip as the mad king is accompanied by his fool, "one daft in strength, the other in weakness." Nor is it around the protagonist alone that Melville is prepared to weave "tragic graces." His solemn prayer to the democratic God invokes the Spirit of Equality that is evinced by "the kingly commons." Though Andrew Jackson is its Messiah in the political sphere, it was also the source of inspiration for the master allegorist, Bunyan, and for the founder of the novel, Cervantes. But Melville's celebration of the common man is not so unboundedly hopeful an affirmation as Whitman's. The qualities he ascribes to his "meanest mariners, and renegades and castaways," are dark as well as high; the rainbow he undertakes to spread over them will illuminate "their disastrous set of sun."

In the narrator Melville finds his fullest voice, and completes the identification suggested in *Redburn* between his runaway self and that scriptural wild man against whom every other man's hand was raised. Fenimore Cooper, in *The Prairie*, had called his squatter Ishmael Bush. Ishmael, the self-styled, is not only Melville in his definitive role; he is the self-isolating individual, less sympathetically represented by Hawthorne in Wakefield, "the outcast of the universe," and by Poe in William Wilson, "outcast of all outcasts most abandoned." The Pequod's sole survivor, having been resurrected from the vortex by clinging to the coffin that proves his life-preserver, Ishmael must unburden himself like the Ancient Mariner. Enthralled, he relays to us the hypnotic spell of Ahab's egomania; on the other hand, he feels a genuine bond of fraternity in the "Siamese ligature," the monkey-rope that literally ties him to the altruistic Queequeg, who is to bequeath him the means of survival. Melville was to make a conventionally sinister presentation of darker breeds in the mutinous slaves of "Benito Cereno" and the feral redskins of *The Confidence-Man*. But *Typee* and *Omoo* had borne witness to his affection and admiration for the Polynesians; and though Ishmael shows initial repugnance, he shares his bed with Queequeg at the inn, learns to accept him as a bosom friend, and recognizes in this tatooed Fiji Islander a "George Washington cannibalistically developed." Thus the motive of Fidus-Achateship, which runs through all of Melville's previous books, is consummated by an object-lesson in interracial brotherhood, crossing the color-line to embrace an alter ego of dark complexion. Each of the Caucasian mates, it appears, has a colored harpooneer: it takes a white "knight" to steer the boat, and a black "squire" to spear the whale. Starbuck ·he first mate, has Queequeg; Stubb has the Gayheaa Indian, Tashtego; and Flash the full-blooded African, Dagoo. A streak of lightning, across the pitch-black sky, involves the latter in a tense midnight dialogue:

DAGOO

What of that? Who's afraid of black's afraid of me! I'm quarried out of it!

SPANISH SAILOR

(*Aside*) He wants to bully, ah!—the old grudge makes me touchy. (*Advancing.*) Aye, harpooneer, thy race is the undeniable dark side of mankind— devilish dark at that. No offence.

DAGOO (*grimly*)

None.

And the choric scene breaks off, when a white squall comes up, with the small black boy, Pip, shivering and praying to the big white God.

After the first lowering, when little Flask stands on the shoulders of the gigantic Dagoo, Ishmael cannot refrain from commenting: "The bearer looked nobler than the rider." That emblem may have presented itself to Melville via Hawthorne; for just such an invidious pair was portrayed in Bridge's *Journal of an African Cruiser*; and there the white man tumbled from the Negro's back. The comment of Bridge-Hawthorne is more explicit but less forthright: "An abolitionist, perhaps, might draw a moral from the story, and say that all, who ride on the shoulders of the African race, deserve nothing better than a similar overthrow." Melville-Ishmael scores the san kind of point by more implicit example, when the frightened Pip jumps overboard and is nearly abandoned by his boat-mates, since—as Stubb tells him—the whale they have been chasing would be worth thirty times what Pip would fetch on the Alabama auction-block. Pip's is the extreme case; yet, as Ishmael fatalistically wonders, "Who ain't a slave?" The motley crew of nondescript blubber-boilers has been recruited from vagabonds and pariahs, desperados and misfits, the underdogs of many countries and races, not one out of two American-born. Their most visionary member happens to be the old Manx sailor, "a man from Man"—that is, from the Isle of Man. Every man aboard is an islander in his own peculiar way, "each Isolato living on a separate continent of his own." Yet when they are rowing, or working together, thirty men are as one, all of them "federated along one keel." The implication could be summarized in the aphorism that Ernest Hemingway would echo from John Donne: "No man is an island." The Pequod, even more than the Neversink, is a microcosm of the social order, a heterogeneous group of individuals whose united energies are harnessed toward a controlling aim.

Melville is fond of citing precedents from French Revolutionary history. The watcher at the masthead emulates Napoleon on his column above the Place Vendôme, with folded arms, not caring whether the streets of Paris below are ruled by Louis-Philippe, Louis Blanc, or Louis the Devil. Louis-Philippe had been overthrown by the Revolution of 1848; Louis Blanc had tried next to introduce socialism; whereupon Louis Bonaparte staged his diabolical *coup d'état,* notoriously a current event at the moment. Looking farther afield toward the Russian Empire, while discerning a hint for the tragic dramatist, Ishmael looks ahead prophetically to the problem of "irresistible dictatorship." His perception that moral superiority is incompatible with domination over others, that the true elite therefore remains anonymous while its aggressive inferiors grapple for power, has been amply borne out by Hitler's "leader-principle." The authoritarianism of Captain Ahab, sultanic as it may sound, is incidental to his overriding motivation: he lords it over his men, as Starbuck perceives, in order to be a democrat with respect to the powers above. The contrast between the forecastle and the cabin is the dialectic between society and solitude, which Emerson had borrowed from Edmund Burke. As the most rugged of individualists, Ahab can be historically placed among those captains of industry and freebooters of enterprise who, at the public expense, were so rapidly transforming the country and the age. Significantly viewing the wake of the Pequod, in his sunset monologue, he envisions his ruthless purpose as the track of a railroad, even then being laid across the plains and along the canyons of the West. We are reminded too that the ill-fated ship is an investment for its snug Yankee stockholders, though its seamen are risking their lives for a minimal share of its profits— a long lay. "For God's sake, be economical with your lamps and candles!" Ishmael begs the comfortable reader. "Nor a gallon you burn, but at least one drop of man's blood was spilled for it."

Melville, who had previously lodged a protest by deserting the Acushnet, is thoroughly realistic in his survey of the whaling industry. He quotes Daniel Webster's remark that Nantucket, its island capital, "is a very striking and peculiar portion of the national interest." But to economics, as to politics, Melville applies the unvarying touchstone of ethics. Turning sea-lawyer, he discusses the whale as a piece of property; but the question of its ownership introduces a legal distinction, which is fundamentally an ethical one, between "fast-fish" and "loose-fish." Fish are loose when they are independent, as men's minds and opinions should always be. However, in an epoch of spreading colonialism and imperialism, too many free-lances are made fast; the British Empire dominates India, and the United States is jeopardizing the independence of Mexico. Melville's ideology, which is oratorically expressed in such allusions and digressions, is decisively acted out by "The Town-Ho's Story." That parable, which was separately published in two periodicals shortly before the book appeared, is interpolated at the second of nine encounters with other whaling ships, seamarks on the Pequod's uncertain itinerary. During the gam, the fraternization between the crews of the Pequod and the Town-Ho, the whole of the story was not publicly told; the "secret part," which links the two ships together and makes the whale's intervention so providential, was communicated by three white seamen to the redskin Tashtego, who blurted it out in his sleep. Ishmael has interwoven "this darker thread," choosing to retell the tale as he rehearsed it to an incredulous party of Spanish friends at the Golden Inn of Lima—a city which is proverbial with Melville both for its whiteness and for its corruption, and hence for the ambiguity of appearances.

The Town-Ho, a sperm-whaler out of Nantucket, takes its name from the shout that goes up when a whale is sighted; yet the expression, in passing, seems to glance landward, townward, backward at citified man. The chapter gives the homesick Ishmael a chance to salute the inland waterways, notably the Great Lakes and the Erie Canal. The desperate hero, Steelkilt, "a tall and noble animal," is a Lakeman; his boldest accomplices are a pair of Canallers; whereas the brutal villain, the mate and part-owner, Radney, is an islander from Martha's Vineyard, an unfederated Isolato. Melville, the lifelong champion of elective affinities, was learning to depict the special antipathy that draws one man to another, as Claggart would be drawn to Billy Budd. The conflict between Radney and Steelkilt is framed by larger conflicts, and accelerated by rhythms of suspense; for the hull is dangerously leaking, and the sailors are taking turns to man the pumps. Under the sadistic goading of Radney, Steelkilt rebels and others follow his lead. Thus the temptation to mutiny, which Starbuck resists on the Pequod, is realized aboard the Town-Ho—though not so catastrophically as it will be on the slave-ship of Benito Cereno. Again the language is revolutionary: the mutineers are Sea-Parisians, the decks are barricades. But when Steelkilt is hoisted from his "entombment" in the hold ("a place as black as the bowels of despair"), and when his faithless companions are strung up like "the two crucified thieves," the nimbus of purer example hovers over him. Ought we, then, to assume that "The Town-Ho's Story" is Melville's "Parable of the Grand Inquisitor?" He had anticipated Dostoevsky's idea in *Mardi*, when the philosopher Babbalanja said of Alma (or Jesus Christ): "As an intruder he came, and an intruder he would be this day; on all sides he would jar our social system."

What can the secret be, hissed out by the Lakeman, which is powerful enough to prevent the Captain from flogging him? That does not deter "the predestinated mate," though he is already bandaged and pale from the blow that Steelkilt has dealt him. Yet it may be Radney's vengeful act that summons up the White Whale, who seizes him and drags him down into the foam, where their "two whitenesses" are fatally blended together. Moby-Dick thereby not only avenges Steelkilt, but also—as we have learned from the babbled confidence of Tashtego—saves him from taking revenge into his own hands. He does not commit a murder, as Billy Budd will unintentionally; yet, having gone so far as to plot one, Steelkilt can hardly be identified with Jesus. Nevertheless, there is something Christlike in his announcement, when he finally gains the upper hand over the Captain, "I come in peace." He would seem to be under the whale's protection; whereas to Radney, and of course to Ahab, the whale is the agent of cosmic retribution. Moby-Dick seems to be a *deus ex machina* for the Town-Ho; on the Pequod he will become a *diabolus ex machina*; but, though Steelkilt cannot be Christ, Ahab is a sort of Antichrist. The happy ending of the episode completes its reversal of the story at large. Through its protagonist it brings to the foreground, in bold relief, those subordinate lives which sink into the background whenever Captain Ahab stumps his deck. The frantic democracy of the Town-Ho reaffirms what is stated in the negative through the totalitarian regime of the Pequod. Steel-kilt—who would have been Charlemagne, "had he been born son to Charlemagne's father"—stands forth as the book's most authentic hero, Melville's representative of the Godhead at work in every man, that Spirit of Equality which manifests itself through the kingly commons.

This conception of a social pantheism, as it were, is the nearest that Melville comes to a positive resolution of his inquiries. Speculation at the highest level, where the Captain overtops the crew, pushes through nature toward the supernatural. "Doubts of all things earthly and intuitions of some things heavenly"—such is Ishmael's skeptical credo, which makes him "neither believer nor infidel." The subject-matter facilitates his immersion in natural phenomena, in the fauna and flora of the ocean, and in the struggle for life as the naturalist of the Beagle, Charles Darwin, had begun to conceive it. The book itself is an encyclopedia of the science of cetology, as well as a manual of the technique of whaling. Yet whales are assigned, by one of its schemes of taxonomy, to various schools of philosophical thought. Ishmael aloft on the mast, high above waves that seem to be Cartesian vortices, reels with the heady exaltation of Platonic idealism: "Methinks that what they call my shadow here on earth is my true substance." Even the whale has its transcendental emanation in the spirit-spout, which so fascinated the Hawthornes. Nothing exists in matter without being duplicated in mind; nature is linked to the soul of man through analogies; and Ishmael, in pointing out those correspondences, sublimates the adventure from a physical to a metaphysical plane. There it becomes a gigantic psychomachia, the plot of which is—in a favorite word —predestinated, though not necessarily by the dogmas of orthodox Calvinistic theology. Ishmael's own analogy is a mat which is being woven by the woof of free will on the warp of necessity. Queequeg's sword, by intervening casually, performs the function of chance in contributing to the emergent design.

The pattern of destiny seems to unfold itself in signs and portents at every stage of the way. But *omen* is not in the Captain's dictionary; he dares the gods to speak outright, and not in darkling hints or old wives' tales. The warning at the outset is delivered by a ragged stranger whose designation, Elijah, identifies him with that prophet of the Old Testament who denounced the abominations of Ahab. Ahab, King of Israel, defied God by worshiping idols and took the law into his own hands by appropriating his neighbor's vineyard. Captain Ahab, at once "ungodly" and "godlike" in his lawless defiance, is also prefigured by Prometheus and Lucifer: "I am darkness leaping out of light." Though he claims to be Fate's lieutenant, acting under orders, he challenges Fate and questions the order of the universe. He is enveloped in terrible rumors of blasphemy ("that deadly scrimmage with the Spaniard afore the altar at Santa"). Heaven seems to have retaliated through the stroke of lightning that, according to sailors' gossip, seared him from head to toe. His vendetta has its provocation in the wound inflicted by Moby-Dick. The lost leg of flesh and blood has been replaced by an artificial limb of ivory. "On life and death this old man walked." Yet, figuratively speaking, that is the plight of all mortals. Ahab, dismasted, bears a darker and deeper trauma of a more intimate nature; his whalebone leg, in a mysterious accident, seems to have pierced his groin and wounded his manhood; but that state-secret is only half revealed. Consequently, all the woes of existence, all the hostile forces he has felt, the storm that Peter Rugg challenged, he has personified in the impersonal image of the whale. When Starbuck—the exponent of conscience—objects to his plan for wreaking vengeance upon a dumb beast, Ahab replies with a definition of his worldview and a confession of his attitude:

All visible objects, man, are but as pasteboard masks. But in each event—in the living act, the undoubted deed—there, some unknown but still reasoning thing puts forth the mouldings of its features from behind the unreasoning mask. If man will strike, strike through the mask! How can the prisoner reach outside except by thrusting through the wall? To me, the white whale is that wall, shoved near to me. Sometimes I think there's naught beyond. But 'tis enough. He tasks me; he heaps me; I see in him outrageous strength, with an inscrutable malice sinewing it. That inscrutable thing is chiefly what I hate; and be the white whale agent, or be the white whale principal, I will wreak that hate upon him.

This is the challenge of a disillusioned transcendentalism, which is impatient with material surfaces, eager to probe as far beyond them as possible, and doubtful as to the results of such an exploration. If the existential gesture proves nothing else, it asserts an identity; with "Bartleby," the wall will strike back and crush that identity. The zeal for knowledge carries Melville farther than Hawthorne, for whom it so often turned out to

be self-condemned. Ahab seems to be motivated by the
spirit of science, when he views his mighty adversary
as a riddle to solve or a sphinx to outwit. "Of all the
divers thou has dived the deepest," he concedes. Hence
to catch Moby-Dick would be to have sounded the
depths. The hieroglyphic furrows upon the whale's
brow might well invite the conjectures of another
Champollion—or the ratiocinations of an Auguste Dupin. It is inviting to sympathize with the protagonist
in his function of investigator, lured and eluded as he
is by the "devilish tantalization of the gods." The devil's
compact with Faust has its moral equivalent in Ahab's
consecration of the harpoon. The climax of that ceremony is virtually a black mass; the sacrilegious incantation (*"Ego non baptizo te in nomine patris, sed in
nomine diaboli"*) is indeed, as Melville confessed to
Hawthorne, the secret motto of a book which has been
broiled in hellfire; and the notes for this passage under-
score the difference between black (or goetic) and
white (or theurgic) magic. The weapon that is to spear
the white whale must be baptised in the blood of the
three dark-complexioned harpooneers, as if that polarity
were inherent in nature. Moreover, Ahab has his own
harpooneer—or should we say his shadow, or his demon?—in Fedallah, the "gamboge ghost" who has been
smuggled aboard in the misty dawn, with his boatload
of spectral oarsmen from the Philippines, and who remains "a muffled mystery to the last."

It is the Parsee, Fedallah, who injects "the diabolism
of subtlety" into the cross-purposes of reason and madness in Ahab's megalomania. Though the captain's eye
may awe the crew, it is Fedallah's which domineers
over Ahab. The Parsee cult of fire-worship intermingles

with the snake-worship of the Ophites and with the aura of other pagan rites. The basic premise of the Manicheans, that the devil may be no less powerful than God, is entertained as a working hypothesis; while the problem of which side is good and which is evil, though presented in terms of black and white, is by no means oversimplified. In contrast to that nostalgic sentence comparing the sea to the mainland, we have this outlandish description of the ship:

> As they narrated to each other their unholy adventures, their tales of terror told in words of mirth; as their uncivilized laughter forked upwards out of them, like the flames from the furnace; as to and fro, in their front, the harpooneers wildly gesticulated with their huge pronged forks and dippers; as the wind howled on, and the sea leaped, and the ship groaned and dived, and yet steadfastly shot her red hell further and further into the blackness of the sea and the night, and scornfully champed the white bone in his mouth, and viciously spat round her on all sides; then the rushing Pequod, freighted with savages, and laden with fire, and burning a corpse, and plunging into that blackness of darkness, seemed the material counterpart of her monomaniac commander's soul.

We have had a premonition when Ishmael blundered into a Negro church, "and the preacher's text was about the blackness of darkness." Soon he found his way to the Spouter Inn, so ominously presided over by one Peter Coffin, where he was greeted with a blackened picture of the Leviathan. But this was counterbalanced by a rusty harpoon, from a whale which was slain off the Cape of Blanco, and by objects of carved whale-ivory known as *skrimshander*. Melville interweaves his blacks and whites as carefully as the contrasting strands of hemp and manilla; yet when he pauses to give his obsession full scope, he concentrates his grandiloquent inquiry upon "The Whiteness of the Whale." In "this white-lead chapter about whiteness," Ishmael shows the bedazzled reader through his Virtuoso's Collection. Though he richly heaps up illustrations, the essential quality becomes more and more elusive as he undertakes to define it, until it finally seems to fade away into an appalling sensation of panic before the unknown and the unknowable. "Therefore, in his other moods, symbolize whatever grand or gracious thing he will by whiteness, no man can deny that in its profoundest idealized significance it calls up a peculiar apparition to the soul."

The symbolism of terror is universal. Otherwise, Death would not ride a pale horse in Scripture, and the Ancient Mariner would never have been bedeviled by an albatross. The glitter of Antarctic snow and ice, we may not irrelevantly remember, was the single mystery that Poe had left unresolved. W. H. Hudson would explain it as animism, "the mind's projection of itself into nature," our predisposition to be terrified by the exceptional. This may account for the stimulus it lends to visions or hallucinations like that of Hans Castorp in *The Magic Mountain*. One effect of taking mescaline, Henri Michaux has recently testified, is an impression of "absolute white, white beyond all whiteness." Truly, Melville seems justified in characterizing such an impression as "a dumb blankness, full of meaning, . . . a colorless all-color of atheism from which we shrink." Tracing its multiple connotations through the *chiaroscuro* of his alternating heroines, or from the lost innocence of *White-Jacket* to the deadly pallor of "Benito Cereno," may we not add one more paradox to the many that Ishmael has already accumulated? May we not surmise that Ishmael's whiteness, by virtue of a culminating paradox, is blackness in perversely baffling disguise? "Even blackness has its brilliancy"— and the most brilliant spectacle of all is the blackness of whiteness. All other whales are of Ethiopian hue; and Moby-Dick is set apart from them by his albinism, as they are set apart by their magnitude from all other created things. Their element is "the black sea," which conceals a multiplicity of secrets, "the dark Hindu half of nature." The organisms it breeds are predatory and cannibalistic; its vultures are sharks; and the God that made them, says Queequeg, is "one damn Ingin." If the so-called white man's burden is "ideal mastership over every dusky tribe," then the dusky races, in their closeness to nature, display an innate mastery of their own. Crossing the Equator, unappalled, they can hear the singing of mermaids—or is it the moaning of the drowned?

That the biggest fish should end by getting away is the conventional *dénouement* for a fisherman's yarn. That this particular monster of the deep should confound his pursuers, with a flip of his atom-smashing tail, was foreordained by the very conditions of the three-day chase. It is not for Ahab to cry *"Eureka!"*

Canst thou draw out Leviathan with an hook? . . .
Canst thou fill his skin with barbed irons? . . .

When the voice spoke out of the whirlwind to Job, the whale—which Puritans would identify with the devil—was the final instance of God's inscrutability:

> He beholdeth all high things: he is a king over all the children of pride.

The sacrifice of so many lives to the unrelenting ambition of one man—the moral could not be clearer or more humane. The upshot of that one man's experiment—that crazed explorer who breaks his quadrant and ignores his compasses—will forever remain in philosophic uncertainty. For, if Moby-Dick holds any answer to the enigmas that perplex mankind, any key to the whispered disclosure of Steelkilt, any clue to the "talismanic secret" that still bemuses Pierre, he disappears into the depths without yielding it up. Perhaps the secret may be that there is no secret, Melville speculated in one of his letters to Hawthorne. And again: "Why, ever since grandfather Adam, who has got to the meaning of his great allegory—the world?" Since, in sober fact, there is no such animal as an albino whale, Moby-Dick is utterly unique by definition. Since he is an irreducible symbol, an archetype of archetypes, there is no cogency in the varying labels with which his interpreters have attempted to tag him. To evade reduction into categories is the essence of his character. As a sperm-whale he concretely embodies a generative principle, which is intimated by the sexual interplay of the ninety-fourth and ninety-fifth chapters. But as a sport, *lusus naturae*, he is a preternatural being; he is everything and nothing, the absolute, "the great gliding demon of the seas of life." Doubtless, to apprehend him would be to understand the ways of God; but that is also true of picking the unplucked flower in Tennyson's crannied wall. Melville's book is not a mystery, to paraphrase C. S. Lewis on *Hamlet*: it is a book about a mystery. And, as Justice Holmes has testified about it: "Not Shakespeare had more feeling of the mystery of the world and of life." Like the multivalent doubloon that Ahab offers for his capture, *Moby-Dick* must have a different meaning for every man. What every man seeks in the water is what he may find in his narcissistic reflection, "the ungraspable phantom of life."

But few men seek the visage of reality by striking through the pasteboard masks of appearance; and fewer still would dare to fulfil that impulse if they suspected that whiteness was blankness, possibly nothingness. Colonel Lawrence of Arabia, who may have been such a man, is said to have reserved an exclusive shelf for those books which he considered diabolic. There were only three; and when we learn that the other two were *The Brothers Karamazov* and *Thus Spake Zarathustra*, we are more precisely aware of what may be meant by the diabolism of *Moby-Dick*. It is a tension sustained between doubt and belief. Our orphaned souls oscillate from the one to the other, and must await the repose of the grave to learn the secret of our paternity, Ishmael opines. "He can neither believe, nor be comfortable in his unbelief," Hawthorne commented, in his *English Notebooks*, after walking and talking with Melville by the seashore near Liverpool, "and he is too honest and courageous not to try to do one or the other." Five years after the publication of *Moby-Dick*, he was on the point of giving up his literary career. He seemed "overshadowed," Hawthorne noted, expressing the hope that Melville soon would "brighten." That was the last meeting between the two. Melville's journey took him to Palestine; and when he recounted it in *Clarel,* he went back over his earnest discussions with Hawthorne (whom he called Vine), reproaching his austere friend for "non-cordialness." A few years afterward, Hawthorne was dead, and Melville was reproaching himself:

> To have known him, to have loved him
> After loneness long;
> And then to be estranged in life,
> And neither in the wrong . . .

And the monody goes on to delineate a Hawthornesque landscape in the drypoint of black and white. Now the recluse is homeless, the vine conclusively chilled:

> By wintry hills his hermit-mound
> The sheeted snow-drifts drape,
> And houseless there the snow-bird flits
> Beneath the fir-trees' crape:
> Glazed now with ice the cloistral vine
> That hid the shyest grape.

Hawthorne's death is emblematized in much the same imagery that *Clarel* employs to voice the muted anguish of Melville's survival:

> Though black frost nip, though white frost chill,
> Nor white frost nor the black may kill
> The patient root, the vernal sense
> Surviving hard experience.

What seems so remarkable in retrospect is not the separation of Hawthorne and Melville, but their conjunction at the strategic midpoint of the nineteenth century and of their respective careers. As the irony of circumstance would have it, the adventurous Melville was beginning to introvert his talent, while the sequestered Hawthorne was just about to set forth upon his belated travels. The shock of recognition may have been somewhat unilateral; yet it was enough to drop "germinous seeds," as Melville characteristically put it, into his soul; and this was the miraculous year in which *Moby-Dick* was germinating. His impressions of Hawthorne's work, both in his review of *Mosses from an Old Manse* and his letter on *The House of the Seven Gables,* read like a declaration of his own intentions. It is in the latter book that he glimpses "a certain tragic phase of humanity," the visible truth that can only be told by contradicting the devil. "For all men who say *yes* lie; and all men who say *no,*—why, they are in the happy condition of the judicious unencumbered travelers in Europe; they cross the frontiers into Eternity with nothing but a carpet-bag,—that is to say, the Ego. Whereas those *yes*-gentry, they travel with heaps of baggage, and, damn them! they will never get through the Custom House." This two-sided remark, addressed to a man who had lately retired from a post in a custom-house by a man who was to spend his later days as a customs inspector, has an especially striking light to cast on the second chapter of *Moby-Dick,* "The Carpet-Bag," where Ishmael sets forth upon his journey through "blocks of blackness." Melville himself was traveling light when he visited Hawthorne at Liverpool, as his host recorded, "taking with him, by way of luggage, the least bit of a bundle"—an ego which had failed to encounter its double.

Continuing his solitary pilgrimage to the Holy Land,

Melville recorded in his journal at Joppa that he experienced "the genuine Jonah feeling." That had been the feeling of Melville's youthful voyagers, Redburn and White-Jacket; and it runs in a strong undercurrent through *Moby-Dick*. The bar at the inn is spanned by the jaw of a whale; the bartender is hailed by the drinkers as Jonah. One of Ishmael's excursions subjects the Bible story to an exegetical scrutiny. Most important, it is the text for "The Sermon," the chapter from which the book takes its ethical bearings. The setting is a Whaleman's Chapel at New Bedford, lined with the cenotaphs of men lost at sea; the small congregation of sailors, their wives, and their widows, is scattered like "silent islands." The preacher, Father Mapple, with his sailor-like turns of speech and behavior, had one or two living models; but he has a salty eloquence which is Melville's own. His homily is, of course, a prefiguration, a "heralding presentiment" of the hazards in store for Ishmael. The hymn that precedes it stresses the antithesis, which the sermon pointedly amplifies, between "the black distress" of the sea and the radiance of sunlight. It may well be Father Mapple who imparts to Ishmael the gift for perceiving symbols in ship's gear: thus the lamp that hangs so straight in Jonah's cabin betokens the light of conscience. Such a lamp in a dissimilar vessel, the riverboat of *The Confidence-Man*, will be symbolically extinguished at the end. The lesson of duty, as Father Mapple expounds it, is "two-stranded." Jonah, the "God-fugitive," is "a model of repentance" for all who refuse to heed a difficult command. But Father Mapple, like Hawthorne's Father Hooper, can also direct his preaching at himself. Jonah, the "pilot-prophet," is the exemplar for those who have been singled out "to preach the Truth to the face of Falsehood."

The peroration sums up Jonah's dilemma by balancing two sequences of alternatives. "Woe to him who seeks to please rather than to appall!" Yet, on the starboard hand: "Delight is to him who gives no quarter in the truth, and kills, burns, and destroys all sin, though he pluck it out from under the robes of Senators and Judges." The omen will be fulfilled by the misnamed Delight, heavily damaged by Moby-Dick himself, the last of the nine ships that cross the path of the Pequod. The alternative, Woe, would be challenged by Pierre in the guise of a black-visored knight; but Pierre would fail in his effort to strike through that visor; and Billy Budd will mutely inculpate himself by striking out against palpable injustice. Which then is true, which is the truth, Proust would inquire: the tragic vision or the joy of life? Ishmael contemplates this crucial question as he stands before the flaming tryworks, and warns us not to gaze too long into the fire—the flame of suffering. He deprecates our tendency to ignore jails, hospitals, and graveyards, to talk more about operas and less about hell, and to dismiss melancholy authors as sick men. In their defense he argues:

> The sun hides not the ocean, which is the dark side of this earth, and which is two thirds of this earth. So, therefore, that mortal man who hath more of joy than sorrow in him, that mortal man cannot be true—not true, or undeveloped. With books the same. The truest of all men was the Man of Sorrows, and the truest of all books is Solomon's, and Ecclesiastes is the fine hammered steel of woe.

Elsewhere Melville points out that the Galapagos tortoise is, in equal measure, black and bright. Here he instances the Catskill eagle, which not only soars through "the sunny spaces" but dives into "the blackest gorges." Ishmael will dive; he will know the lonesomeness of the castaway, like the half-witted Pip, whose sea-change has endowed him with wondrous insights. And Ishmael will soar; with the coffin as his means of life-in-death, he will rise to the surface, like Jonah being vomited forth from the whale. After the ostracism, the resurrection. The last word, "orphan," brings us back *da capo* to the terse exordium: "Call me Ishmael." The narrator, surviving alone to tell his tale, becomes a spokesman for the modern writer in all his restlessness, his self-consciousness, and his alienation. The Victorian Samuel Butler once termed himself "a literary Ishmaelite." He had been anticipated by Melville; and he would be succeeded by the generation of Stephen Dedalus and Tonio Kröger.

Among the "fish documents" that Melville used, the most suggestive was Owen Chase's account of the wreck of the Essex, stove by a whale. After that disaster, Captain Pollard, the master of the Essex, was never entrusted with the command of another ship. He was a night-watchman on Nantucket, when Melville stopped at the island shortly after the completion of *Moby-Dick*. Following a conversation between the two men, Melville jotted down in his journal: "Noah after the flood." He was to recall the same impressive figure, in *Clarel*, and to wonder: "A Jonah is he?" He might have been wondering about his own eclipse, and the anticlimax of his later career. He had some reason to feel that his vocation had been, in Father Mapple's phrase, "to sound those unwelcome truths in the ears of a wicked Nineveh." An analyst of the poetic imagination, Gaston Bachelard, has formulated—in another connection—what he labels "the Jonah complex." M. Bachelard seems to have in mind that spiritual malady which the late George Orwell has somewhat more incisively diagnosed in his essay on Henry Miller, "Inside the Whale." This is the widespread and appealing fantasy of a return to pre-natal bliss, "a womb big enough for an adult," a cushion of blubber between the irresponsible self and reality. But for Jonah, resisting his call, the fish was not a vehicle of escape; it was an instrument of Providence; and his three days and three nights in "the belly of hell" were a prayerful ordeal. The Jonah complex, we might more properly say, is the outlook of the reluctant prophet, brought to recognize his responsibilities, forced to propound unwelcome truths, and treated without honor by his compatriots and contemporaries. Literary history, which has produced a whole succession of Jonahs, makes amends as best it can by posthumous veneration.

Unhappily, it may be as Orwell implied, that writers in our time have increasingly tended to stay inside the whale. To carry out the unpopular mission of Jonah is to realize an intolerable truth: "that all deep earnest thinking is but the intrepid effort of the soul to keep the open independence of her sea." Whereas the comfort and safety of the land conspire against the autonomous individual, whose epitaph is Ishmael's chapter on Bulkington. Moreover, a way of life conceived by Poe as a battle of wits, or by Hawthorne as a conflict of conscience, presupposes an intellectual dynamic which can scarcely be counted among our blessings today. On the whole, the heritage of Melville has been a cultivation of his weaker qualities; his penchant for the subjective and the rhapsodic has deliquesced into the torrential outpourings of Thomas Wolfe; his involvement with his materials has made it easier for autobiography and reportage, thinly disguised, to masquerade as fiction. The bequest from Poe that has been most widely enjoyed is, inevitably, the detective-story—a convention which permits us to externalize, if not to exorcise, our sense of guilt and our foreboding of death. It was Hawthorne's good fortune to find a continuator, as well as a biographer, in Henry James. But James begins, where Hawthorne ended, with the problems of Americans in Europe; and his expatriation bears out his assumption that romance is no longer compatible with the American scene. His devotion to the memory of his cousin, Minnie Temple, makes the death of a young and beautiful woman as poignant a theme for him as it was for Poe. The opposition between blonde and brunette is quite as characteristic of James as it was of his predecessors, and could be traced through his works to its twilight phase in *The Wings of the Dove*, where the "dusky hair" of Kate Croy opposes the "exceptionally red" hair of the pale Milly Theale.

Actually, his first tale, "The Story of a Year," is an allegory from the sidelines of the Civil War, in which the transitions between war and peace are conveyed by images of darkness and brightness respectively. The heroic theme of the war itself would be celebrated, retrospectively and impressionistically, in the prose of Ambrose Bierce and Stephen Crane. It was too late for Melville, though he touched upon the subject fragmentarily in a volume of poems, *Battle-Pieces, and Aspects of the War.* In his preface he approached the collective experience from an Aristotelian point of view: "Let us pray that the terrible historic tragedy of our time may not have been enacted without instructing our whole beloved country through terror and pity." He discerned the protagonist of that tragedy in Abraham Lincoln, and looked up to "the father in his face" as Billy Budd would look up to Captain Vere; but Lincoln was to be Whitman's captain, not Melville's. The original sin that brought about the national catastrophe, as the Abolitionists of *The Liberator* had insisted, was slavery. Even Poe had sensed the power of that blackness, and concealed an intimation of it in the Ethiopian hieroglyphics chanced upon by Arthur Gordon Pym. Melville made the situation explicit when the dying Benito Cereno, asked what the shadow was that hung over him, responded: "The Negro." The issue was not exhausted by Harriet Beecher Stowe. Mark Twain could resolve it compassionately, when Nigger Jim was being hunted down by officers who inquired of Huckleberry Finn: "Is your man white or black?" Huck's reply— "He's white"—may well be regarded as a white lie, for which Huck later excuses himself by saying: "I knowed he was white inside." But there remains another aspect to this ethnic transference, an innate blackness in the white man, which Robert Penn Warren has perceptively evoked in his narrative poem, *Brother to Dragons*:

He saw the dark hand set the white dish down.
He felt the darkness growing in his heart.
He saw the dark faces staring, and they stared at him.
He saw poor George as but his darkest self

And all the possibility of the dark that he feared,
And so he struck, and struck down that darkest self.

It may be that the continual presence of darkness
in human shape, as a tangible reminder of the fears
and impulsions that it has come to symbolize, helped
to create a sensibility which seems distinctively Southern, and which has been contributing more than its
share to contemporary literature. "A man sees further
looking out of the dark upon the light than a man does
in the light and looking out upon the light," William
Faulkner writes in his short story, "*Ad Astram.*" Surprisingly enough, Faulkner's first book, a sequence of
poems, may be said to look out from the light; and yet
its title, *The Marble Faun*, signalizes much more than
a coincidence; for the outlook of the poet-novelist, like
that of Hawthorne's prototype, has developed in the
dark. Insofar as that vantage-point has a continuity, it
is one which went underground in the aftermath of
the Civil War, when the Golden Day of Transcendentalist hope yielded so rapidly to the Gilded Age of financial exploitation. The Gold Rush had begun the great
undeception, for Melville as it had for Poe, with the
triumph of brightness in its most materialistic and
illusory form:

> Gold in the mountain,
> And gold in the glen,
> And greed in the heart,
> Heaven having no part,
> And unsatisfied men.

What dazzles men can blind them, Ishmael—echoing
Goethe—had warned. The source of light itself can

darken the vision of its beholders, such as Hemingway's pertinacious fisherman in *The Old Man and the
Sea.* "All my life the early sun has hurt my eyes, he
thought. Yet they are still good. In the evening I can
look straight into it without getting the blackness. It
has more force in the evening too. But in the morning it is painful." To bring out the differences between
evening and morning, between our twentieth and nineteenth centuries, we need only juxtapose this passage
and the closing sentences of *Walden:* "The light which
puts out our eyes is darkness to us. Only that day dawns
to which we are awake. There is more day to dawn. The
sun is but a morning star." It is even more revealing to
reconsider Thoreau's version of the American dream in
the context of F. Scott Fitzgerald's conclusion to *The
Great Gatsby,* with its chastened realization that our
future has suddenly became our past. "For a transitory
enchanted moment man must have held his breath in
the presence of this continent, compelled into an esthetic contemplation he neither understood nor desired,
face to face for the last time in history with something
commensurate to his capacity for wonder." But now, as
the continent shows its night-side, the dream is behind
us, "somewhere back in that vast obscurity beyond the
city, where the dark fields of the republic rolled on under the night."

For our dreamers, America was a garden, an agrarian
Eden, which was losing its innocence by becoming
citified. Melville had located his City of Woe in London or Liverpool; Poe had tracked down imaginary
crimes in the streets of an imagined Paris; and Hawthorne had exposed sins most luridly among the ruins
of Rome. With the development of industrialism and

the concurrent growth of American cities, the mental climate was changing from romantic to realistic. Things were in the saddle, as Emerson—not always sanguine—lamented; for things were no longer emblems of ideas. They were things-in-themselves, and they rode mankind into the twentieth century at a constantly accelerating pace. Even Henry James, in *The Ivory Tower*, made an attempt—interrupted by his death—to set a novel once more in his native country, and to depict "the black and merciless things that are behind the great possessions." Meanwhile the analytic approach and the systematic technique of the European novelists were being applied to local and regional situations. "Away with old romance!" shouted Whitman, calling for new voices "to exalt the present and the real." Hawthorne, the apologist of the romance, had shrewdly made his rising young American, Holgrave, a practitioner of photography. Fiction, in its consequent effort to keep up with fact, aided and abetted by science and commerce, has depended more and more upon documentation, cross-section, journalism. Theodore Dreiser could be merciless in his exposure of the urban conditions that determine the sordid tragedies of our daily headlines. But, though the Critical Realists had the courage to say *no*, their work is altogether too negativistic because they lacked imaginative autonomy. Working in the theater, Eugene O'Neill could grope toward a symbolic dimension again, and could attain more tragic potency than our other dramatists because he too saw life as a *Long Day's Journey into Night*. For our contemporaries, as for the late Wallace Stevens, "Domination of Black" has been an occasional intermission in a much gaudier spectacle. Yet Ezra Pound,

after having revitalized a poetic tradition and partici-
pated in a foreign catastrophe, can cry from the depths
that man is

> A swollen magpie in a fitful sun,
> Half black half white.

This is the last extreme of Manicheanism, and few of
us would wish to share its utter despondency. The
dissidence has grown shriller as the minority has grown
smaller, and as the majority—at the other extreme—
has thundered *yes* with electronic resources of amplifi-
cation. The culture that made an Ishmael of Herman
Melville made a millionaire of P. T. Barnum and a
madonna of Mary Baker Eddy. Americans take their
tragedy lightly, Henry Adams complained; and his complaint was borne out by the relegation of Hawthorne's
romances, Poe's tales, and Melville's narratives to the
children's shelves of the public libraries. It is equally
probable that, conditioned to a regime of anesthetics
and anodynes, we take our trivialities too seriously.
Against the mounting pressures of conformism, we are
left with only the quiet watchword of Bartleby: "I
would prefer not to." Against the *yes*-gentry, in their
wishful campaigns to affirm by denying the negative, to
spread the self-deceptions of positive thinking, or to
suspend our hard-won disbelief in the incredible, it may
not be enough to repeat "Nevermore." But if we listen
to Mr. Smooth-it-away, whose other names are legion
today, we shall find out that he is the devil in disguise;
he will conduct us to the brink of hell by what purports
to be a Celestial Railroad. Luckily, the parable stops
at that point, with Hawthorne exclaiming: "Thank
Heaven it was a Dream!" Every nightmare has a happy

ending, so long as we can wake up, so long as Pierre can say: "It is all a dream—we dreamed that we dreamed we dream." It is a consolation to recall that the Book of Jonah does not terminate in the destruction of Nineveh, "that great city." The Ninevites, who could not tell their right hand from their left, nevertheless repented and were saved. The avenging prophecy, somewhat to Jonah's chagrin after all his thankless disquietude, went unfulfilled because its warning had proved so effective. It had undoubtedly exaggerated, as art must, when it tries to convey the truth. It had also missed something, as criticism must, when it is looking for other things. "The picture you see doesn't consist of the things you see and say words about," Sherwood Anderson has written in *Winesburg, Ohio.* "There is something else, something you don't see at all, something you aren't intended to see. Look at that one over here, by the door here, where the light from the window falls upon it. The dark spot by the road that you might not notice at all is, you see, the beginning of everything."

Castles and Culture

GOETHE, in a poetic greeting to the United States, congratulated her on possessing no ruined castles. America was better off than Europe, as he went on to explain, because the new world lacked such useless reminders of feudal strife. Consequently he voiced the hope that, when a breed of native poets arose, they would be able to dispense with ghost stories and legends of robber barons. Most Europeans of good will and enlightenment have, in some measure, shared this American dream. The map of an uncharted hemisphere betokened a fresh page of history, an escape from the confining institutions of what Tom Paine characterized as an "old world overrun with oppression." And if democratic revolution tended to shut off the past, Alexis de Tocqueville pointed out, it opened up the future to poetry. The European imagination, from Chateaubriand to Kafka, has looked toward the western horizon whenever it turned from the citadels of constraint and artifice back to nature or forward to Utopia.

Meanwhile the American imagination seems to have been embarrassed and somewhat obsessed by the idyllic virginity of the terrain, the very blankness of the *tabula rasa*. "Natural scenery" needed the embellishment of "poetical association," according to Washington Irving, the first American to gain a secure position in English letters—a modest but comfortable niche between Goldsmith and Dickens. Hence Irving's career became a sentimental journey in search of the picturesque and the retrospective, a realization of the longing expressed in his *Sketch-Book* "to tread . . . in the footsteps of antiquity,—to loiter about the ruined castle." One of his landmarks was a castle in Spain, the Alhambra; another, closer to home, was Bracebridge Hall. When he returned to the local color of his native region, he celebrated New York as an old Dutch colony. His characteristic spokesman, Rip Van Winkle, sleeps through the present, dreams of yesteryear, and awakes a bearded and bewildered wanderer in an epoch which has passed him by.

From the other side European curiosity, whenever it dwells upon American literature, is naturally attracted by the indigenous. Here the pioneer, in spite of himself, was Fenimore Cooper. As it happened, Cooper was a country squire who devoted some of his less popular novels to the rights of the landed gentry. He spent some years in England and on the Continent, attempting to challenge Scott and Dumas upon their own ground. But the transatlantic popularity of his frontiersman hero led him to revisit the pathless forest and to round out his five-volume Leatherstocking cycle. Cooper's redskins had an even greater impact: predatory rivals rather than noble savages, they reappear only thinly disguised in Balzac. Yet their creator, in a book discreetly addressed to English readers and entitled *Notions of the Americans,* lamented that his country had no peasantry to write about. "No annals for the historian," his lament continued, "no manners for the dramatist, and no obscure fictions for writers of romance."

This attitude, struck repeatedly by American writers through the nineteenth century, is formulated in a famous passage from the volume on *Nathaniel Hawthorne,* contributed by Henry James to the "English Men of Letters" series. James was preparing his own career as an English man of letters when he catalogued those "items of high civilization" so essential to the novelist and so absent from the American scene: no castles, of course, nor cathedrals, no thatched cottages nor ivied ruins, neither the paraphernalia of a court nor the monuments of an aristocracy—nor, indeed, to be devastatingly specific, any Oxford, Eton, Epsom, or Ascot. But James was also exemplifying the romantic logic that had set Hawthorne's final novel in Italy because, as the preface to *Transformation (The Marble Faun)* attested, "romance and poetry, ivy and lichen and wall-flowers, need ruin to make them grow." Whereas among his own compatriots, even then commencing their Civil War, Hawthorne incuriously could perceive "no shadow, no antiquity, no mystery, no picturesque and gloomy wrong."

But contemporary realism was for twentieth-century novelists; Hawthorne expressly considered himself a romancer. His contribution was the development of a sense of the past, the rediscovery of Gothic New England. His legendary sketches, *Mosses from an Old*

Manse, were homegrown in the Concord habitation that had previously sheltered Emerson's cosmic optimism. Hawthorne treated the Puritan background at length in *The Scarlet Letter*; he was to deal with Transcendentalist speculation in *The Blithedale Romance*. The middle novel in this trilogy, *The House of the Seven Gables*, records the tension between those two spheres. The decaying house with its ancestral curse, its secret panel, its mysterious portrait, and its buried treasure—what is this but Hawthorne's ruined castle? The seventeenth-century dwelling still shown to visitors in Salem today was for him "an emblem of aristocratic pomp amid democratic institutions." In describing a flight from its shadows into the sunlight via the newly constructed railroad, he seems to describe his own hesitations between tradition and modernity.

Hawthorne's lifelong preoccupation with domiciles is reflected in the titles of his books—not least in that book of English impressions which he called, with mixed emotions, *Our Old Home*. He was confirmed as an unregenerate Yankee by his later years as consul at Liverpool; yet he was haunted by the recurrent fantasy of an American returning to England and seeking the estate of his ancestors. This is the subject of several unfinished romances, and represents a kind of legacy from Hawthorne to James. The latter starts in *Roderick Hudson* where *Transformation* left off: with the fascinations and corruptions of Rome for the young American artist. These are embodied in the sinister smile of Gloriani the sculptor, a Bohemian and presumably a charlatan. It is not until the ripeness of *The Ambassadors*, and the recognition-scene in Gloriani's garden, that the meaning of "the terrible life behind the smile" is revealed—the secret of art lived, life felt, and feeling mastered.

"The splendor falls on castle walls . . ." Tennyson's trumpet-call, faintly reverberating in Northhampton, Massachusetts, summons Roderick Hudson from innocence toward experience. Daisy Miller begins by visiting the Castle of Chillon, and ends by dying—like an early Christian martyr—of overexposure in the Coliseum. James's heroines, from Isabel Archer to Milly Theale, gradually learn that Europe is more than an esthetic spectacle; it is a moral involvement in which they become the tragic protagonists, inheriting riches and victimized by intrigues. Education, culture, civilization itself is no grand tour of an endless art gallery, but a pursuit of the knowledge that good and evil are not respectively aligned on the western and eastern sides of the Atlantic. Thus, between Mr. Newman in *The American* and Prince Amerigo in *The Golden Bowl*, the hemispheric values are transposed. What is wrong with the United States, it follows, is not the lack of ivy or thatch, but the thinness and flatness of the psychological landscape.

James deplored those unimpeded vistas which Goethe had welcomed. European poets might complain of coming late into a world too old. James, reversing the plaint, had come too early into a world too young. Lacking "the tone of time," the richness of tradition itemized in his list of hallowed symbols, what was left for the writer of fiction? Simply the whole of life, retorted William Dean Howells. In giving up the foreign service to chronicle the small beer of American domestic life, Howells had abandoned the ruined castle—as it were— for the *parvenu* town house put up on the water side

of Beacon Street by his Boston businessman, Silas
Lapham. And James could approve, perhaps envy, the
course that his friend had taken. One of his own earliest
stories, "A Passionate Pilgrim," involves a sickly American who wants to see Oxford and die. Literally achiev-
ing his ambition, he dies amid the spires and quad-
rangles, but not before his last words have looked homeward:

> There's a certain grandeur in the lack of decora-
> tions, a certain heroic strain in that young imagina-
> tion of ours which finds nothing made to its hands,
> which has to invent its own traditions and raise
> high into our morning air—with a ringing hammer
> and nails—the castles in which we dwell.

This affirmation is less typical of the expatriate James
than of his fellow Americans. For a full answer to his
critique, an invidious comparison between American
progress and the housing conditions of an antiquated
and unsanitary Europe, we should have to turn to
The Innocents Abroad or *A Connecticut Yankee at
King Arthur's Court*. But Mark Twain had no conver-
sance with Epsom or Ascot, though he had gambled
with miners during the California Gold Rush; though
he had not studied at Eton or Oxford, he had been
educated at the pilot's wheel of a river-boat; and in his
account of that liberal education, *Life on the Mississippi*, he dedicates a chapter to this problem under the
suggestive heading of "Castles and Culture." Passing
by the state capitol of Louisiana, he is provoked by the
gingerbread medievalism of its architecture, which bears
so little organic relationship to the community or the
period. (The skyscraper that has since replaced this

edifice, built under Governor Huey Long, has provided a setting for recent novels by John Dos Passos and Robert Penn Warren.)

Here Mark Twain attacks a favorite target, the debilitating influence of Sir Walter Scott's romances upon the mores of the South, and more broadly speaking, the spurious cultural pretensions of the Southern plantation. Under the guise of fiction he goes farther; the self-styled King and Duke, who are exposed as a bad actor and a cheap gambler in *The Adventures of Huckleberry Finn,* constitute a satire on royalty and nobility as measured by Mark Twain's faith in the common man. On the other hand, in *The American Claimant,* a young lord demonstrates his basic manhood by becoming a cowboy. There may well be a sense in which every writer is either a Don Quixote or a Sancho Panza: either a knightly idealist who insists that each inn is a castle, or a realistic squire who treats any castle as if it were an inn. In this respect, as in so many others, the relation between Henry James and Mark Twain is complementary.

Huckleberry Finn's confessions terminate in his resolve to "light out" before Aunt Polly can catch him and civilize him. Huck's declaration of independence, however, is tempered by an acknowledgment of continuity: "I've been there before." It is hard to say which conflicting impulse, wanderlust or nostalgia, dominates the American temperament. Hawthorne manifests a homing instinct, while Herman Melville seems embarked upon an outward journey; yet the paths of the two men crossed in mid-career. On his first voyage Melville, too, had sought castles and cathedrals; but the British ports displayed slums and warehouses; and henceforth he pursued a more distant quest in the other direction. Among his "wooden-walled citadels of the deep," Benito Cereno's slave-ship is compared with a chateau, and the mutinous Town-Ho with the Bastille. On such a stage, against a timeless backdrop, man in the open air, reliant upon his own efforts and unaccommodated by heraldic trappings, is both a national hero and an epic theme.

The English novel, from *Waverley* to *Brideshead Revisited*, revolves around great houses and conjures with the perquisites of a settled order. For these America, always on the move, has few equivalents; her log-cabins are the milestones of exploration, her homesteads the expedients of subsistence, her skyscrapers the inventions of science. Her schoolboys, memorizing an earnest poem by Oliver Wendell Holmes, exhort one another to leave the "low-vaulted past" and build "more stately mansions." Accordingly, her millionaires have reared their crenellated battlements at Newport or reconstructed abbeys in Hollywood—reconstructions hardly substantial enough to resist the volleys of Aldous Huxley or Evelyn Waugh. A far cry, all this, from the hut that Henry Thoreau built near Walden Pond, or from the advice he offered to other American builders: first create your castle in the air, then put a foundation under it. The rate and scale of later developments made it increasingly difficult to preserve such an accord between the speculative and the practical.

Ralph Waldo Emerson had propounded a manifesto for original genius when he asserted that beauty and truth were quite as indigenous to Massachusetts as to Tuscany or the isles of Greece. But Walt Whitman was more ambiguous when he invited the Muses to

migrate in person from Greece and Ionia to the isle of
Manhattan, and especially to the Philadelphia Exposi-
tion of 1876. In demanding that the sign *To Let* be
hung on German, French, and Spanish castles and Italian collections, it is not clear whether he regarded
American culture as a competition with or an importation from "the elder world." Successors, at all events,
have continued to face the same dilemma. Typically,
the late Sinclair Lewis took his Dodsworth abroad and
poised that well-meaning automobile manufacturer between two equally insistent muses. One of them tells
him, "American life is so thin, so without tradition."
And the other says, "Create something native . . . dismiss the imitation chateau."

But, as the distance between hemispheres is shortened,
the difference between alternatives is neutralized. American criticism has cultivated a taste for such elaborate
products of European literature as Edmund Wilson
exhibits in *Axel's Castle.* The younger generation of
Americans now writes such plaintive testaments as Robert Lowell has deposed in *Lord Weary's Castle.* Anglo-
American poetry moves freely "between two worlds become much like each other"—and who, if not T. S.
Eliot, has the authority to modernize the well-worn
expression of Matthew Arnold? A more surprising witness is Ernest Hemingway, than whom no writer has
ever seemed more intransigently American. Yet most
of his fiction takes place in other lands: the West In-
dies, Africa, Italy, France, and particularly Spain. It is
as if Huck Finn, after having lit out, grown up at last,
and long been expatriated, discovered that the bells of
Europe were tolling—and, Mr. Eliot would add, the
towers of civilization were falling—for him.

By this time the United States has accumulated, for better or worse, her own store of ruins and ghosts. Her darkest memory, in spite of Mark Twain, is what has made the South such fertile ground for writers today. Insofar as the ruined castle stands for the pride and guilt of authentic tragedy, its specifications are met by that gloomy mansion which Colonel Sutpen built on slave labor in *Absalom, Absalom!* But William Faulkner, as he declared in accepting the Nobel Prize a few years ago, is less concerned with regional traits than with universal passions. In this he resembles his fellow Southerner, Edgar Allan Poe, whose ruined castle was the haunted palace of the mind itself, so terrifyingly disintegrated in "The Fall of the House of Usher." Such terrors, Poe confessed, were "not of Germany but of the soul." How, then, could Goethe ever have foreseen that this brave new world would soon bring forth the most Gothic of all romancers?

General

THE MOST convenient guide to further reading is the three-volume *Literary History of the United States*, New York (1948), which includes competent chapters on Hawthorne, Poe, and Melville in the first volume, and detailed bibliographies in the third. The most influential series of critical revaluations has been D. H. Lawrence's *Studies in Classic American Literature*, New York (1923). F. O. Matthiessen's *American Renaissance*, New York (1941), contains rich sections on Hawthorne and Melville, considered in relation to one another and to other figures of their time. Perry Miller's *The Raven and the Whale*, New York (1956), presents a solid and entertaining picture of the literary world in which Poe and Melville figured. Of Professor Miller's studies in New England culture, one which has particular significance for American symbolism is his edition of Jonathan Edwards' *Images, or Shadows of Divine Things*, New Haven (1948). The rare book entitled *The History of the Kingdom of Basaruah*, as edited by Richard Schlatter, Cambridge, Massachusetts (1946), may well be regarded as the first American work of prose fiction. An early argument for the importance of the theological background was advanced by Paul Elmer More in "The Origins of Hawthorne and Poe," *Shelburne Essays*, First Series, New York (1904). Charles Feidelson's *Symbolism and American Literature*, Chicago (1953), is a helpful introduction to the relationship it spans. The concept of innocence, a logical counterpart to the theme of blackness, has been traced through the nineteenth century by R. W. B. Lewis in *The American Adam*, Chicago (1955). In *The Enchafèd Flood*, New York (1950), W. H. Auden discourses suggestively on "the romantic iconography of the sea," with considerable emphasis upon *Moby-Dick*. F. I. Carpenter was one of the first to discuss the alignment of Hawthorne's and Melville's heroines, in "Puritans Preferred Blondes," *New England Quarterly*, IX (1936). The darker side of a more sanguine writer is indicated by Sholom J. Kahn in "Whitman's 'Black Lucifer'," *Publications of the Modern Language Association of America*, LXXI (1956). Elliott Coleman's English translation of Georges Poulet's *Studies in Human Time*, Baltimore (1956), appends a short but penetrating chapter on "Time and American Writers." A recent European interpretation, which finds a spiritual unity in Hawthorne, Poe, and Melville, is Luigi Berti's *Storia della Letteratura Americana*, Milan (1950). "The Broken Circuit," an article by Richard Chase in the current *Anchor Review*, II (1957), seems to parallel the point of view taken here. A bibliographical survey of "The Use of Color in Literature," by Sigmund Skard in the *Proceedings of the American Philosophical Society*, XC (1946), shows how much has already been done, and suggests how much remains to be done, through that approach. Among the many items it lists, a special relevance may attach to the little known article of F. B. Gummere, "On the Symbolic Use of the Colors Black and White in the Germanic Tradition," *Haverford College Studies*, I (1889). In the studies of Gaston Bachelard, relating poetry to psychology by way of the elements, there are some stimulating excursions on Melville and especially on Poe: *L'Eau et les Rêves*, Paris (1942); *L'Air et les Songes*, Paris (1943); *La Terre et les Rêveries du Repos*, Paris (1948). Max Bense, in *Aesthetica*, Stuttgart (1954), touches on some of the metaphysical implications in the work of Poe and Melville.

Hawthorne

THE STANDARD TEXT of the collected works is still the Riverside Edition in twelve volumes, edited by Hawthorne's son-in-law, George Parsons Lathrop. The manuscripts of

The American Notebooks, New Haven (1932), and *The English Notebooks*, New York (1941), have been ably re-edited by Randall Stewart. Professor Stewart has also written the most dependable biography, New Haven (1948). *Nathaniel Hawthorne: Representative Selections*, edited by Austin Warren in the American Writers Series, New York (1934), is notable for its introduction and its critical bibliography. In Julian Hawthorne's two volumes, *Nathaniel Hawthorne and his Wife*, Boston (1885), reminiscence is enriched with correspondence not otherwise collected. The letters of Hawthorne discussing the murder trial that might have inspired *The House of the Seven Gables* are printed by Edward B. Hungerford in the *New England Quarterly*, V (1933). The posthumous romance, *Dr. Grimshawe's Secret*, has been republished in a trustworthy edition by Edward H. Davidson, Cambridge, Massachusetts (1954). The half-forgotten *Journal of an African Cruiser*, which Hawthorne edited for Horatio Bridge, New York (1845), deserves at least a marginal place in the canon. "Hawthorne's Spectator," the home-made periodical he conducted at the age of sixteen, has been reprinted by Elizabeth L. Chandler, *New England Quarterly*, IV (931). In *Hawthorne as Editor*, University, Louisiana (1941), Arlin Turner has identified and reproduced Hawthorne's early contributions to *The American Magazine of Useful and Entertaining Knowledge*. Professor Turner has also elucidated the background of English reading in "Hawthorne's Literary Borrowings," *Publications of the Modern Language Association*, LI (1936). The dissertation of Jane Lundblad, *Nathaniel Hawthorne and European Literary Tradition*, Upsala (1947), relates his work to continental precedent. In a discussion which focuses on "My Cousin, Major Molineux," Roy Harvey Pearce makes some interesting points about "Hawthorne and the Sense of the Past," *Journal of English Literary History*, XXI (1954). Leo Marx points out reflections of the industrial revolution in the imagery of Hawthorne and of Melville, in "The Machine in the Garden," *New England Quarterly*, XXIX (1956). A latent theme is heavily underscored in *Haw-*

thorne's Faust: A Study of the Devil Archetype, by William Bysshe Stein, Gainesville, Florida, (1953). *Hawthorne's Fiction: The Light and the Dark*, by Richard H. Fogle, Norman, Oklahoma (1952), examines that basic dualism in terms of artistic effect. An earlier discussion of the same problem is "Color, Light, and Shadow in Hawthorne's Fiction," by Walter Blair, in the *New England Quarterly*, XV (1942). A psychological interpretation, "The Dark Lady of Salem," along with essays on related matters is to be found in *Image and Idea*, by Philip Rahv, Norfolk, Connecticut (1949). Anthony Trollope's appreciation, "The Genius of Nathaniel Hawthorne," first appeared in the *North American Review*, CXXIX (1879); its occasion was the appearance of Henry James's *Hawthorne* in the English Men of Letters Series.

Poe

It is a scandal to American scholarship that there is no satisfactory edition of the complete works. The Virginia (or Monticello) Edition, seventeen volumes edited by James A. Harrison, New York (1902), has long been outdated by the advance of textual and bibliographical knowledge. There is a sound edition of Poe's *Letters*, in two volumes edited by John Ward Ostrom, Cambridge, Massachusetts (1948). The biography by Arthur H. Quinn is a rich mine of careful documentation. *The Life and Works of Edgar Allan Poe*, by Marie Bonaparte, translated by John Rodker, London (1949), is "a psychoanalytic interpretation"—rather more sensitive than most—bearing the imprimatur of Freud himself. *The Mind of Poe*, by Killis Campbell, Cambridge, Massachusetts (1933), is a useful collection of articles dealing with the canon, views on slavery, and other relevant topics. The three important appreciations by Charles Baudelaire may be most conveniently obtained in the Pléiade edition of his translation, *Histoires Extraordinaires*, edited by Y. G. Le Dantec, Paris (1951). *Les Poêmes d'Edgar Poe*, Paris (1928), translated by Stéphane Mallarmé, includes the translator's commemorative sonnet. Paul Valéry's pretentious essay on *Eureka*, in the first volume of *Variété*, Paris (1924), seems less illuminating than scattered remarks by the same poet-critic elsewhere. Authoritative, though all too brief, is the account of Poe's French influence in T. S. Eliot's Library of Congress lecture. "From Poe to Valéry." *Hudson Review*, II (1949). W. H. Auden has made an attractive selection, and contributed a sensible introduction, in the Rinehart Series, New York (1950). *The Histrionic Mr. Poe*, by N. Bryllion Fagin, Baltimore (1949), paints a convincing portrait of its subject against a theatrical background. *Biblical Allusions in Poe*, by W. M. Forrest, New York (1948), traces and tabulates one of the main resources of Poe's style. In "The Use of Color Words by Edgar Allan Poe," *Publications of the Modern Language Association*, XLV (1930), W. O. Clough has made a statistical count which is utilized in the present study. Dostoevsky's Russian introduction has been made available in English by Vladimir Astrov in "Dostoevsky on Edgar Allan Poe," *American Literature*, XVI (1942). In "A Reinterpretation of 'The Fall of the House of Usher'," *Comparative Literature*, IV (4), Leo Spitzer connects that tale with sociological determinism and various other intellectual currents. The elusive figure who holds the key to *The Narrative of Arthur Gordon Pym* is described by Robert F. Almy in "J. N. Reynolds: A Brief Biography with Particular Reference to Poe and Symmes," *Colophon*, II (1937), and further by Aubrey Starke in "Poe's Friend Reynolds," *American Literature*, XVI (1944). In "Poe's Imaginary Voyage," *Hudson Review*, IV (1952), Patrick F. Quinn considers *The Narrative of Arthur Gordon Pym* in the light of some recent French reconsiderations. Allen Tate's "Our Cousin, Mr. Poe," *Partisan Review*, XVI (1949), is a personal revaluation which—it may be hoped —heralds a full-length study.

Melville

A DEFINITIVE EDITION of Melville's collected works is a desideratum which has yet to be supplied. The volumes already issued under the joint auspices of Hendricks House and Farrar and Straus seem to go out of print before new ones are available, though they comprise a *Moby-Dick* with an encyclopedic apparatus, edited by Luther S. Mansfield and Howard P. Vincent, New York (1952), and a *Pierre* with a brilliant introduction by Henry A. Murray, New York (1949); other volumes are *Collected Poems*, edited by Howard P. Vincent, Chicago (1947), *The Piazza Tales*, edited by Egbert S. Oliver, New York (1948), and *The Confidence-Man*, edited by Elizabeth S. Foster, New York (1954). In the meanwhile, the sixteen volumes published at London (1922–4) must still be accorded the title of Standard Edition. In the case of *Billy Budd*, the only reliable text is that of Jay Leyda in the compact selection edited for the Viking Portable Library, New York (1952). Mr. Leyda's two-volume *Melville Log*, New York (1951), is a model of its kind, an author's biography as revealed through a generous assemblage of pertinent documents. It can be supplemented, particularly in the sphere of family history, by Eleanor Melville Metcalf's *Herman Melville: Cycle and Epicycle*, Cambridge, Massachusetts (1953). The volume of *Representative Selections* in the American Writers Series, edited by Willard Thorp, New York (1938), still serves its purpose as a handbook and a chrestomathy. Among the numerous critical biographies, perhaps the most thoughtful and sympathetic are those of William Ellery Sedgwick, *Herman Melville: The Tragedy of Mind*, Cambridge, Massachusetts (1944), and of Newton Arvin in the American Men of Letters Series, New York (1950). Melville's actual experience has been closely followed, and compared with his books, in such studies as *Melville in the South Seas*, by Charles R. Anderson, New York (1939). The subtle interplay between fact and fiction is most painstakingly analyzed by William H. Gilman in *Melville's*

Early Life and Redburn, New York (1951). Merrell R. Davis has disentangled much of the intricate allegory in *Melville's Mardi: A Chartless Voyage,* New Haven, (1952). The volume of *Moby-Dick Centennial Essays,* edited by Tyrus Hillway and Luther S. Mansfield, contains fruitful contributions by Perry Miller, Henry A. Murray, Henry Nash Smith, and others, Dallas (1953). The principal interpolation in Moby-Dick, "Melville's 'The Town-Ho's Story'," is cogently discussed by Sherman Paul in *American Literature,* XXI (1949). "Melville's 'Benito Cereno' and Captain Delano's Voyages," by Harold H. Scudder, *Publications of the Modern Language Association,* XLIII (1929), collates that story with its documentary source. "Herman Melville's 'I and My Chimney'," by Merton M. Sealts, *American Literature,* XIII (1941), brings out the autobiographical reverberations of an apparently slight sketch. John W. Schroeder's "Sources and Symbols for Melville's *Confidence-Man,*" *Publications of the Modern Language Association,* LXVI (1951), is a courageous attempt to crack a tough nut. In a voluminous book, *Melville's Quarrel with God,* Princeton (1952), Lawrance Thompson over-argues a tenable point, a justifiable piece of devil's advocacy. Charles Olson's *Call Me Ishmael,* New York (1947) is a lyrical presentation of factual data and of Shakespearean echoes. George C. Homans, in "The Dark Angel," *New England Quarterly,* V (1932), broached a theme which has still to be fully explored.

1800. Wordsworth, *Lyrical Ballads* (Second Edition).	
1801. Chateaubriand, *Atala*.	
	1804. Born at Salem, Massachusetts, July 4.
1808. Goethe, *Faust* (Part I).	1808. Father dies in Dutch Guiana.
1814. Scott, *Waverley*.	
	1816. Family moves to Maine.
1819. Irving, *A Sketch-Book*.	1819–21. Attends school in Salem.
1821. Cooper, *The Spy*.	1821–25. Attends Bowdoin College.
1827. Manzoni, *The Betrothed*.	
1828. Webster, *American Dictionary of the English Language*.	1828. *Fanshawe*.
1830. Hugo, *Hernani*.	
1835. Tocqueville, *Democracy in America*.	
1836. Emerson, *Nature*.	1836. Edits *American Magazine of Useful and Entertaining Knowledge*.

1809. Born in Boston.
1810. Death of father.
1811. Death of mother.
Brought up by Mr. and
Mrs. John Allan of
Richmond.

1815–20. In England.

1819. Born in New York City.

1826. Attends University of
Virginia.
1827. *Tamerlane and Other
Poems.*
1827–28. Joins U.S. Army.

1829. *Al Aaraaf.*
1830–31. At West Point.

1830. Family moves to
Albany.

1831. *Poems.*
1831–35. In Baltimore.

1832. Death of father.

1833. Begins career as
magazine writer with
"Manuscript Found in a
Bottle."

1836. Marries his cousin,
Virginia Clemm. Moves
to Richmond. Editor,
*Southern Literary
Messenger.*

CHRONOLOGY	HAWTHORNE
1837. Whittier, *Poems.* Dickens, *Pickwick Papers.*	1837. *Twice-Told Tales.*
	1838. Engaged to Sophia Peabody.
	1839–40. Measurer in Boston Custom House.
1840. Dana, *Two Years Before the Mast.*	1840. *Grandfather's Chair.*
1841. Carlyle, *Heroes and Hero-Worship.* Emerson, *Essays: First Series.*	1841. Member of Brook Farm Community.
1842. Balzac, *The Human Comedy* (Foreword).	1842. Marriage. Residence in Old Manse at Concord.
1840–44. *The Dial.*	1844. Birth of daughter, Una.
	1846. Birth of son, Julian. *Mosses from an Old Manse.*
	1846–49. Surveyor in Salem Custom House.
1847. Marx and Engels, *Communist Manifesto.* Emerson, *Poems.* Longfellow, *Evangeline.*	
1848. Thackeray, *Vanity Fair.* Lowell, *Biglow Papers.* Thoreau, *Civil Disobedience.*	
1849. Parkman, *The Oregon Trail.*	

POE	MELVILLE
1837–38. New York. *The Narrative of Arthur Gordon Pym*.	1837. Teaches at district school.
	1838. Studies engineering at Lansingburgh Academy.
1839. Philadelphia. Editor of *Burton's Gentleman's Magazine*.	1839. First voyage on merchantman Saint Lawrence to Liverpool.
1840. *Tales of the Grotesque and Arabesque*.	1840. Trip to Middle West.
1841–42. Editor of *Graham's Magazine*.	1841. Ships on whaler Acushnet for South Seas.
	1842. Jumps ship at Marquesas. Also visits Tahiti.
1843. Wins prize for "The Gold Bug." *Prose Romances*.	1843–44. Returns from Honolulu to Boston or frigate United States.
1844. Moves back to New York. Literary critic of the *New York Mirror*.	
1845. Proprietor of *The Broadway Journal*. *Tales of Mystery and Imagination. The Raven and Other Poems*.	
1846. Libel suit against T. D. English.	1846. *Typee*.
1847. Virginia dies of tuberculosis at Fordham.	1847. *Omoo*. Marries Elizabeth Shaw. Lives in New York.
1848. *Eureka*. Engagement.	
1849. Richmond. Dies in Baltimore.	1849. Birth of son, Malcolm. *Mardi. Redburn*. Journey to London.

CHRONOLOGY	HAWTHORNE
1850. Dickens, *David Copperfield.* Wordsworth, *Prelude.*	1850. *The Scarlet Letter.*
	1850–51. Living at Lenox, Massachusetts.
	1851. Birth of daughter, Rose. *The House of the Seven Gables. The Snow Image.*
1852. Harriet Beecher Stowe, *Uncle Tom's Cabin.*	1852. Moves to "The Wayside," Concord, Massachusetts. *A Wonder Book. The Blithedale Romance. Life of Franklin Pierce.*
	1853. *Tanglewood Tales.*
	1853–56. United States Consul at Liverpool.
1854. Thoreau, *Walden.*	
1855. Longfellow, *Hiawatha.* Whitman, *Leaves of Grass.*	
1857. Flaubert, *Madame Bovary. Atlantic Monthly* founded.	
1858. Holmes, *The Autocrat of the Breakfast Table.*	1858–59. In Italy.
1859. Darwin, *The Origin of Species.*	
1860. George Eliot, *The Mill on the Floss.*	1860. Return to "The Wayside." *The Marble Faun.*
	1863. *Our Old Home.*
	1864. Dies on trip with Franklin Pierce at Plymouth, New Hampshire.
1868. Louisa May Alcott, *Little Women.*	

POE	MELVILLE
1850. *Works.*	1850. *White-Jacket.* Moves to "Arrowhead" near Pittsfield, Massachusetts. 1851. Birth of son, Stanwix. *Moby-Dick.* 1852. *Pierre.* 1853. Birth of daughter, Elizabeth. 1855. *Israel Potter.* Birth of daughter, Frances. 1856. *The Piazza Tales.* 1856–57. Mediterranean journey. 1857. *The Confidence-Man.* Lecturing. 1860. Journey to San Francisco on brother's clipper-ship Meteor. 1863. Moves to New York. 1866. *Battle-Pieces.* 1866–85. Inspector of Customs at the Port of New York. 1867. Death of Malcolm.

1869. Mark Twain, *The
      Innocents Abroad.*
      Tolstoy, *War and Peace.*
1871. Whitman, *Democratic
      Vistas.*

                                      1872. *Septimius Felton.*

1873. Mark Twain and
      Charles Dudley Warner,
      The Gilded Age.
1876. Henry James, *Roderick
      Hudson.*
1879. Henry James, *Daisy
      Miller; Hawthorne.*
      Ibsen, *A Doll's House.*
1880. Adams, *Democracy.*
      Zola, *The Experimental
      Novel.* Dostoevsky, *The
      Brothers Karamazov.*
1881. Henry James, *Portrait
      of a Lady.*
1883. Howells, *The Rise of   1883. *Dr. Grimshawe's Secret.*
      Silas Lapham.* Mark
      Twain, *Huckleberry
      Finn.*

1888. Bellamy, *Looking
      Backward.* Bryce, *The
      American
      Commonwealth.*
      Whitman, *November
      Boughs.*
1890. Emily Dickinson,
      Poems. William James,
      *The Principles of
      Psychology.*
1891. Bierce, *Tales of Soldiers
      and Civilians.* Howells,
      Criticism and Fiction.
1895. Hardy, *Jude the
      Obscure.* Crane, *The
      Red Badge of Courage.*
1900. Conrad, *Lord Jim.*
      Dreiser, *Sister Carrie.*

1876. *Clarel.*

1886. Death of Stanwix.
1888. *John Marr and Other
      Sailors.*

1891. *Timoleon.* Death.

1924. *Billy Budd.*

Index

A NOTE ON THE TYPE

THIS *book is set in* ELECTRA, *a Linotype face designed by W. A. Dwiggins* (1880–1956), *who was responsible for so much that is good in contemporary book design. Although much of his early work was in advertising and he was the author of the standard volume* LAYOUT IN ADVERTISING, *Mr. Dwiggins later devoted his prolific talents to book typography and type design, and worked with great distinction in both fields. In addition to his designs for Electra, he created the Metro, Caledonia, and Eldorado series of type faces, as well as a number of experimental cuttings that have never been issued commercially.*

Electra cannot be classified as either modern or old-style. It is not based on any historical model, nor does it echo a particular period or style. It avoids the extreme contrast between thick and thin elements which marks most modern faces, and attempts to give a feeling of fluidity, power, and speed.

Designed by HARRY FORD.